D0272650

FORGOTTEN
VOICES

Also available in the Forgotten Voices series:

Forgotten Voices of the Great War
Forgotten Voices of the Great War (illustrated)
Forgotten Voices of the Somme

Lest We Forget: Forgotten Voices from 1914–1945

Forgotten Voices of the Second World War
Forgotten Voices of the Second World War (illustrated)
Forgotten Voices of the Blitz and the Battle for Britain
Forgotten Voices of the Holocaust
Forgotten Voices of the Secret War

Forgotten Voices of the Falklands

FORGOTTEN VOICES

OF
D-DAY

IN ASSOCIATION WITH
THE IMPERIAL WAR MUSEUM

RODERICK BAILEY

EBURY
PRESS

3 5 7 9 10 8 6 4

Published in 2009 by Ebury Press, an imprint of Ebury Publishing
A Random House Group company

Introduction © Winston S. Churchill 2009
Text © Roderick Bailey and Imperial War Museum 2009
Jimmy Green and Lawrence Hogben material used by kind permission of Dangerous Films
Photographs (unless otherwise indicated) © Imperial War Museum 2009

The Random House Group Limited Reg. No. 954009

Addresses for companies within the Random House Group can be found at
www.randomhouse.co.uk

A CIP catalogue record for this book is available from the British Library

The Random House Group Limited supports The Forest Stewardship Council (FSC), the
leading international forest certification organisation. All our titles that are printed on
Greenpeace approved FSC certified paper carry the FSC logo. Our paper procurement policy
can be found at www.rbooks.co.uk/environment

Mixed Sources
Product group from well-managed
forests and other controlled sources
www.fsc.org Cert no. TT-COC-2139
© 1996 Forest Stewardship Council

Printed and bound in Great Britain by Clays Ltd, St Ives PLC

ISBN 9780091930110

To buy books by your favourite authors and register for offers visit
http://www.rbooks.co.uk

Contents

Author's Preface

On the morning of Tuesday, 6 June 1944, Allied forces began landing on the northern coast of Nazi-occupied France. The first airborne troops arrived by parachute and glider just minutes after midnight; by dawn, a vast seaborne assault force was fighting its way ashore. The Normandy landings, the largest, most complex and ambitious operation of their type ever attempted, were a turning point in the Second World War. The long-awaited Second Front had opened and the liberation of Western Europe had begun.

Drawing on the Sound Archive records of London's Imperial War Museum, this book is concerned with the British contribution to D-Day. It is a compilation of eyewitness testimonies and impressions, of personal and personalised accounts of episodes that occurred on that day and during the long months of preparation that preceded it.

One of the greatest strengths of the museum's vast collection is that it includes accounts from men and women whose experiences are not widely known yet are rich in unusual and unexpected detail. So, against Lord Mountbatten's memories of the early problems faced by the most senior of planners, we have the recollections, for example, of a young WAAF aircraftwoman who packed parachutes in the run-up to D-Day and worried about the consequences of doing too many too quickly. Royal Navy seamen speak of the disastrous night in April 1944 when German E-boats caused havoc and heavy casualties among American landing craft training off Slapton Sands in Devon: a hushed-up episode that remained little known for decades. A conscientious objector describes his work as a parachute medic who dropped before dawn into Normandy. Here, too, is the modest account of the only man to win a Victoria Cross on D-Day.

Some of the most important and powerful testimonies come from Royal

Navy officers and seamen caught up in the terrible carnage of Omaha Beach, where American troops went ashore in the face of fierce enemy opposition. The fact that British personnel were present and did important work on Omaha rarely features in histories of the day's events there.

Perhaps the most poignant account is that left by Tom Treanor, a war correspondent. Treanor was an American – the only one quoted in this book – and his description of going ashore on Utah beach was recorded for broadcast just hours after his return from Normandy on the night of 6 June. He was killed two months later when his jeep was crushed by an Allied tank on a road north of Paris.

Given the snapshot-style of the Forgotten Voices series and the nature of oral history, this book cannot of course touch on every aspect of D-Day. What it can do is shed light on the vast and varied range of roles performed by British civilians and servicemen during the long build-up period and on D-Day itself, and raise the voices of men and women whose testimonies might otherwise go unheard. By underlining Britain's contribution in this way – in the words and through the experiences of individual participants – the book may also help to restore some balance to the popular image of D-Day. As it has been portrayed in recent films and non-fiction, that image does not always give the British the credit and attention they deserve.

Roderick Bailey, January 2009

Acknowledgements

My greatest debt is to the men and women who have chosen over the years to record their memories and impressions both of D-Day and of the build-up to that tremendous event. I should also like to acknowledge the role of the Imperial War Museum in collecting and preserving those testimonies. Within the Museum, I should like to thank Margaret Brooks, Richard McDonough and Richard Hughes of the Sound Archive; I am grateful also to Nick Hewitt, Alan Wakefield, Abbie Ratcliffe, Madeleine James, Sarah Paterson and Victoria Wylde and to the many Reading Room staff who have patiently produced tapes for me. Thank you to Dangerous Films, Susan Langridge of the Green Howards Regimental Museum, Jamie Callison, Lyn Smith, Alexandra Pesch and Judith Moellers. Thank you, too, to Ken Barlow and Charlotte Cole, at Ebury, and to Gillon Aitken, my agent. Every effort has been made to trace copyright-holders and I apologise to those whom I was unable to locate.

Roderick Bailey, January 2009

Introduction by
Winston S. Churchill

Few, who visit the military cemeteries of Normandy, can fail to be moved by the row upon row of gleaming Portland stone memorials, standing in silent witness to the heroism and sacrifice of the British, Commonwealth and American soldiers, who laid down their lives that Europe might be free. However often one may visit them, it is impossible to come away from these often vast, always immaculately maintained, British and American war cemeteries without feelings of sadness, of gratitude, but also of intense pride. One cannot help but reflect on these young men – average age in their early twenties, but some mere teenagers fresh out of school – whose lives were so cruelly cut short in the flower of their youth. In the words of the Kohima epitaph: 'For your tomorrow, we gave our today'.

Unlike the American crosses with name, age and rank, the British war graves often carry messages from 'mum and dad', a wife or a sweetheart, in addition. None could be more poignant than the tribute I came across from the parents of a nineteen-year-old, who had died on D-Day:

> To the World he was One ...
> To Us he was the World

But *Forgotten Voices of D-Day* brings to life, with a brilliance, vividness and immediacy, the memories and experiences, the thoughts and humour, of so many of their comrades, who came through the ordeal, and lived to tell the tale.

Roderick Bailey, a distinguished historian and former Winston Churchill Memorial Trust Fellow has, with this work, done signal service to the memory and heroism of those who took part in the greatest seaborne and airborne invasion of history, only a dwindling band of whom are still with us today.

This work would never have been possible but for the foresight and painstaking effort of the Imperial War Museum which, over many decades, has recorded the oral testimony of many hundreds of the participants in these dramatic events, which moulded the course of history and paved the way directly for the downfall of the Third Reich – participants of every rank, from the Montys, Mountbattens and Ikes down to the humblest, or not so humble, private soldier. Through it all, the courage, camaraderie and humour of the ordinary British 'Tommy' comes shining through.

The D-Day invasion involved an armada of nearly 7,000 warships and landing-craft, while in the air more than 11,000 aircraft participated. By nightfall, some 132,715 Allied troops had been put ashore. Hollywood revels in depicting D-Day and the ensuing Battle of Normandy, in movies such as *Saving Private Ryan* or *Band of Brothers*, as an overwhelmingly, if not exclusively, American affair. Indeed in the former, the only reference to British involvement was a curt: 'Where are Monty's boys – they're late!' But the reality was rather different. As these pages make clear, even on Omaha Beach, the Royal Navy played a vital, though unsung, part in getting the Americans ashore.

Overall, the number of British troops – including from the British Dominions and Commonwealth – who landed on the beaches and landing-grounds of Normandy on D-Day, was equal to that of the Americans. Only beyond the end of June 1944 did the number of US troops in action worldwide begin to surpass that of Britain and her Commonwealth, which had borne the burden for nearly five long, painful years of war.

How easy it is with the benefit of 20/20 hindsight, with which we are all endowed, to believe in the inevitability of historical events. We therefore *know* that the invasion was bound to succeed. But that was certainly not how it appeared to the decision-makers of the day, most especially to the British prime minister, Winston Churchill, who harboured searing memories of the disaster that had attended the British, Anzac (Australian and New Zealand Army Corps) and French forces as they attempted to land, nearly thirty years earlier, on the beaches of the Gallipoli peninsula. As they waded ashore, they were caught by underwater obstacles and barbed-wire entanglements, while being raked by withering machine gun fire from the entrenched and well prepared Turkish defenders. Some battalions suffered 70 per cent casualties and Allied casualties, up to the moment they were forced to evacuate nine months later in January 1917, totalled 252,000.

On invasion-eve, the night of 5 June 1944, the Prime Minister dined alone with his wife, before making his way to the Map Room to examine the final dispositions for the attack. As Sir Martin Gilbert records in his official biography (Vol. VII, p. 794):

Shortly before she went to bed, Clementine Churchill joined him in the Map Room. 'Do you realize,' Churchill said to her, 'that by the time you wake up in the morning twenty thousand men may have been killed?'

In the event – thanks in large measure to successful deception and surprise, combined with masterly preparation – Allied casualties on D-Day were nothing like as grave as Churchill had feared. They amounted to no more than 10,000, which included 2,500 dead – a mere tenth of those of the British Army who died on on 1 July 1916, the first day of the Battle of the Somme.

By the end of June, over 850,000 Allied soldiers had been put ashore and were engaged in the Battle of Normandy, which cost 209,000 Allied casualties, including more than 53,000 dead.

So long as the British and American nations endure, the feats of these ordinary men who, in the face of unbelievable danger, performed extraordinary acts of heroism to liberate Europe from the scourge of Fascism, will live for ever in the hearts and memories of a grateful people.

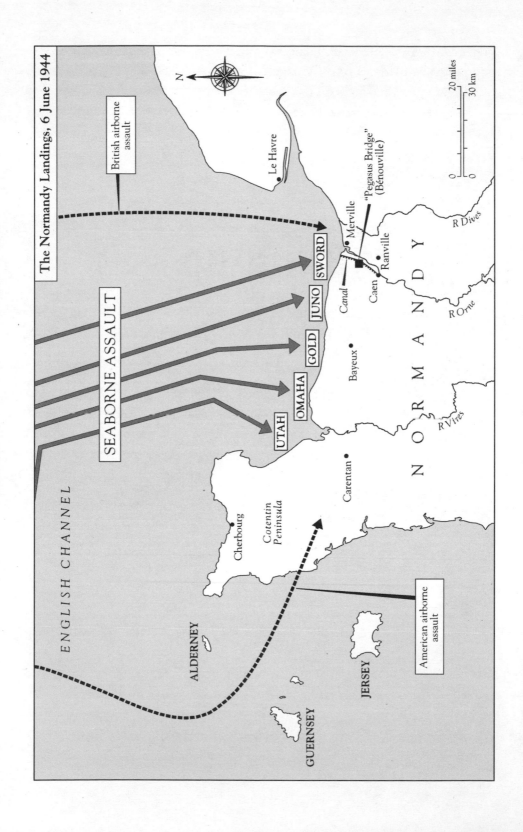

The Normandy Landings, 6 June 1944

N

ENGLISH CHANNEL

SEABORNE ASSAULT

British airborne assault

Le Havre

SWORD

JUNO

GOLD

OMAHA

UTAH

Merville

"Pegasus Bridge" (Bénouville)

Ranville

Canal

Caen

R Dives

R Orne

R Vires

Bayeux

NORMANDY

Carentan

Cotentin Peninsula

Cherbourg

ALDERNEY

GUERNSEY

JERSEY

American airborne assault

20 miles

30 km

Build-up

A seaborne landing on a heavily defended enemy coast is about the most hazardous operation of all.
I think everybody was terribly aware of this all the time.

Planning for D-Day began years before the invasion took place. Indeed, British thinking about ways and means of returning to the Continent started almost as soon as the British Army had been evacuated from Dunkirk in 1940. From the start, however, British planners were faced with a paucity of resources. Serious planning for an invasion became feasible after the United States entered the war in December 1941; only then, with the input of American men, material and expertise, did an invasion of Western Europe seem possible.

By the end of 1943, the Normandy coast had been identified as offering the best chance of a successful landing, and a massive invasion force, mostly of American, British and Canadian troops, was assembling in Britain. By then, too, the senior commanders for the operation had been appointed. An American, General Dwight D. Eisenhower, was placed in overall charge as Supreme Commander. Britons had the next senior roles. As head of 21st Army Group, General Sir Bernard Montgomery was put in charge of all ground forces to be used in the invasion. Admiral Sir Bertram Ramsay and Air Chief Marshal Sir Trafford Leigh-Mallory would command the Allied naval and air forces respectively. Air Chief Marshal Sir Arthur Tedder was appointed Eisenhower's deputy.

Between them and their subordinate officers, the final plan for the invasion was settled. The night before D-Day, a vast armada of ships carrying the seaborne invasion force was to cross the Channel, drop anchor off the Normandy coast and prepare to land the troops after dawn. Two

American airborne divisions would land by parachute and glider to secure the invasion's western flank, while one British airborne division would go in to secure the eastern flank. Preceded by a heavy air and naval bombardment of the enemy's defences, the seaborne force of six Allied infantry divisions – three American, two British and one Canadian – would then land on five pre-selected beaches. By the end of the day, it was hoped, five beachheads would be established, four beachheads would be linked and the troops would have started to make good progress inland. The invasion was code-named Overlord. Its initial phase – the establishment of a firm foothold on the Normandy coast – was code-named Neptune.

Throughout the months running up to D-Day, elaborate measures were taken to confuse and mislead the Germans as to the intended invasion point and to complicate the enemy's ability to react when the landings came. Considerable thought was given to developing methods of getting safely and effectively ashore and breaching Hitler's defensive Atlantic Wall, the feared barrier of anti-invasion obstacles, batteries, bunkers, minefields and fortifications which the Germans had built and sewn along the entire coast of northern France. Among the most innovative devices were General Sir Percy Hobart's 'Funnies' – specialised vehicles designed to clear and breach a host of different obstructions – and the Duplex-Drive (DD) amphibious tanks.

By the spring of 1944, preparations for the invasion were reaching a peak. Troops in training took part in several large-scale landing exercises; to assist them, a number of south coast villages were evacuated. These exercises were not always problem-free and the worst incident happened on 28 April, when German E-boats intercepted American landing craft training off the Devon coast.

PLANS AND PRELIMINARIES

Vice Admiral Lord Louis Mountbatten
Chief of Combined Operations, London, 1941–43
I was recalled from Pearl Harbor, where I was working with the American fleet temporarily, to take up the job in charge of Combined Operations by Mr Winston Churchill.

The very first day I reported to him, he said, 'You are to prepare for the invasion of Europe. For unless we can go and land and fight Hitler and beat his forces on land we shall never win this war. You must devise and design the appliances, the landing craft and the techniques to enable us to effect a landing against opposition and to maintain ourselves there. You must take the most brilliant officers from the navy, army and air force to help plan this great operation. You must take bases to use as training establishments where you can train the navy, army and air force to work as a single entity. The whole of the south coast of England is a bastion of defence against the invasion of Hitler: you've got to turn it into the springboard for our attack.'

This was October 1941, when the whole of our allies in Europe had been overrun and captured and conquered and the Russians looked like being defeated and the Americans weren't in the war. What a hell of a decision to make: to prepare for the invasion then.

Then, when Churchill went over to meet President Roosevelt a week after the Japanese attack on Pearl Harbor, they made their very brave decision: Europe first. We would beat the Nazis there before we crushed the Japanese, which, as the Japanese had just attacked them, was a courageous decision for the Americans. And when General Marshall came over to see the British chiefs of staff he was enthusiastic about the idea of taking part in this invasion which I'd been ordered to plan. But he didn't seem to be able to appreciate that we couldn't stage it as quickly as he had hoped. We hadn't got the landing craft or the other things to go with it, hadn't got the men trained.

Major Goronwy Rees
21st Army Group planning staff
As far as the planning was concerned, it was an essentially British operation. Of course we had American officers with us and they worked very closely with us but the original conception of the plan was a British one and the detailed planning of it was also, I would say, about ninety per cent British. Of course you had to learn to work with the Americans and this is not an easy thing. Their methods of planning and conducting war are really terribly different from ours.

I think the fundamental difference between the way we make war and the way the Americans make war is that we were always conscious of how very small our resources were. We knew, for instance, that if we lost a division it would mean a disaster to us. Whereas the Americans were quite prepared to produce another division, there was an infinite number of divisions in the pipeline, and they regarded people as expendable in a way that we didn't. Not only men, but also material. Our resources were very limited and we simply could not afford to waste things in the way that the Americans could. On the other hand this had great advantages in the sense that the Americans produced material that was beyond our means and their engineering instruments could perform feats in a time and at a speed which we could never dream of.

Vice Admiral Lord Louis Mountbatten
Chief of Combined Operations, 1941–43

The absolutely crucial thing for an invasion is to get the troops across the water and for that you want landing ships and landing craft, and those we just didn't have. They had to be designed; they had to be built in large quantities at a time when all the shipbuilding facilities were required to fight the Battle of the Atlantic. But we managed to get permission to get smaller yards to start building the landing craft and then we started converting merchant ships to landing ships. And above all, when the Americans came in, I persuaded General Marshall right away to double all the orders I'd placed in America. That's how we built up the landing craft at a time when nobody wanted them to be built up.

Brigadier David Belchem
21st Army Group planning staff

The basic reason why Normandy was chosen starts with the air support requirements of the army. The preoccupation of the army is close support from the air. This is carried out by fighter-bombers and at this period of time the range of our fighter-bombers was very limited. Therefore, since there were not enough aircraft carriers, it meant that the air force had to operate from bases in the south of England. This in turn meant that the invasion area had to be chosen between a point somewhere between the south of Holland and the Belgian coast and what we call the Cherbourg Peninsula, which is called the Cotentin Peninsula in France. That was the beginning of the story because this defined the length of coast on which you had to choose the point of assault.

Another part of the choice of Normandy was that you've got to have suitable beaches. You've got to have the possibility of getting straight inland and getting as far and as deep as you possibly can as quickly as possible. And you've got to defend, from immediate interruption, the follow-up forces arriving on the beach. This is why obviously you don't choose to land at the bottom of a cliff at Calais or Dieppe or where have you. And the plan for the subsequent development, of course, was partly dictated by the favourable nature of the zone of Normandy, because we could envisage a lodgement area from where we could get up to the Seine and the Loire. The armed forces would be grouped while more aircraft, installations, dumps and all the rest of it were brought in and ports opened and then you would get tidy and ready for the next stage, which was the advance on Berlin.

Vice Admiral Lord Louis Mountbatten
Chief of Combined Operations, 1941–43
The problem of staying ashore is a very difficult one because of the weather conditions in the Channel. You couldn't expect more than three or four consecutive days with weather fine enough to supply the beaches, so obviously we thought we'd have to take a port. That's why we tried Dieppe. But we found in Dieppe that we couldn't actually capture a port without using such heavy bombardment as would destroy the facilities we wanted to use, so the obvious thing was to bring our own artificial harbour with us, which we called Mulberry, and which everybody thought was absolutely crazy.

Brigadier Arthur Walter
21st Army Group planning staff
The bright boys, and they were British, entirely British, thought up the idea of an artificial harbour in which they built the pieces in England, towed them a hundred miles to the beaches and put them down piece by piece by piece like that. That was 1942. But it wasn't until the Quebec Conference in 1943 that Mr Churchill and the British chiefs of staff sold the idea to the Americans, that the only way you could have an invasion was by building an artificial harbour.

Brigadier Bruce White
Director of Ports and Inland Water Transport, War Office
After the Quebec Conference we went to Washington where the meeting for

German photograph of knocked-out tanks and burning landing craft after the failed Allied raid on Dieppe, 19 August 1942.

the Overlord programme was discussed and a final meeting was held at which General Marshall, who was Chief of the Combined Staff, went through the whole of the preparations that were being made for the invasion and turned to me asking whether the provisions in the form of Mulberry harbours could be accomplished in the time which was remaining. On this occasion I represented the UK and stated that this could be accomplished provided the Americans could supply us with timber, of which we had a shortage, and also tugs, of which we had an insufficiency. It was really a terrific shot in the dark, I might say. Coming back, I thought, 'My God, I'll get hung for this all right if it doesn't work.'

I've often been asked why the word Mulberry was used in connection with the Mulberry harbours. The simple answer is that following my return from America I found on my table at the War Office a letter which had no security and was headed 'Artificial Harbours'. I felt this was a possibility where security might be broken and therefore approached the head of the security branch at the War Office and requested a meeting at which I explained the case, and the chairman asked me what I would like to be done. I said utilisation of a code word would give me the security I would wish for. Turning to the junior officer behind him, he asked what was the next name from the code book and the officer replied, 'Mulberry.'

Captain Alan Adcock
Directorate of Ports and Inland Water Transport, War Office
The outer wall of the harbour was to be formed by large concrete caissons, which were of course to be constructed in this country and towed across and sunk in line. They were some two hundred feet long and the biggest ones were sixty feet high and fifty-six feet wide or thereabouts. The design and construction of these was really a prodigious work; 147 of them were built and hadn't even been designed before the beginning of October 1943. And they were designed and built and floated round to the south coast ready for D-Day between then and April 1944: seven months.

The construction was handled by a special department set up by the Ministry of Supply which was staffed not by civil servants but by men drawn from the big contractors' offices who were used to handling supply and organisation of construction work. It was headed by Jack Gibson of Pauling, one of the big contractors of that day; he was knighted for his effort. And he

A concrete Phoenix caisson being towed by a tug to an assembly point prior to D-Day. The plan was for each caisson to be towed to the Normandy shore after D-Day, where it would be flooded until it settled on the seabed, forming a section of the breakwater of a Mulberry harbour.

managed to persuade, somehow or other, twenty-four of the big contractors of the day, including many that are still well known, people like McAlpine and Costain, Bovis and Taylor Woodrow and so on, to take part in this construction.

I might say that there were one or two contractors who were approached to do it and they refused because they said it couldn't possibly be done in the time and the whole scheme would be a complete flop. But twenty-four of them did agree to do it and they were allocated sites all over the country, and the Ministry of Supply was given wide powers to get materials and labour and they actually got a few men released from the forces to go back to their old firms to help with the construction. But it was a miracle that it was all done in the time.

Major Goronwy Rees
21st Army Group planning staff
We'd had to plan for a long time without knowing who's going to carry out the plans and at last General Eisenhower was made Supreme Allied Commander and General Montgomery was appointed to command the operation in its first days. And Monty came back with the huge prestige of Alamein behind him and with all his boys with sand in their boots and bush shirts and God knows what.

Sergeant Frank Higgins
Royal Military Police
I was stationed with a detachment at St Paul's School, Hammersmith, when it was the General Headquarters of the Home Forces. Our particular duty was the safeguarding of the Commander-in-Chief. Montgomery joined us in January 1944 and our detachment of Military Police then took over the duties of accompanying him on his visits and the security of his mess and his own quarters which were in a block of flats in Hammersmith.

There was always one of us on duty at his flat and, in the case of evening meals, one of us would always be on duty at the mess because invariably there would be entertaining of various officers and staff officers from the navy and the air force. There was always one policeman attached to him when he journeyed from the flat to the headquarters itself and one policeman was always stood by at headquarters while he was there in case he was required.

And it fell to us to do security checks on entering the headquarters: examining passes and credentials of visiting officers. Unless it happened to be your day's leave you were bound to come across him during the day.

I think his black beret and his two badges, the dress that he assumed, rather brought him out as a bit of a showman. When you saw him in his service dress and his ordinary red tabs and brass hat he looked a totally different person. In his beret and his battledress he always seemed to look more military and more commanding than ever he did in his service dress. With his battledress and his beret he stood out a mile.

He was a great showman. He loved show; he really loved it. I'd never seen him more happy, actually, than when we visited factories. They always said that Monty wasn't a woman's man but the ladies in factories really used to go mad about him and he seemed to lap it up. There again, it was his showman's abilities that brought that on. He really loved the crowd.

A lot of people didn't like him, didn't like his manner. He was very brusque and curt in his way of speaking. The high-pitched voice always made him appear to be talking down to one and although I don't think it was his manner it was just the way that one took it.

General Eisenhower I found a very likeable person. I did come across him quite a bit, especially after we'd moved to Portsmouth. I did a lot of night duty at Portsmouth and Eisenhower seemed to be spending a lot of time in London and he used to arrive back in the early hours of the morning, showing very fully all his credentials even though no one could mistake him. He was always very nice. If he came in of an evening and we'd be there, he'd have a little talk with you, pass some comments on London or somewhere where he'd been. It used to break the monotony for someone in that position to talk to a lowly sergeant, as it were. It was always quite nice to have a chat with him.

Brigadier David Belchem
21st Army Group planning staff
There arose differences between Montgomery and Eisenhower from time to time. Eisenhower was a political general whereas Montgomery was a cold, calculating, ruthless combat general. It's very seldom that a general is both of these categories at the same time. The combat man sweeps aside any factor other than those concerned with helping to win the war as quickly as possible with the minimum of casualties. The political general has a rather different

task. He's dealing, shall we say, with public opinion, problems in England and the United States. He's dealing with the statesmen – he's dealing with Roosevelt, with Churchill, with de Gaulle – and things of this kind. He's also concerned with holding together a team which inevitably includes a number of personalities who could be difficult. In this case he's concerned with Bradley, Patton, Montgomery, the air commanders, sometimes 'Bomber' Harris. Therefore he cannot always agree with the much more direct approach of the combat general and this obviously at times caused differences of opinion.

Lieutenant Charles Mills
Naval planning staff
There was tremendous expectancy and always confidence, perhaps more confidence, when Monty arrived to take command of the land forces in the Allied landings and it then went from three, what we called assault areas, to five. He said that three wasn't enough, this wasn't good enough, and he went to the Chiefs of Staff and he said there must be five.

Brigadier David Belchem
21st Army Group planning staff
With Montgomery the primary principle of war was concentration. When you've chosen the right point you put every mortal thing you've got into that area.

Major Patrick Barrass
2nd Battalion, Essex Regiment
Monty decided to put two more divisions in and the Airborne, thank God. I mean, if it had only been three divisions we'd have been boxed in and pushed back into the sea again without any trouble at all.

DECEPTION AND DESTRUCTION

Vice Admiral Lord Louis Mountbatten
Chief of Combined Operations, 1941–43
To prevent the enemy from building up reinforcements so quickly that they could push you back into the sea, you have to do two things. First, you had to

have a deception plan, to make the enemy think you're going to land somewhere else and make him build up all his reinforcements and his defences there. That was easy in our case. It obviously was the Pas de Calais, the straits of Dover, the shortest way across. Not only did all the German generals think we were going to go there but all the British generals wanted to go there. Secondly, having got them all concentrated on the wrong place, you then had to prevent them from being moved to the right place when they discovered their mistake. For that purpose you wanted weeks of interdiction: bombing, destroying roads, bridges, railway junctions, tunnels and everything. For that purpose the whole of the main British and American bomber commanders had to be turned on to the job way ahead of the actual D-Day.

Hugh Astor
MI5 *officer*

I was working for MI5, which was responsible for security in this country, and the section I was working for was B1A which was responsible for capturing German agents and then, whenever possible, running them as double agents.

By 1943 it was realised that all German agents operating in this country were under our control and this opened the possibility of using deception. The agent fits into it by virtue of the fact that he's providing a channel of communication. He's been recruited by the Germans, he's been sent over here by the Germans, the Germans believe that he's operating freely, and you've therefore got a direct line of communication with his German controllers.

The deception plan for Overlord was brilliantly thought out. The mastermind, really, was David Strangeways. The cover plan created an imaginary army and we gave the Germans the impression that we had available almost twice the number of troops that were in fact in existence. It was quite interesting at the end of the war when we went through all their files and found they had recorded with details all these imaginary units, the names of their commanding officers, their divisional signs, call signs and all the rest of it; where they'd been stationed at different times, what training they'd had, what equipment they'd had. All of this was imaginary and passed on by us. The effect of that was that we were able, up to a point, to persuade them that the Normandy landings, when they started, were a diversionary attack and that the main force was still in East Anglia waiting to go across the Channel to Calais.

Only two agents were really used for the deception plan for Overlord. One was Garbo; the other was Brutus. The others played very small parts; they were sort of beating the triangle in an orchestra, just to fill in details from time to time. In the case of Brutus, what I had done was to report in very great detail the position of all the British troops, how they were equipped, how they were commanded, what training they'd had, and the emphasis was always to put them in the East Anglia area.

We were fortunate that senior people, starting with the Prime Minister and Montgomery, believed wholeheartedly in deception and they were therefore prepared to pay a price to make the deception credible. They accepted that you had to give quite a lot of real information in order to make the deception material look credible. When you come to think of it, you can give away an awful lot of accurate information without revealing your plans and without actually helping the enemy. You can say who the commander of such and such a unit is, you can give his name, address and all the rest of it, you can say what training that unit has had, but it's not until that unit is in an assault position that the information becomes delicate.

Pluto and Mulberry were the two things which made the Normandy landings possible and they were therefore the two top-secret elements in all traffic and we could say an awful lot but never, ever touch on those two things. Our worry always was that the Germans would have aerial reconnaissance which would show them these great concrete things being constructed or these great drums which were going to be used for the pipeline. In fact they never did spot them and we were spared any embarrassing questions. But we were all worried that sooner or later we would be asked, 'What are these drums being used for?' so we had to have various cover plans up our sleeve for dealing with that.

All the people that write about double agents – there've been quite a number of books written about Garbo and Brutus and so on – all assume that the leading part has been played by the agent, that they invented the traffic, that they invented the deception plans and so on. But of course that's completely unreal. To have a deception plan you've got to know the real plan. Well, nobody knew the real plan except for a very small number of people. Some would know the place, others would know the date, others would know the composition of the invading force, but very few people knew the whole story. And those that did were code-named Bigoted: it meant that they had access to all the information. My colleagues and I, who were carrying out these deception plans, had to be Bigoted. We had to know the full story in order to give the deception plan.

Major Goronwy Rees
21st Army Group planning staff
Again, I think, this is a lesson learned from Dieppe: we hadn't realised at Dieppe how absolutely essential it was to have an absolutely overwhelming weight of firepower both from the air and from the land. Air Marshal Harris, who still thought that he could win the war on his own, had to be persuaded to use his heavy bombers to attack the German road and rail communications. I think he resisted very strongly, as he thought it was really a diversion from the whole point of the war, but he was made to do it and it was done enormously effectively. This happened equally with the French Resistance, because the French Resistance had vast plans for what they were going to do on D-Day. I had to go to SOE and ask them what their plans were and had to tell them that, from our point of view, we wanted the French Resistance to interfere with the German road and rail communications. This meant them giving up a great many dearly beloved plans of theirs but they did it and, again, they were very effective.

Major Wilhelm Mohr
Norwegian staff officer, 2nd Tactical Air Force
It started in the late summer of '43. From that time we felt very much that the direction of choosing targets and activity were planned as part of the invasion to come and as you got closer towards Christmas there was more and more of that. And I must say the people who did the planning must have been pretty brilliant because it was known later that Hitler had very much set his mind that Calais was going to be the point. We were attacking radar stations primarily in the Pas de Calais area to make him think that this is where we would concentrate. One thing we had as very much a prime job was to push the enemy's air defence backwards, make him have longer distances to cover and so on, but again we did that more in the Calais area than we did in the Normandy area. But you've got to do it there, too. Otherwise they would sort of start wondering.

Pilot Officer Herbert Kirtland
Halifax bomber wireless operator, 76 Squadron, RAF

Instead of strategic targets like Nuremberg and Stuttgart and Frankfurt and Berlin they started to be railway marshalling yards, places like Le Mans and Aachen, that would deny the Germans the opportunity to get their troops and panzers where they were needed if and when we invaded.

We had a very hairy trip to Aachen, I remember. We were attacked but we didn't know what it was that attacked us, nobody identified it; we got no hits but the gunners fired their guns. Flak was very heavy and the mid-upper gunner had a chunk of flak as big as my fist come through the turret and embedded itself in the bottom right-hand gun, which, if it hadn't, would have split him open. And a few minutes after that, Carl was literally flying this thing through the target area and all of a sudden I could hear the noise of another aircraft, which you normally couldn't hear, and the mid-upper gunner said, 'Fucking hell!' Another Halifax had drifted over the top of us, as near to a collision as anything. We could hear his engines and he'd nearly taken the turret off. We got away with it, we got back with no damage, but we'd been fired on by fighters, we'd been hit by flak and we'd had a near-collision all in the space of a few minutes over the target.

With hindsight you know now what the pattern was but you didn't really know then. You were just a cog in a vast wheel and the CO didn't say, 'All right, lads, we're now getting ready for the invasion.' But they were different sort of targets and your own common sense told you, 'If we are planning to invade Europe, this is probably what we ought to be doing.' I think we were pleased they were slightly shorter trips, obviously. But they were just as hairy.

Group Captain Denys Gillam
Commanding officer, 146 Wing, RAF

I was commanding 146 Wing, which was a five-squadron Typhoon wing at Thorney Island. For a month, probably two months, we were operating against German radar stations with rockets and bombs but mostly rockets. Our job was to eliminate the German radar in the Channel with the exception of two stations which were deliberately left in order to spoof the invasion. This was a very expensive time in that we lost about three wing commanders and about five squadron commanders in just over a month. Of course the radar stations were all in the coastal belt where the heaviest flak was. But we did it very successfully and managed to do the job so they were all out of action with the exception of two that were deliberately left.

Lieutenant-Colonel David Strangeways
Chief deception officer, 21st Army Group

You've got to be ruthless in this kind of thing. It's horrible. I used to feel miserable about this. You knew you were sending a fellow on a reconnaissance which wasn't a real reconnaissance, he might get bumped off, but this you've got to do. Because, if you don't do it, then many, many more are going to get bumped off.

Major Patrick Barrass
2nd Battalion, Essex Regiment

There was a lovely story going round; I don't know how true it is. They sent people ashore in darkness to bring back samples of the beaches, so that they could assess whether they were firm enough to take tanks and so forth, and the story goes that somebody left a trowel behind and this was found out and then a bomber was loaded with trowels and sent down the coast dropping them all down the coast so that the position wasn't given away. I can believe it, actually, when I come to think of all the preparations that were done before D-Day to be absolutely sure that nothing leaked anywhere.

Sergeant Frank Higgins
Royal Military Police

We were met one day by members of the Intelligence Corps and they informed us that there was an officer coming from London. He would be arriving by car, he was to be immediately fitted out with the uniform of a sergeant of the Intelligence Corps, he was to accompany us on all visits to places that General Montgomery was going and he was going to study his mannerisms and his way of talking. And that was the man who actually became Monty's double and who went to Gibraltar, just prior to the invasion, where we presume he hoodwinked the Germans and the Spaniards into thinking that he was on Gibraltar when he was in fact in Portsmouth preparing for the start of Overlord.

Major Goronwy Rees
21st Army Group planning staff

I don't think I've ever worked harder in my life than I did during that year. And I think it was always in everybody's mind that unless one really did one's best and really went into every possible difficulty and tried to overcome every possible problem, the operation really could turn into an enormous disaster. Really, a seaborne landing on a heavily defended enemy coast is about the most hazardous operation of all. I think everybody was terribly aware of this all the time.

One felt all the time that something might be given away and without some element of surprise the operation would have been an even more hazardous one than it was. It meant that the staff had to be restricted to a very small number and one of the results of this was, of course, that people were asked to do quite unexpected kinds of jobs. It was a terrible responsibility I felt. I really used to be amazed when I walked around the streets of London, thinking, 'Here am I, the only person here that actually knows the dates of this operation, where it's going to happen, the forces involved. I must be of infinite value to the enemy and unless I'm very careful I really am going to get myself in the most terrible trouble.'

I felt this most of all at the very end of the planning when it had all been done and the whole thing had been translated into operation orders and there, at last, was the great operation order: a thing about that thick. Of course it had to be signed by the three commanders. Monty signed it at St Paul's and then I was given it and told to take it to Air Marshal Leigh-Mallory and to Admiral Ramsay for them to sign. And being very foolish, I didn't take a car from the pool, I can't think why I didn't, I walked out of St Paul's and took a taxi and then I thought, 'My God, how absolutely terrible. Here am I, alone in this taxi, riding through London and very absent-minded and I'm quite capable of leaving the operation order here.' Thank heaven I didn't, though once I'd left a large part of the plans on a bus in London and only by running back faster than I've ever run in my life did I catch the bus up and find it on the seat where I'd left it.

So I went round to Norfolk House where they both were. Admiral Ramsay took one look at it, signed it. Air Marshal Leigh-Mallory insisted on reading the whole bloody thing from start to finish, trying to correct commas. I had to say, 'You know, it's impossible to alter anything more, it's all been agreed.' Finally he signed it.

ALLIES

Brigadier Harry Hopthrow
Director of Fortifications and Works, War Office

I had no sooner got established as director than we attended an urgently summoned conference in the main War Office addressed by a Deputy Quartermaster General. He said, 'I have to tell you, gentlemen, that a force of one million men is coming to this country and as far as Works are concerned you will have to accommodate them.' He said, 'I can't tell you from what country,' but I don't know why, because what other country could it be than the States? And we'd only been engaged on that for about a week and they increased it to a million and a half. We had to provide accommodation not only for their men but also for their stores, hospitals and everything. Well, this put a terrific load on to the organisation. Nevertheless, it was the sort of thing that appealed to me, a big job like this.

Wem is a place in Shropshire and that was where we built the first of their general depots and then we built four more Wems using the same bills of quantities, the same designs, as far as they fitted into the new sites they found for them. They were always referred to as Wems. A Wem had 450,000 square feet of covered accommodation and 375,000 square feet of uncovered accommodation. In addition there were eleven miles of road to one Wem and five miles of full-gauge railway. And we built five of them, for general storage, for the Americans. They built one or two places themselves.

The Americans always wanted more than we gave them and they always had elaborate equipment. For instance, one time we saw a trainload of barbers' chairs coming; they had to have these first-class barbers' chairs and so forth. They had much higher scales of accommodation than we had. We were building for the British troops, too, we had to provide for them; of course some of them went into old barracks and old camps but we had lots of things to build for them.

I had a very good opposite number to me in the American Army, Colonel Berrigan, and their Engineer Corps was much more highly skilled in big work than ours because they'd given them jobs like draining the River Mississippi and that sort of thing. So they were into big stuff from the very beginning. We found they couldn't build roads very well. I don't know why, because they've got some very good roads in America. But if you left it to the Americans and they came across a field and they wanted a road on it, they'd requisition a load of gravel and just pour the gravel on top of the grass. Well, of course, that didn't last very long before the grass came through and they were back to where they'd started. On the other hand, they were extraordinarily good at building railway bridges: they were marvellous. And, of course, we had differences in nomenclature, which was a bit difficult. But Berrigan was a marvellous chap. He and I were hand in hand all the time; I had no problems with him, ever.

Sergeant Major Jack Black
112th Light Anti-Aircraft Regiment, Royal Artillery
You could see the build-up round about you. Even by the summer of 1943 you could see the build-up. We saw the Americans with all their trucks; and our trucks began to have the white star painted on the roofs. You'd have been blind if you hadn't noticed that there was something coming up.

Sergeant Kenneth Lakeman
Royal Corps of Signals
I remember the first lot of Americans and Canadians coming in. I had been asked to collect one of our Arial motorcycles from the workshops and on my way back I was stopped at a crossroads by a military policeman. This was just outside Camberley: Frimley Green. There was a Canadian convoy coming along and after a while he stopped the convoy and waved me on and the convoy didn't stop. Here was I, careering along on a motorbike, and this huge Canadian truck coming full blast at me, so I took evasive action and drove straight through this hedge. And I always think this is British mentality at its best: I went through this hedge on the bike and landed up in this garden and there was a dear lady there pruning roses and without turning a hair she looked at me and said, 'Are you all right? Would you like a cup of tea?' I thought that was bloody marvellous. She said it had happened several times. She'd had a tank through her garden on one occasion.

Wren Messenger Margaret Seeley
Women's Royal Naval Service, HMS Squid (Royal Navy shore station, Southampton)
I remember bicycling up to Winchester and bicycling all around Southampton and the roads were lined with American troops, stationary.

The Americans arrive: a United States Army private, John Ziaja, of Adams, Massachusetts, not long off the boat.

They'd all sort of converged, all these huge American lorries full of GIs, and they all whistled at us and threw us Mars bars and bits of chocolate. It was a question of either being on your dignity and bicycling on or getting off your bicycle and grovelling in the ditch and picking up the candy, which of course we did because we were on rationing. One just waved at them and thanked them and went on our way. But the Americans were everywhere.

Edna Dron
Land Army Timber Corps, Tiverton, Devon

I remember our first introduction to Americans. A friend and I were sitting in the YMCA and this gang of Americans came. I think it was their first night there and they came up to us and asked if we were in the Home Guard: they saw the strange uniform; we thought it was a cheek! But they were very friendly and they had lots of dances which we went to and I suppose they provided a lot of the social life there.

The Americans had plenty of money and they had big mouths and they'd shout about it. They had plenty of food. They had the PX: that was the American place where they got all these goodies, cigarettes and things like that. But they were a good crowd of people to enjoy yourself with. For many of them, I suppose, it was their first time away from home. They were homesick, I think, most of them.

Corporal George Richardson
6th Battalion, Durham Light Infantry

We went down to Cambridge and got into trouble with some American forces. Every time the DLI [Durham Light Infantry] met up with the Americans usually a little war went off because the British women wouldn't look at us. We'd been told we were somebody by both General Smuts and General Montgomery; everybody had told us we were heroes and we'd be welcomed back home as heroes. We came back home and nobody wanted to know. The only reason that our troops were finding fights with the Americans was because they had a lot of money and they were going around with half a dozen medals on and had never been in action.

It went on for a few weeks until we were told we were receiving a visit from the Supreme Commander, General Eisenhower. We assembled on a big green, a full brigade turnout in a three-sided box, the brigadier at the front with a microphone, all the COs all perfectly lined up, blancoed up, spit-and-polished up. Eisenhower came up and got partly along, not far from me; kept stopping and pointing at the medals and saying, 'I bet you're proud of this'. Wasn't receiving any answers back. And I heard him say, 'Ah, shit. This is not what I've come for.'

He went back, over to the microphone, and he says, 'I want to speak to you men. Come round here.' And not an officer or man moved. He turned round to the brigadier and says, 'I want to speak to these men. I want them to come forward.' And the brigadier said, 'I'm afraid they'll not take any orders from you, sir.' And he said, 'But why not?' The brigadier said, 'I'll do it,' and he just shouted to the COs, 'Break off your men and bring them forward.' And from what I hear the brigadier said, 'The British Army doesn't take any orders from an American general.' Of course, the old brigadier was more or less of the same opinion as all our COs and every man jack of us. We'd seen a lot of action and been brought home and the Yanks had invaded England while we were away. That was the opinion of everybody.

He told us then that we were good troops, he knew that we'd seen a lot of action, we should be proud of our Africa Star that we'd rightly earned, we'd come over and we had a bigger job to do yet: we had to clear the Germans from occupied Europe. And to do that we had to cooperate with the American Army. And he said, 'No way can you cooperate with the American Army if you're going to be meeting them in the streets and fighting with them in England. I want you to be friends and find out that you can be friends. I want you to go down into Cambridge and the first Yank you come to, go up to him and shake hands and say, "Hi, Yank. I'm pleased to meet you. How are you doing in your unit?" And you'll probably find out that the American soldier will meet you on your own terms.' And after that we broke off. I think we were given an extra large tea and rum ration.

Sergeant George Self
8th Battalion, Durham Light Infantry
Eisenhower came to see us and gave us a lecture about the American soldier: why were we always bickering at one another? And he said, 'When we get to the other side, they will show you how to fight.' That was the worst thing he could have said. That night in Southampton there was blood flowing down in rivers.

Sergeant Major Jack Black
112th Light Anti-Aircraft Regiment, Royal Artillery
We met the odd one when we were on leave and found them perfectly all right. I don't think there was the animosity that people have said there was towards them. The only thing that grieved us was the fact that they had much better facilities. I mean, when you went on to a gun site where the Americans were and you heard they had ice cream freezers and that sort of thing, it galled you slightly. Plus the fact they had the manpower. Where we had ten men on a Bofors gun, there was about twenty of their fellas manning the equivalent gun that they had. It was a good job we had them like that, mind.

TOOLS AND TRAINING

Sub Lieutenant Peter Bird
Landing Barge Vehicle (LBV) commander
When Louis Mountbatten was appointed chief of Combined Operations he commandeered about a thousand Thames lighters. In the early days they decided that these lighters would be loaded up with stores, ammunition, food, and they would be towed over by tugs and put on an enemy beach. That was at a time, in 1942, when we had very few landing craft of any sort, no purpose-built landing craft. But when the Americans came into the war we got possibly a thousand Chrysler marine engines and they decided to convert these 'dumb' lighters.

They put in a ramp in the stern, a watertight bulkhead, twin Chrysler marine engines and a steering wheelhouse box thing on the starboard side, aft, and, of course, a rudder for steering the vessel. Most of the coxswains were ex-Thames lightermen who, I understand, were on a special contract of about a pound a day and were regarded as millionaires by the rest of them; but they were on a finite contract, allocated to this LBV flotilla. Some of the coxswains, of course, were as old as my father but they were all jolly good types and I got on with them very well.

They were called Landing Barge Vehicles because originally they'd envisioned that we'd have a loaded three-ton lorry that we would take to an enemy beach and put ashore over the ramp. But as purpose-built landing craft came into being, and I think most of them came from America, we got LCAs,

LCMs, all types of landing craft, and we then reverted to unloading stores from ship to shore because that was our basic design. We could carry perhaps eighty, ninety, even a hundred tons of stores and put them on the beach.

Able Seaman Bob Shrimpton
Asdic operator, HMS Belfast (Royal Navy Cruiser)
We went into the Clyde for some modification and we saw all these landing craft everywhere. We said, 'What are those?' because we'd never seen any before, and the petty officer said, 'They look like landing craft to me.' 'Well, where are they going?' 'Wouldn't know. Probably Italy or something.' It's only afterwards that little memories slot together and you realise just what was going on.

Leading Seaman John Tarbit
Landing Craft Assault (LCA) coxswain
Every week there was a hundred being detailed and sent to a training camp for landing craft and I got called up in this. I went down to the Chief Petty Officer in the drafting office and said, 'What are you doing? What about my naval career?' He said, 'Away you go lad, there's a war on.' So that took care of me for the next few years. I felt a bit perturbed about that, as I didn't know what to expect; I thought they only put the dropouts into Combined Operations, those that aren't good for anything else. But I enjoyed it. I automatically became a coxswain and I qualified for leading seaman at the same time. We did the training and we spent several months waiting because (a) there was nothing for us to do, there was no operations to do, and (b) there weren't enough landing craft at the time, they were still being built.

Sub Lieutenant Herbert Male
Landing Craft Tank (LCT) crew
There were so many people being required at that stage for the invasion fleet that they had an offshoot place in Lochailort, in Scotland, and I was sent there for my commission. Not only was it a school but it was a toughening-up process. It was assumed that the living conditions would be so spartan aboard landing craft that we had to be tough physically as well as mentally and they put us through assault courses, wading frozen rivers, climbing mountains, as

well as doing all our schooling for commission. There were weekly exams and if you failed you went back to sea.

Sub Lieutenant Anthony Swainson
Combined Operations

I was switched off training landing craft crews and sent with ten other guys to a very special briefing. It was behind closed doors; there was a sentry outside to keep everybody at bay. It transpired that we were to be trained to take landing craft over to Normandy with big tanks full of liquid high explosive. We would pump it into the sea, throw a charge over the side and beat it, hoping it would explode and blow up all the mines before the landing. We realised very early on that this was complete suicide. We more or less made our wills and said goodbye to everybody. We were thoroughly depressed by this.

We used to practise down near Bournemouth, on the beaches, firing these hoses into the sea. We never filled them up with liquid high explosive. Liquid high explosive was terribly volatile: if it was just touched by a bullet the whole thing would go up in flames. But Montgomery came down to see us doing a final rehearsal one day and luckily the south-west wind was blowing fairly strongly and all the hoses got intertwined with each other and he said, 'Stop, stop, stop. We'll kill more of our own troops then the enemy,' and he cancelled the whole project. But that was a job for suicide, finish, kaput; it was the most ghastly and worrying experience. But good old Monty, he stopped it on safety grounds.

Midshipman Rene Le Roy
Landing Craft Obstacle Clearance Unit

The Navy thought we must stop casualties on the initial landing. They couldn't say that the beach obstacles would be destroyed in all the bombardment so they prepared small teams which would try and cut out as much of the beach areas as possible. That was the role.

The officers and the petty officers were all volunteers but we couldn't get any men so I went down to Portsmouth barracks with Lieutenant Hargreaves to see the base commander. The defaulters all fell in, in a large assembly hall, a little bit like *The Dirty Dozen*. They were told that anybody who volunteered to join these gentlemen on special services would come out of Portsmouth prison.

An American aerial reconnaissance photograph of beach defences in Normandy taken exactly a month before D-Day. Men working on the defences can be seen lying flat and running for cover, alarmed by the sudden presence of the aircraft.

I collected twenty-six men. They all came out pasty-faced, some pimply-faced, looking quite rough. I had to take them to HMS *Dolphin* where they had to go in the thirty-foot diving chamber to see if pressure affected their ears and I lost three of them – they had trouble with their ears so they went back to barracks. Then we did a simulated escape from a submarine to see if they could face up to going in a chamber and get out of it and how they reacted. They all thought this was rather fun, you know. 'Where do we go next?' I ended up with eighteen but lost some in London who deserted. And then I took the rest of them up to Cumberland, to the demolition school.

By then they were still quite a ropey crowd of boys. They didn't want discipline, didn't want anything. And I remember the first day at the explosive school – they were all sitting at their desks – and a naval lieutenant came in, the explosives officer, and none of them stood up when he came in and I thought, 'Oh God. We're going to start off with this all the time.' But he ignored it and he said, 'Right, I'm going to talk first about how you set off an explosion. You have your explosive, your cortex, your time fuse; you have this and that.' And he was going on and on about it and you could see everybody just picking their noses, playing with their faces; they couldn't care less.

Then he said, 'Right,' and he produced a small amount of explosive and laid it on each of the desks and put the time fuses on the desks and the cortexes on the table. And he said, 'Now, gentlemen. Go out and make a bang.' And that completely changed them. They turned round and said, ''Scuse me, guv. Can you run through that again, please? Can you give another little explanation?' That was the changing point. So they went out and they all made bangs and they all came in and said, 'That was bloody marvellous!' In this two-week period they progressed to blowing up anything you could think of, including trees and safes. And there was one lad who said, 'This is like a bloody refresher course. I've been in once for this.'

They did their training down at Appledore – severe training – and they changed. You suddenly saw them become quite elite fellows. They were smart. Boots were smart. Gaiters were smart every morning on parade. They even cropped their heads because we had a lot of perspiration and it was difficult washing and I was telling them about accidents and cuts on your head and things and how it's easier to deal with shaved-head fellows. There was tremendous humour amongst them all; there were quite a few cockney types who had the most weird sense of humour. And they did respect rank from a point of view, they did understand, but they never called me 'Sir'. They called me 'Guv'. And that was strange for someone at my age, eighteen. In those days I was six foot three and used to box so I think they were rather not wanting to mix in any roughhouse or anything and I think that's how we kept discipline.

Lieutenant Ian Hammerton
Sherman Crab flail tank commander, 22nd Dragoons

We had a visit from General Hobart, who was the 79th Armoured Div's GOC. He gathered everybody round him and said, 'I have some news for you. You have heard of the Lord Mayor's Show?' And everybody's heart stopped beating. 'You know that people come round afterwards to clear up the mess? Well, your job is going to be the very opposite. You're going in front, to clear up the mess. You are going to be mine-clearers: flails.' Nobody had ever heard of them. The bottom dropped out of their world. They were stunned, absolutely stunned.

To find out how these things worked, I was sent back to my old battalion in Suffolk, who were experimenting with flails, Snakes and Scorpions and all the other strange menagerie of things, in the Orford training area, a part of Suffolk that was sealed off, highly secret. Some of the villages were evacuated, boarded up, and there they'd built replicas of the Atlantic Wall – pillboxes, bunkers, walls, minefields, wire, anti-tank ditches, the lot, full-sized – and we practised breaching them.

The Crabs were the flail tanks. The flail consisted of a number of chains offset around a long cylinder which was mounted on a jib on the front of the tank and driven direct from the tank engine. The jib could be raised or lowered by hydraulics and the driver had control of that, and at either end of the flail rotor were cutter blades for cutting through barbed wire. The chains we used to start with were rigid chains like a motorcycle chain ending in a broad chain end, so it gave it weight. That was later changed to oval chains with a heavy ball on the end. When you blew mines you might blow half a dozen before you blew the ends off the chains and then you had to stop and change them. They were simply fixed with a bolt and a split pin and we carried spare chains on the outside of the tank.

A Sherman Crab flail tank at work.

STT 9486

Trooper Joseph Ellis
Churchill Crocodile tank driver, 141st Regiment, Royal Armoured Corps

We had the Churchill tank which was converted into a flame-thrower tank. Originally the Churchill tank had a two-pounder gun and two Besa machine guns, one at the top and one at the bottom. We finished up with a Mark VII Churchill tank and a 75-millimetre gun, still a Besa in the front, a two-inch mortar and down at the bottom they took the Besa out and put a flame gun in. This was attached up to a trailer with pipes underneath, thick rubber reinforced pipes, and the trailer was fixed on the back with an elbow joint and filled up with 150 gallons of flame-throwing fuel, which was a mixture of soap, petrol and rubber. Petrol burns, soap spreads and rubber sticks, so if you got it on any part of your clothes and you tried to get it off it would stick to another part. Only way you can get it out is for somebody to roll you on the floor and douse it completely. If you switched it on to work as a flame gun, when the fuel came through, it ignited and it went 180 yards.

Major Allan Younger
Commanding officer, 26th Assault Squadron, Royal Engineers

Our role, as with all the other assault squadron roles, was to land in front of other troops on the beaches in order to clear away obstacles and enable particularly tanks following behind to keep up with the infantry and go on inland and take the proper bridgehead. In each squadron we had four troops. Each troop contained six AVREs, Assault Vehicles Royal Engineers, and on those AVREs were various improvisations for getting over or through whatever obstacles we expected to meet.

These improvisations included a thing called a fascine, which was a huge bundle of chestnut paling about ten or twelve feet across; it was held on a little ramp in front of the tank and could be released and fill up a ditch. It included an assault bridge, which could be dropped and then the tank could go up it, and so on. We had a thing called a Petard, which was a code name for a spigot mortar, which fired a charge of about twenty-five pounds a limited distance; I think about fifty yards was the maximum range. The object of this was to break up concrete, so that if you met a wall, for instance, and you couldn't get over it in any other way, you could smash it down.

We were all very new to driving tanks around. We got a draft of drivers from the Royal Armoured Corps who had driven tanks before and so this got us off to a good start; and they were good lads, too. To start with we had to practise the launching of these obstacles, the command of tanks, use of wireless, keeping together and so on. Then we started to do assault landings, both to get to know the naval people who would take us and also to do some practice in that type of warfare which none of us had ever done before.

We did the first of these in the winter in Scotland. We were based on Fort George, Inverness, and we did, I think, two quite major assaults on beaches along the coast there. The navy took us somewhere out into the North Sea in mid-winter, it wasn't a particularly attractive experience, and then back towards the coast during the night and we landed about dawn on some isolated beach area of Elgin.

Most of these were pretty catastrophic exercises, all sorts of things went wrong, but we were learning. Vehicles broke down. Coming off a landing craft when the sea is rough isn't particularly easy and sometimes we'd get a vehicle, an AVRE, broken down in the actual entrance of the landing craft, LCT, and it had to be towed off and so on. We would launch our bridge against something or other and the bridge would slip. I remember one tank climbing up one of the bridges fell off and turned upside down and I think a couple of chaps got quite badly hurt doing that. But we were learning all the time and getting better. And by the time D-Day came around we were really quite good.

Trooper Ronald Mole
Sherman tank gunner/wireless operator, 4th/7th Royal Dragoon Guards
We were moved out to a gorgeous place called Fritton and that was where we got the first feel of the DD tank. This had a canvas screen that was inflated with two oxygen bottles which were located in the bow of the Sherman, four metal struts, two either side, and thirty-two air bags which were inflated at two thousand pounds' pressure per square inch. There were two brass propellers at the back of the Sherman and when a button was pressed these dropped and engaged the drive and once you were in the water you could steer thirty starboard, thirty port, just as if you were in a craft.

Corporal Patrick Hennessy
Sherman tank commander, 13th/18th Hussars
The big problem with the DD tank is that if that screen gets holed then that tank will surely sink because there is nothing to keep it up and you've got

Royal Engineers train at clearing paths through bays of replica enemy 'Element C' obstacles (also known as Belgian Gates).

thirty-two tons of metal sitting there. The slightest accident to that screen would let the water gush in and the tank would sink. So we went down to Gosport, to the submarine school down there, and the submariners decided to teach us how to escape from a sunken vessel.

Well, the Royal Navy used something called the Davis Escape Apparatus. It's a fairly large, bulky piece of equipment stuck to the chest and they found this useful in escaping from sunken submarines. But the Davis Escape Apparatus wouldn't do for us because we couldn't get through the hatch so they invented a new thing known as the Amphibious Tank Escape Apparatus. It worked on the same principle, which was a bag on the chest, an air bottle on the back, nose-clips, goggles and a mouthpiece. They told us how to use this and taught us all the dangers of coming up from depth too quick: the bends and this sort of thing.

The grand finale of this training came two days later when they took us into a building where there was a large pit dug in the earth some forty feet deep. At the bottom of the pit stood a tank, a Valentine tank in those days, and down the side of the pit was a ladder. Wearing only our denims and gym shoes and with our escape apparatus, we went down the ladder, walked across to the tank and got in and took up our crew positions: the driver in his seat, the gunner in his, etc. etc. and we had a naval instructor with us.

Now, as we sat there, sluice gates were opened and water came pouring in and we were told to sit where we were quite calmly and we were not allowed to put on the breathing apparatus until the water had hit chest height. When this happened we put in the mouthpiece, pulled down the goggles and put on the nose-clip and began breathing as the water rose above us. We had to sit there until the instructor told us to move and all the time the water rose until we were sitting under forty foot of water. Then, one by one, we received the signal and calmly and quietly, so the book says, each man came up through the hatch and went to the top and climbed out.

If a tank should sink the heaviest part of that tank is the turret and it seems obvious that the turret would sink down to the bottom tracks-up; and if that should happen, of course, there is no possibility of getting out of the hatch. Nevertheless, this is what we were given, this is what we were trained on and I suppose the civil servants were pleased to say, 'We've given you an escape. What are you worried about?' Of course, it wouldn't work in practice. And in practice, when tanks did sink, I never heard about one man who escaped.

Above and below: A Sherman Duplex-Drive (DD) tank with its screens lowered and raised.

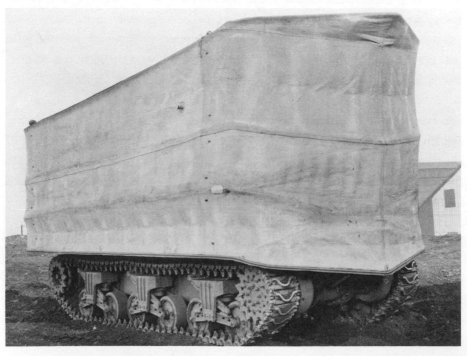

Captain John Semken
Sherman tank commander, Sherwood Rangers

We found ourselves with a very ugly sort of mutiny developing, which took the form of people saying that they couldn't muster the courage to do these trips in escape apparatus, they couldn't bring themselves to do it and so on. Like all mutinies the thing was smoothed over and the chaps became reconciled to it.

Trooper Ronald Mole
Sherman tank gunner/wireless operator, 4th/7th Royal Dragoon Guards

Once we felt fairly confident, or at least it was decided that we were competent, we moved down to Fort Monkton at Gosport and did our first sea operation from Stokes Bay. It was a night swim and we slipped into the water and travelled about three miles up the Solent in line ahead. All one could see was a small red and green light as you were following the vehicle in front, about ten, fifteen yards behind. When that light started to disappear, obviously they were turning, so we were looking then for a little white light on the beach and you turned in and homed in on that. But it was rather a hair-raising experience in the dark, first time at night, up to your knees in water, because these craft were very blunt nosed – they didn't ride the wave, they just bumped into it – and of course water came over the top and the poor old driver down below was getting electric shocks because he had a twelve-volt battery by his elbow. That was our initiation to a night swim.

Private Frederick Perkins
5th Battalion, Royal Berkshire Regiment, attached to 3rd Canadian Division

We were training with the 'Funnies': the flails, the Crocodiles, the tanks with bridging on them, tanks with great rolls of wooden bobbins which they dropped in ditches and went straight over the top of them. All those kind of 'Funnies' were brought in and as soon as they arrived they were covered over with canvas sheets so that the public couldn't see them. The public were actually ordered to have all their blinds drawn and if they had to go to work they had to be gone to work before the exercises started: it was all top secret, the 'Funnies'. The DD tanks, the Duplex-Drives, the swimming tanks, they came in as well. Even us infantry didn't know what the DD tanks were. So when we saw them, we thought, 'What is this, monsters coming out of the sea? Tanks swimming?' We couldn't believe it, really.

Major David Warren
1st Battalion, Royal Hampshire Regiment

We prepared ourselves by going to the Combined Training area at Inverary in Scotland where we learned the various techniques of landing from assault craft and so on. Having carried out two assault landings before, one in Sicily, one in Italy, the naval side of it was familiar. We did know about landing craft and how to travel in them and how to get out and so on.

Sergeant James Bellows
1st Battalion, Royal Hampshire Regiment

We were the most experienced men in the British Army on invasion training and the instructors were all men who had never left the country. It was really funny. I had to take my signallers down for a lecture and leave them in this Nissen hut with a corporal from the Royal Corps of Signals and when I came to collect them this poor corporal is nearly in tears. I said, 'What's the matter?' He said, 'Your men have been taking the mickey out of me, sergeant.' I said, 'Why? What happened?' He said, 'When I started to teach them about waterproofing their sets, they started laughing.' I said, 'Well, that's understandable,' and I told him what they'd actually done. He said, 'And I'm supposed to tell them what to do?' I said, 'All the equipment you've got here, they've used in action. Not once. Twice.' 'Well, sergeant,' he said. 'I'd appreciate it very much if you'd let them teach me.' Which is what they did for the remainder of the time in Inverary. One of the things they taught him was how to waterproof a pocket watch and still tell the time. He said, 'Well, how do you do that?' All you do is get a French letter, as they were called in them days, put your watch in, get the air out, tie a knot and there you've got your watch waterproofed and you can still tell the time. Simple little things and he appreciated it.

Lieutenant David Wood
2nd Battalion, Oxfordshire and Buckinghamshire Light Infantry

It was a time when everybody was trying to inspire us with military thoughts. When you went on to the assault course, people screamed, 'Remember Hong

Kong!' or 'Remember Singapore!' And at one stage, but not when we were there, they had buckets of entrails and the like, so that you actually had blood splashed on you and you felt even more aggressive than you otherwise might have done.

Brigadier The Lord Lovat
Commanding officer, 1st Special Service Brigade
A demonstration was laid on where the brigade landed at Angmering and fought their way across very difficult country. We landed under smoke in the same craft as the ones we actually went ashore with on D-Day. This is rather an important point as you've got to know the sailors as well as yourself, the sailor being responsible for getting you ashore, and if you aren't in complete tune there can be misunderstandings. Anyway, we landed on the coast at Angmering in three waves under the cover of smoke launched from two-inch mortars and swept inland and did it very quickly. I remember the third wave that came in seized all the cars of the spectators. They reckoned they were getting rather far behind in the sweeping inland movement, seized the cars, much to the rage of the drivers and the people who owned them, and formed a mobile column that followed the main advance, which had to cross the Arun below Arundel Castle and get to the gap in the Downs above the town. And this we managed to do in a very much shorter time than was generally expected. It was a good thing of its kind and it surprised the brass hats in the War Office who came down to watch the whole affair, although there were a good deal of hard feelings as smoke bombs fell among the higher generals.

Sapper Thomas Finigan
85th Field Company, Royal Engineers
There were quite a few accidents during the training. I remember a particular occasion when we were carrying Bangalore torpedoes ashore. A Bangalore torpedo is a two-inch pipe, roughly about ten to twelve foot long, full of explosives, and that was pushed through a barbed wire entanglement and you set it off and it used to blow the wire apart. We had an infantry battalion of the King's Liverpool Irish who used to look after us – once sappers are in minefields and you're under fire you have to have someone to protect you, you don't take your arms into a minefield – and we were on the beach for about ten days and one of these Bangalore torpedoes went up and it killed several

men. We were getting up in the morning and having our wash when it went off. It was a matter of about a hundred yards down and it was quite gruesome. What came out in the inquiry was that they were using it over a fire when they were boiling their water in cans, they were using it as a support over the fire. I think there were seventeen that died.

Lance Corporal Alan Carter
6th Battalion, Green Howards
We were on this invasion training and our artillery were firing. I was going up this slope, there was a bloke in front of me and the rest of the blokes were behind me, and the artillery fired a shell and it dropped short. It caught this lad, shrapnel in his arm; and off went my steel helmet on to the ground. I picked it up, put it on, never looking at it, and turned round to the rest of the blokes and said, 'Who the hell's buggering about here?' I thought they'd thrown a grenade or something. And I looked at one bloke and he had a face of horror, open-mouthed. He said, 'You'll never get killed in France. Look at your steel helmet.' I took it off and there was a hole where a bit of shrapnel had gone that you could get your fist through.

Captain John Sim
12th Battalion, Parachute Regiment
We were out on two nightly exercises a week, moving about the countryside, lugging our equipment, attacking positions, digging in, and we had quite a number of parachute exercises which was good. The aircraft were available, all sorts of aircraft, and we had battalion night drops in the Salisbury Plain area and the odd brigade exercise as well, so we were really put through our paces. One of the hardest physical tests we all had to go through, even the CO, was a fifty-mile march in full fighting order carrying all our equipment, all our weapons, our mortar shells and so on, fifty miles within twenty-four hours. The average was twenty-two hours. Our morale was high: this tremendous adventure coming towards us.

Private Philip Crofts
7th Battalion, Parachute Regiment
We did constant cross-country runs, constant route marches, constant road run-and-walks, constant manoeuvres. We did very little parade-square drill.

Practically the only drill we did was battle drill. We were always doing something. Everything seemed to be geared up for one purpose. It was the most intense period of training I've ever had in my life for anything.

Private Ernest Rooke-Matthews
9th Battalion, Parachute Regiment

As time went on we got to the point where we started doing training on specific tasks: attacking a bridge, defending a hillside, attacking a battery. All the different things that might well have come. Then we went on a special exercise where they had actually constructed a mock battery at a place called Inkpen and we were doing night attacks on this battery. And that – we didn't know then, of course – was what the powers that be had decided would be one of the major tasks.

Private Harry Clarke
2nd Battalion, Oxfordshire and Buckinghamshire Light Infantry

We attacked so many bridges at night that we formed the opinion then that we would be attacking a bridge at night. It became so fixed in our minds. This went on for some months and finally we went to Exeter for ten days where we practised countless times each day. We formed up in platoons to simulate glider landings and we attacked a bridge. Each time we took a different position so that we were ready to take on any role should we land out of turn. If we were first to land, we would take the bridge. Second to land would take on the inner defences. Third to land would rush over the bridge and reinforce the first platoon. And this went on for eight to ten days and we were thoroughly sick of it at the end because we'd continued to do it until we were absolutely perfect in every detail. At that time of course we did not know what it was all about but we had a good idea that it was for the invasion.

Aircraftwoman Ivy Button
Parachute packer and repairer, Women's Auxiliary Air Force

At Ringway we were packing the parachutes for the paratroops when they were going to invade. When we first started we didn't have to do it so fast. But of course when they were getting ready to invade France they were training hundreds of men. We first did about eight an hour but then, as they were training all these men, they sort of kept on increasing the amount until we were rushing all the time. And by the time we'd done, oh, eighteen an hour, we all felt that you just couldn't put your mind to it as exactly as you should. We didn't feel we should have had that responsibility. So when they tried to put it up more we all got together and said we didn't want to do it. We didn't feel we should be responsible for maybe causing somebody's death by a parachute not opening. So we stuck to our guns and the CO agreed with us in the end.

Sergeant Bob Rose
Glider Pilot Regiment
We had to do the PR job where we went round the factory and talked to all the workers in the factory. 'These are the boys who are going to fly your aeroplanes,' and all the rest of it, and we were making dates with these girls but we never went back there again. Then we'd go in the MD's office and have a small whisky. 'Small whiskies for fliers,' he used to say. Then we'd collect the brand new aircraft.

Sub Lieutenant Roderick Braybrooke
LCT crew
We were training with British troops, picking them up from Southampton, loading and going across to Studland Bay because the beach at Studland was similar to what we could expect the other side. I think it was Churchill tanks, mainly, we were taking and dropping off and they'd go on up the beach. This was an ongoing thing.

Corporal John Lanes
Sherman tank commander, Sherwood Rangers
We used to sail down and land on Hayling Island. We did that two or three times. They wouldn't allow the tanks to go inland, they just used to get out of the craft and on to the beach and stay there, so whenever we went somebody would always bring a football and we'd have a kick-about. We were having a kick-about one day on the beach, because there was nothing we could do, and a brigadier came up and said, 'What do you think you're doing? Don't you realise there's a war on?' We'd just come back from Africa after four years.

United States troops disembarking from Landing Craft Assault (LCAs) during combined Anglo-American invasion manoeuvres on the Devon coast.

Commander Felix Lloyd-Davies
HMS Glasgow (Royal Navy cruiser)

We started carrying out bombardment practices off the south coast of Devon which were live practices carried out mainly by American troops to practise the landings for Normandy. Part of the south coast was evacuated and we opened fire with live ammunition over their heads and undoubtedly it helped them a lot.

Betty Tabb
Civilian, Slapton, Devon

My sister heard the rumour in the shop when she went to get some groceries and she said to Mum that we were all going to have to move and of course Mum says, 'That's nonsense talking like that. Where we going to go?' And she says that's what she heard in the shop. There was a meeting called then in the village hall and that confirmed that there was going to be an evacuation of the area for the American training.

My parents just couldn't believe it. I mean, Mum just said, 'Well, no, it's not going to happen because it can't. What are we going to do? Where are we going to go?' But it had to be so. So, of course, everybody had to get their thinking caps on and think, 'Well, where are we going to go?' If you couldn't get anything yourself the authorities would help but they did want you to try and get yourself fixed up, if possible, because, as you can imagine, there were hundreds trying to move. Thousands, I suppose, really. Quite an area it was.

Ordinary Seaman Leslie Tabb
Royal Navy seaman from Slapton, Devon

There wasn't a lot of damage done to the village, structural damage. I think the church got knocked about a bit. There might've been one or two corners of houses knocked off by tanks. There was a lot of looting went on. You might wonder what there was left to loot but a lot of people left things behind. When they went away, they thought, 'Oh, we'll be back again in a while.' So, if there was anything that they could do without, they'd left it stored in a cupboard under the stairs and thought, 'Oh, well, it'll still be there when I come back.' I think the people that done the looting were the people who'd come to rebuild and paint the places, not the Americans. I can't see what the Americans would've wanted with what people left, old ornaments and whatever, you know. Not when they were going to war.

Slapton parish church, Devon. When the village and surrounding area were evacuated to permit training exercises in preparation for D-Day, churches and historic monuments were padlocked, ringed with barbed wire and designated out of bounds. To further identify this church as 'untouchable', a white strip, visible here, was painted on the roof.

Sergeant Edwin Sinclair
Instructor, 12th Field Training Regiment, Royal Artillery

We were doing exercises which obviously pointed to an invasion. The Second Front was on everybody's tongue; the politicians were talking about it. We were getting pep talks from generals and various other people; we were meeting in cinemas all over the country periodically for pep talks. One general said, 'The war's a fucker; everybody thinks it's a fucker. Monty's a fucker but Monty's the fucker who can finish the fucker.' That was told to us on the stage of one of the cinemas where we attended one of these pep talks; some general came out with it. I thought myself it was a fairly apt saying for the time.

I think the general attitude of the British Army was that with American support – we could not have done it on our own – we could definitely invade Europe and we could actually beat the Germans. Up to then we'd been having rather a hard time. We were practically scrambling our way up Italy and places like that and the Germans were holding us in various places. Stalin was pushing forward with the Russian Army. But at that time I think the anticipation of the Second Front had been built up. I think everybody was more or less ready to go. I'm not going to say that if somebody had come up to me and said, 'Would you volunteer to go and open the Second Front?' that I'd have jumped in. Personally I was willing to go along with the rest if we were ready. And the people who were in charge of us then were a different brand of people from the people who were in charge of us at the beginning of the war – we'd pulled Monty back into England for the Second Front. Most of the troops had great confidence in their leaders at that time. I know I had that feeling that if we've got to do it, let's go and do it.

Major Peter Martin
2nd Battalion, Cheshire Regiment

All the officers had to assemble one day in a cinema and General Graham, who Monty used to refer to as 'A gallant old warhorse' and was a delightful person, stood up and addressed us. He said Monty had been in grave doubt as to whether the 50th or the 51st Highland Division should be one of the initial assault divisions in the invasion of Europe and, in the end, Monty had tossed for it and he, General Graham, was delighted to say that Fifty Div had won and would therefore have the very great honour of leading the invasion of

Europe. Whereupon there was a colossal boo from all around the cinema. I felt really quite sorry for General Graham but I think the division felt it had done its stuff by now and that it was time somebody else took a turn. We couldn't really see why we should be the spearhead when there were so many divisions in the United Kingdom who had not seen a shot fired so far. However, we consoled ourselves with the thought that good old Fifty Div, veterans of the Sicily landings, were of course the obvious ones to select if you wanted to guarantee a successful landing.

Private Richard Atkinson
9th Battalion, Durham Light Infantry
There was a lot of moaning went on. 'Not fair. Not again. How about somebody else having a go?' Things like that. But the usual soldiers' moan and we knew we had to get on with it. There's nothing we could do.

Sergeant John Clegg
Centaur tank crew, 1st Royal Marine Armoured Support Regiment
The British Fifty Div had been brought back and most of them hadn't been given any leave. The thing that you could see on the side of their lorries as they went down the road was: 'No Leave, No Second Front.' I don't know whether they did eventually get any leave or not but that was their slogan. One couldn't blame them, really. I mean, they'd done their job in Italy and North Africa. To think that the Second Front was looming and they were going to be involved in that without leave, at least. One can imagine, you know, telephoning your wife or sending a card saying, 'I'm in England but I'm not going to be able to see you.' So of course it wasn't fair. But life has never been fair.

Sergeant Joe Stevens
33rd Field Regiment, Royal Artillery
Montgomery visited us at Hawick and prior to his coming we were all paraded. The surveyors put out white lines of tape, we all stood on the tape, the divisional commander came on to the parade ground as though he was Monty and went down the whole line of senior officers shaking hands. The next day we were taken out again, we were all lined up on the tapes, and before Monty arrived the tapes were all taken away.

Then Montgomery came on to the parade in a jeep and stood on the bonnet and he said, 'Gather round me, men.' He didn't shake hands with anybody and we all pushed forward and knocked the brigadiers and the brass hats all out of the way. He said, 'Look upon me like a boxing promoter. And if I were to tell you that you were going into a fight and it was going to be a walkover, I would ill-advise you. But we're going to Europe, everybody knows we're going to Europe; the Germans know we're going to Europe but they don't know when and where and this will be the deciding factor. I wish you all luck.' And then he left the parade. He looked as though he were talking to me. He was talking to everybody, I know, but he looked as though he were talking to me.

Corporal Reginald Spittles
Cromwell tank commander, 2nd Northamptonshire Yeomanry
We had to go and see Monty to give us a pep talk. We was at Rudston village and they lorried us over to this area. He finished off by saying that we would be going on to Germany. 'It will be just like cricket,' he said. 'We're going to knock them for six.' And a little voice behind me said, 'I hope the buggers know this.'

Private Richard Atkinson
9th Battalion, Durham Light Infantry
He'd give you a few fags and spoke to two or three people but he was a general who'd come amongst you, which I'd never seen. They were usually distant figures. He was able to bring everything down to our level and I think we appreciated it, actually. Another thing he did, he wouldn't make a move unless he had everything he thought was necessary: guns, trucks, everything. And that gave you a little bit of comfort. There was no haphazard, half-cocked business. You knew you had a fighting chance, let's put it that way.

Brigadier Sir Alexander Stanier
Commanding Officer, 231st Infantry Brigade
He was marvellous at contacting the troops and I think that's what a commander must do, because if you don't get the men to stand and fight you won't win the battle, however brilliant the plan is.

H 38644

General Sir Bernard Montgomery, commander of all Allied ground forces for the invasion, inspecting and speaking to troops in the spring of 1944.

H 38645

Corporal Andrew Jones
1st/5th Battalion, Queen's Royal Regiment
He liked his training. I think with all the training and what happened afterwards we owe him a great debt. He didn't send us into battles in which he knew there was going to be a great lot of casualties. I don't think he wanted to see things that had happened to him in World War One.

Captain Julius Neave
Sherman tank commander, 13th/18th Hussars
He had a sort of maddening attitude from my point of view in that he knew perfectly well that the loyalty of the officers was absolutely unquestioned but he had to curry favour with the troops in some way or the other which he did by making, as far as he could, the officers look foolish. I found that a very irritating trait. This was demonstrated on this occasion when he did arrive extremely late and found the whole of the garrison of Fort George, which was very considerable, drawn up in serried ranks. He announced in a loud voice that it wasn't what he wanted at all and everyone was to break ranks and gather round his jeep and he would stand on the top. And I knew perfectly well that if we'd been a rabble waiting for him to arrive there would have been the most frightful criticism: 'What is this rabble hanging around and waiting?' In the same way, he would, quite uncharacteristically for a very ascetic man, hand out and throw cigarettes and things out of his car at the troops in a way which I found really rather ostentatiously objectionable. But one forgave him because he was so successful. I think success was the measure. The troops wouldn't have liked him if they'd been unsuccessful.

Driver Roy Hamlyn
282 Company, Royal Army Service Corps, attached to 3rd Canadian Division
The 3rd Canadian Division was lined up on three sides of this enormous great field, drawn up on three sides, and then beheld some of the great generals of the time, Canadians especially, and then King George VI came along. I was quite shocked to see him because he looked a very sick man. Obviously he had been made to look a little bit better than what he really was, with make-up or whatever it is they use, but he was evidently a very sick man. He didn't look left or right but just went through the motions of passing through us.

Major George Chambers
8th Battalion, Durham Light Infantry

We had another inspection. We didn't know who it was, we had no idea, we weren't told, and we were drawn up in these squares awaiting the inspection. The usual thing, of course: you got into the square about half-past eight in the morning and at about half-past ten the general or whoever was coming would arrive so you were standing there, doing nothing, getting bored stiff. And what should come but one great big car with one man inside. No outriders; not like the way Monty had come with his posse of outriders, etc. And out of this car stepped Eisenhower, who then did a Monty – called everyone around – and proceeded to address the troops. At this stage the troops were bored stiff and had had all this so many times before. But, you know, at the end of this speech that Ike gave, the troops burst into spontaneous applause, which was tremendous praise of the man. His personality had got across to the troops. They were a bored and bolshie lot at that particular time.

Company Sergeant Major William Brown
8th Battalion, Durham Light Infantry

He was great. The finest general that ever was, General Ike. There was no bullshit at all about him, you know. But he was immaculate. You'd have thought he was cut out of chocolate.

OPERATION TIGER: THE SLAPTON SANDS DISASTER

Telegraphist Derek Wellman
HMS Onslow (Royal Navy destroyer)

There were various major exercises before the invasion proper. There were three in all, I think. Operation Tiger was one of them and it hasn't received much publicity although it was one of the most disastrous of the war.

We were meant to cover the area where the rehearsal was taking place, which was at Slapton Sands in Devon, though the area covered was mostly in Lyme Bay which stretched from Portland Bill all the way into Plymouth Command, and we were looking for E-boats. The VHF DF [Direction-Finding] operation had moved from U-boat frequencies to E-boat frequencies, but we didn't have much success with them. By and large E-Boats did far less

HM Queen Elizabeth during the Royal Inspection of the 6th Airborne Division, spring 1944.

Standing beside Brigadier James Hill, HRH Princess Elizabeth watches a demonstration parachute jump during the Royal Inspection of the 6th Airborne Division, spring 1944.

communicating by wireless. Occasionally they communicated by radio but only for a few seconds and we weren't in quite the same business of getting bearings and so on of E-boats because they moved very rapidly. We had encountered quite a few of them even before this particular action and tried to keep them at bay.

The disaster occurred because of the two close escorts provided by the Royal Navy: one of them collided with an LST leaving harbour and it was ordered to go back to Devonport for repair and a substitute wasn't provided. In my view that's fairly conclusive as to why the E-boats, who came across the Channel round about the Plymouth area, were able to follow along the coast and get to the stern of this convoy of LSTs without being spotted or driven off. And of course they played havoc, sank two LSTs and set a third on fire and so on.

Peter Nevill
Beaufighter night-fighter pilot, RAF
The 27 April 1944 was my twentieth birthday and this happened at 2.15 the next morning, so I took off on my birthday and this happened the next morning. When I went out on my patrol I saw a lot of landing craft heading towards Lyme Bay. They were on their way into the bay from various places along the coast for this exercise. This exercise was to practise landing tanks and lorries and stores, so these landing craft were all loaded up with these things and the idea was that they would offload them at Slapton Sands in South Devon.

I'd already been told to keep clear because there was an exercise on. Well, we went as far as Start Point and realised that all hell was being let loose in Lyme Bay. There was a ship on fire; there were tracer shells flying in all directions. And I got on to control, 'Hey, there's something wrong happening here. They need help.' They said, 'Keep away, it's an exercise.' I said, 'My God, if it's an exercise, it's an exercise that's really gone wrong,' but I was told to keep away. So what we did instead, we went to the entrance of the bay and looked in to see what was happening, and we realised that there were E-boats in amongst the landing craft.

Ordinary Seaman John Capon
HMS Obedient (Royal Navy destroyer)
On 28 April we was out in the Channel, clearing up. We'd just come on morning watch, we'd come on at midnight, just an ordinary patrol, and I was looking over the side of the pom-pom deck, leaning against the rails, and I saw two orange balls of flame. I says to Wiggy Bennett, and these are the exact words, "'Ere, Wig. Some poor bastard's copped it over there.' And then all of a sudden the sound came back, 'Boom! Boom!' Then we saw tracer. He said,

'Oh, it's an exercise. They're doing it on Lyme Bay.'
Before the morning came we were put at action stations. And then Irwin, he phoned up Dover and told them about it and they said to us, 'Hold your stations'. Irwin wanted to go in to help, he wanted to go in and do what he could, but they said, 'Hold your stations'. And it was just breaking dawn and I looked around and you couldn't see anywhere without a body, without a Yankee turned upside down, dead. There was hundreds and hundreds of bodies.

And all of a sudden comes a chug-chug-chug and up come these seven E-boats. They came up our port side, opened up with their small machine guns, a couple hit our side, and then they came round our bow and down our starboard side, firing their machine guns all the time. We got a couple off but we couldn't lay the guns because we were that close, but once they started getting away we opened fire with the pom-poms. One of them we did catch, we literally carved the bridge off that with the pom-pom, but it was still going, it still joined the others, and away they went.

That was Slapton Sands and that was the most bodies I have ever, ever seen. As far as the eye could see there was bodies. We did pick up one alive. They laid him on the wardroom table and he just popped off of hypothermia. They stripped him off, covered him up with a blanket and that, but he died, poor sod. I can see him now. Good-looking kid. They were only kids. But then again, we were all kids, weren't we?

Able Seaman James Henry Morgan
HMS Onslow (Royal Navy destroyer)
There was a low mist on the water, a two-foot mist, and what they did, they asked for volunteers to go and pick survivors up. So we went, me and this Harris, in the cutter, a stoker and three seamen, and we brought eight back

and then we brought seven back the second time. We were pulling them out, these Yanks. Then they laid the dead bodies out on the galley flats and in front of witnesses they cleared their pockets out of their cash and their identification and all that lot. Even those that were alive we took their money and all that lot off them and we dried it for them, dried all the money for them, and when we brought them back into Portland they took all the dead off. The survivors that could walk marched off.

Telegraphist Derek Wellman
HMS Onslow (Royal Navy destroyer)

We had a number of coffins come on board. They were placed in the coffins and taken off. But the event that stuck in my mind was that the Officer Commanding cleared lower deck, which meant that he had everybody who wasn't on watch round him, and came up with the most extraordinary statement. He said, 'You're not to speak of this event, of what's transpired tonight, not just for the rest of the war but for the rest of your natural lives.' Which struck me as very odd – the use of words more commonly used by judges than anybody else – and I imagined he was reading from some directive that he had. As might be expected, we respected this confidence. Because, obviously, it would have a devastating effect on American morale to know that over 750 of their men, mostly young people of my own age, nineteen, twenty, who had never known anything about warfare, in fact had only recently landed in Britain, had died simultaneously.

Peter Nevill
Beaufighter night-fighter pilot, RAF

We followed two E-boats, which we hoped would be the ones we'd seen before. They went into Cherbourg harbour and we followed in and gave them some rockets. I'm not sure whether we hit them or not. Then we had to get out, quick. The Germans suddenly woke up and all the guns in Cherbourg seemed to be firing at us. We went like hell out of it. Nothing followed us, it seemed, and we got back to base. We had been damaged: we lost a flap on the wing.

We reported and went and had our breakfast and then went to bed. Round about 10.30 in the morning we were woken to go and see the officer in charge. He said he'd reported what had happened and we were told that in no way were we ever to talk about anything that had happened because the Americans wanted to keep it quiet.

Later, whilst I was in hospital, my navigator came to see me and said that they'd taken away my logbook and his logbook. They must have shredded them. That's a terrible thing to do, to take a bloke's logbook away. I mean, they could have taken a couple of pages out, but they destroyed the whole thing.

Countdown

*If there ever were a word, it was 'armada'. I don't know what the
Spanish Armada was like; it must've been a fearful sight.*

By the middle of May 1944, units in Britain earmarked for the invasion
had moved into camps close to airfields and ports. At one minute to
midnight on the evening of 25 May, every camp was simultaneously sealed:
barbed wire went up, guards patrolled the perimeter, nobody was allowed in
or out. During the next few days each unit was briefed on its D-Day tasks.
Then, with the date of the invasion set for 5 June, thousands of men and
vehicles bound for the seaborne assault began to leave the camps for the
south coast ports. Many units were already embarked and at sea when news
came through that the operation was postponed: conditions in the Channel
were too rough. Twenty-four hours later, Eisenhower ordered the invasion
to proceed on 6 June. The waiting was over.

THE CAMPS

Pilot Officer Ron Minchin
Australian Stirling bomber pilot, 196 Squadron, RAF
We knew that our end result was D-Day; we knew that we were training for
D-Day. We were actually getting bigger and bigger exercises with more and
more planes, more and more squadrons, more and more troops, more
and more gliders. And eventually we got up to a point where 38 Group did a
whole exercise full of paratroopers, with gliders, simulating what we'd be
doing eventually on D-Day. And as D-Day approached, of course, the
concentration told us it wasn't far away. It was pretty easy to see, when we

were flying round England, the build-up on the south coast. And there were fighters galore in the air all the time just in case there were any enemy aircraft, to try and keep them away from everything and not see.

Private Frederick Perkins
5th Battalion, Royal Berkshire Regiment, attached to 3rd Canadian Division
The south coast was just unimaginable, really. There were so many lorries, so many men assembled in an area, say, from Dover right the way to Devon, to Slapton Sands, to Brixham. It was just one vast marshalling area of men and materials all the way along.

The marshalling areas were very adjacent to the ports: Portsmouth, Southampton. I myself was in a transit camp to the east of Waterlooville. We were in a pine forest and the tents were pitched among the pine forest. There were thousands of these camps around, it seemed, all handling different divisions.

When we came into the marshalling areas, round about April, we started to get good contact with the Canadians. We made friends with the Canadians and they knew us as their beach group. They made a very, very good impression. We knew they were coming from famous regiments, like the Regina Rifles, the Chaudière Regiment, the Royal Winnipeg Rifles, the Queen's Own Rifles of Canada. The Canadians had taken a heavy toll of casualties at Dieppe and we knew they were going to give a good account of themselves in Normandy.

Sergeant Joe Stevens
33rd Field Regiment, Royal Artillery
We went out on an exercise there and, on returning, Major Wise said, 'Stevens, order them back to the camp.' I put it out on the radio – 'Tell them to get back to camp' – and he said to me, 'Stevens, when we go back into the camp, we're not coming out again, so we'll go and have a beer.' We went into a local pub and as we went in he said, 'Stevens, do you play "Shove Halfpenny"?' Not 'Shove Ha'penny!' I said, 'Yes, sir,' and he said, 'Well, you'd better, because we're taking on the locals.' We had a few hours in there and enjoyed ourselves and then went back to camp.

Armoured vehicles await collection prior to the opening of the Second Front. The figure in the foreground sitting on the wheel-arch with her back to the camera is an ATS mechanic.

Sergeant Edward Wallace
86th Field Regiment, Royal Artillery
All of a sudden barbed wire appeared all the way around the camp. Red caps, blue caps with dogs, patrolling outside. Nobody was allowed to leave, nobody could come in.

Leading Telegraphist Alan Winstanley
Combined Operations Bombardment Unit
If I remember rightly there were a number of civilians in the camp who just got caught in it because they were delivering or doing something and that was their hard luck, they were sealed in like the rest of us. Same with the NAAFI personnel, because most of the NAAFI personnel were locals. They were not allowed to go back home: once the camp was sealed, that was it for them as well. Telephone calls were absolutely out of the question. Letters could be written but naturally they went into the military post-box.

Sergeant Kenneth Lakeman
Royal Corps of Signals
One of our fellows applied for compassionate leave. His mother was seriously ill, in fact she died eventually, but they wouldn't let him out.

Trooper Eric Smith
5th Royal Tank Regiment
You had the odd character who always managed to get out. One or two of our, say, militant characters went into Ipswich overnight and stole bicycles and came back to camp with the bike. The next morning on parade the sergeant major said, 'There was a bit of trouble in Ipswich last night. Some of you characters disobeyed orders and went into Ipswich and the police are coming today to identify you. So those who took part, don't come on parade.' They were terrible, really. Feared nothing. I suppose they'd been through so much, they thought, 'Well, if they put us inside, we'll still be alive. Stick us in prison, doesn't matter.'

Private Jack Forster
6th Battalion, Durham Light Infantry
Instead of having British guards, we had Americans patrolling outside the wire. Well, that upset us. If they'd been British guards I think we might have

not grumbled, you know, but when there's Americans walking by! God knows, we didn't like that.

Private Frederick Perkins
5th Battalion, Royal Berkshire Regiment, attached to 3rd Canadian Division

We knew we were on top security and it was imminent. What made it more imminent was that they decided to get rid of the forage caps we wore and gave us a beret, a khaki beret. They said, 'This stays on your head better when you're running.' They were absolutely right but the berets looked hideous as a military headdress. Then, leading up to D-Day itself, we had what they called the Normandy haircut. That was all off the head, hair taken right off to within a quarter of an inch all over, something like a crew cut. This was to prevent the spread of lice when you couldn't wash. So we went to the barbers and we looked a sight. Everyone was shorn off, like shearing sheep.

Sapper Thomas Finigan
85th Field Company, Royal Engineers

We had a lot of entertainment. We had rather large marquees with twenty-four hours a day film shows. They were on all the time and the films that we saw were before they were released to the general public, they came straight over from America. I think I saw *Going My Way* with Bing Crosby about twelve times. They had several tents with different films going on but that was one film I always liked.

Trooper Ronald Mole
Sherman tank gunner/wireless operator, 4th/7th Royal Dragoon Guards

We had a visit from Charlie Chester and his Stars in Battledress and that I shall never forget. By then, as you can imagine, we were down to our last ninepence for a cup of tea and a cake in the NAAFI. But he was there and he really gave us a good night. For his finale he came on dressed up as Monty himself

Private Frank Rosier
2nd Battalion, Gloucestershire Regiment

We started playing rugby to keep ourselves amused because we weren't doing much; we knocked up inter-company rugby challenges and football

A sergeant of the 1st Battalion, King's Own Scottish Borderers, composes a letter from his unit's tented camp at Denmead, Hampshire.

challenges. Inside our camp were some black Americans cooking our food and the black Yanks were watching us and said, 'We'll beat you at your game and you try and beat us at basketball,' which they played. So we played them at rugby and actually beat them but they got their own back and beat us at basketball. Then came the order that we were not to play with the black Yanks: the white Yanks had objected. As a cosmopolitan cockney used to playing with black children, Indian children, Chinese or whatever as a kid, it was part of my life and I couldn't believe my ears. I was eighteen and I thought, 'That's stupid!' I still can't believe it today.

Sergeant Major Russell King
2nd Battalion, Royal Warwickshire Regiment
We had to stop blokes playing football eventually because there were that many blokes getting crocked playing football they were going to be short of men. I remember quite a few lads getting ankles turned. Not serious injuries but enough to stop them marching.

Sergeant Edward Wallace
86th Field Regiment, Royal Artillery
I can recall on one occasion a sergeant from the London Scottish giving a talk on how to make harmless a German Teller mine and the blasted thing blew up on him, left him in bits, and two or three of his companions who were with him. Those bits were paraded about the camp so that everybody could see what a Teller mine did to you. A lot of them went back into their tents and were violently sick. It didn't affect me because I'd seen so much of it before.

Major John Mogg
9th Battalion, Durham Light Infantry
My commanding officer was Humphrey Woods. He was a highly experienced desert commander having got a DSO and two MCs and been blown up on mines and things. He was slightly deaf in one ear; he was young; he was beloved by his battalion. And he said to me, 'There are three people that are allowed out of camp: you and I and the quartermaster. We will leave the quartermaster behind and you and I shall have dinner.' I said, 'That suits me very well,' and we went to the Haunch of Venison in Salisbury and we had a marvellous dinner, hardly daring to open our mouths because of security. We

certainly didn't talk about anything like planning. But the thing I remember most vividly was when we got to the end of our meal, we were having a glass of port and Humphrey said to me, 'I haven't said this to anybody else but I know that I am going to be killed when we get over to the other side.' I said, 'Come on, you can't know that. That's ridiculous.' I ordered two brandies quickly. He said, 'No, I feel it in my bones.' And here was a chap who'd been through it all, he'd been blown up on mines and everything else, but he somehow felt he was going to be killed. The amazing thing was how unbelievably enthusiastic he was that the battalion should be successful. He rushed around, never stopped. I mean, twenty-four out of twenty-four hours he was working, practically. That was the epitome of courage: to know you're going to be killed and to go on.

Major Peter Martin
2nd Battalion, Cheshire Regiment

I can remember again that unreal feeling that one had before leaving on the invasion of Sicily. Everything was totally normal and the countryside was so gorgeous and in a few days' time one would be going into an absolute charnel house, if my guesses were right.

Sergeant Desmond O'Neill
Cameraman, Army Film and Photographic Unit

I remember going to one unit, I think it was the South Lancashire Regiment, and taking some film of their final preparations for D-Day. I hadn't come across them before. They were laagered down near Roland's Castle in Hampshire, in woods there, and I went into the camp – the whole area was actually one huge camp. Very strict security all the way round.

There was certainly a very excitable, tense atmosphere amongst those chaps. They'd been training presumably for a couple of years and they knew full well that they were going to be the spearhead troops and they knew therefore that there was a good chance of them getting shot. The atmosphere there was totally different to any other unit I'd ever been to. Discipline was strict but absolutely on a hairline. A very peculiar atmosphere. I know that the casualty figures had been given to them, the presumed casualty figures.

We photographed the chaps being instructed as to what was going to happen on the morning of D-Day, where they were going in and the rest. It was all mocked up. I didn't do very much filming apart from taking pictures of these chaps in the camp. They liked it. First of all they'd never seen a cameraman before. Secondly, it was a great divertissement. You know, 'The Mrs is going to see me back in Wigan,' all this kind of thing. I think it was a welcome diversion.

Major Patrick Barrass
2nd Battalion, Essex Regiment
I remember being taken into a big marquee tent where there was a huge scale model of the coast on which we were going to land with every detail you could think of. The enemy positions were there with their guns and machine guns, every little hedgerow, every little tree, all taken off air photographs which were also there, pinned up on great big boards behind. The names of the places on the scale model were all coded, so that Bayeaux, for instance, was called Chicago or something. You didn't get the real names but you got the real area.

Sapper Thomas Finigan
85th Field Company, Royal Engineers
They showed you the actual beach that you was going to land on. The beach was split into three, there was red, green and white, but of course all the names were fictitious. We didn't know if it was going to be northern France, Holland, Belgium or Norway but you knew exactly what beach you were going to land on and you could see all the obstacles that were there. We used to go in there on our own and study these maps so if the ship landed a hundred yards up or down you could know which way to go. You could say, 'That's where I've got to be, that's where my job starts.'

Private Frederick Perkins
5th Battalion, Royal Berkshire Regiment, attached to 3rd Canadian Division
One or two of the men knew where it was because they'd been there on holiday before but they didn't really let on. They could have taken bets on it but they didn't, they rather left it as it was, because they'd have been put in prison if they'd let the cat out of the bag.

Private Francis Bourlet
2nd Battalion, Oxfordshire and Buckinghamshire Light Infantry
I think we'd been there about five days and they started talking about this place as being in France. Then they mentioned it was going to be in Normandy, which didn't mean a great deal to me anyway except for William the Conqueror.

Private William Gray
2nd Battalion, Oxfordshire and Buckinghamshire Light Infantry
It didn't mean a lot to anyone. Nobody had ever been to France. In fact very few had been abroad at that time.

Lieutenant Hubert Pond
9th Battalion, Parachute Regiment
They unrolled, rather dramatically, a large-scale map of the Normandy coast and there, more or less in the middle, was a red dot indicating the battery we were to attack, which was called the Merville Battery. The things that impressed us immensely here were the number of air photographs we were given to help us to decide what to do there. These were taken mainly from low-flying aircraft, at what must have been considerable risk to the pilots, and you really could see the battery and the surrounding countryside with tremendous clarity. There was one, I remember, of a Frenchman waving up at the pilot as he cycled along a road near the battery.

Lieutenant Alan Jefferson
9th Battalion, Parachute Regiment
We were shown a diagram of what our objective was going to be and it looked so formidable that when we saw it everybody laughed. It was four concrete emplacements surrounded by thick wire, ten-foot high, six-foot thick barbed wire, with a minefield and an anti-tank ditch and cattle wire on the outside. A huge, fortified position about a mile from the coast. The model was so good, so clear, that it was possible to trace one's own movement on it. And each day, when a new photograph arrived, the intelligence people used to get a pin and dig out another crater on the model. It was that up to date.

Pathfinders of 22nd Independent Parachute Company, 6th Airborne Division, are briefed at Harwell airfield, Oxfordshire. Their designated role on D-Day was to land in Normandy shortly after midnight and mark dropping and landing zones for the main force of British parachute and glider-borne troops.

Staff Sergeant Peter Boyle
Glider Pilot Regiment
The RAF had made a film, with the model, of the glider going in, round the various turns, to the target. We saw this film as many times as we liked. We could go and watch it and then say, 'Can we have another look? I want to see so-and-so.'

Private Victor Newcomb
Medical Orderly, 224 Parachute Field Ambulance
The confidence with which that information was given to us impressed me. They seemed to have a wealth of information which was deadly accurate or at least was offered to us as a total and accurate assessment of the situation and which we were willing, at that stage, to accept as being absolutely accurate. None of us had any experience of things going wrong.

Private Dennis Bowen
5th Battalion, East Yorkshire Regiment
One of the things that pleased me on this briefing was that here I was amongst these old soldiers and the major, the company commander, who was giving this briefing. We were told that the Germans who will be opposing us will be the 21st Panzers or some such unit and one of the old soldiers who were at the side of me said, 'Oh, well, don't worry about that. We've already done those ones.' They'd already met them in North Africa. So I knew I was among a group of men that knew the enemy and knew their business.

Private Ron Dixon
12th Battalion, Parachute Regiment
There were models, which were quite good, but I can honestly say I didn't take much notice of them. I thought, 'We'll be all together, we'll drop in the same place, there'll always be somebody who knows the way.'

Major Napier Crookenden
Brigade Major, 6th Airlanding Brigade
My brigadier, James Hill, spoke to each battalion and he said, 'You've had the most excellent briefing. You know exactly what's happening. You know your tasks down to the last detail. But gentlemen don't despair if, when you get

there, you find absolute chaos reigns.' And in view of what happened later it was an extraordinarily prophetic remark.

Private Gordon Newton
9th Battalion, Parachute Regiment

As we left the briefing there was a huge bang and a series of explosions and the largest smoke ring I'd ever seen ascended the tented encampment of the Royal Ulster Rifles. Several of them had been de-priming grenades and some of them were anti-tank grenades and had gone off and the chain reaction had killed two of them. It was bedlam. This, to have occurred five days before our intended operation, did very little for morale. We ran over there and the regimental sergeant major said, 'Settle down, you lads. Settle down, settle down. One of those things. You've got a job to do. Try and forget it.'

Sapper William Dunn
AVRE driver, 26th Assault Squadron, Royal Engineers

We had to seal the tanks. Every tank had to be sealed to keep the water out because we were supposed to be dropped into six feet of water when we got to France. Each crew did its own tank. We had to go round with a black compound all round the tank and this compound dried into a very hard sealing. And we had to put extended exhausts and extended air louvres on so that no water got into the air louvres or the exhaust. They were about four or five feet above the tank, these extras, so as you could get through the water. At the other side they were going to be blown off so you could get back to normal: there was a small explosive charge coupled to the turret and the tank commander just pressed a button and blew these things off. It was a good thing to do, doing it for yourself. You knew you were responsible for yourself.

Captain William Mills
Administrative Officer, 9th Battalion, Parachute Regiment

Our vehicles were painted: we had signs allotted to each vehicle, like LH33, TD24, UD and all that. This all meant Upper Deck, Between Decks, Lower Deck. It was all worked out in advance. And also the ship number was on. We didn't know what it meant. All my vehicles were painted MT21.

Private Arthur Dales
Royal Army Service Corps
We were attached to a field security section in a village in South Wales on the Cardiff to Newport road. A bit further along the road was a big American camp and in there was the 2nd United States Infantry Division. They had an Indian head on their shoulder patch, they were earmarked for the invasion and they had been confined to camp in readiness for D-Day. They wanted extra security, so our unit was earmarked under the field security section to provide a twenty-four-hour guard on this camp and we set up a roadblock on this road outside the camp and stopped every vehicle and searched it.

One night I was on duty and I was just walking round by the wire and an American soldier came over and he shouted out, 'Say, Limey! Can you do anything with these?' And he threw over the wire his swimming trunks, packets of cigarettes and some toiletries. There was talcum powder – I'd never seen men's talcum powder before. Well, I wished him good luck because I knew he was earmarked for the beaches. And it must have been about two o'clock in the morning that the gates in the camp opened and convoys of lorries started going down to Barry docks.

Sergeant Neville Howell
73rd Anti-Tank Regiment, Royal Artillery
I remember it was the Saturday evening when we started off. It was extremely cold and there was a little light drizzle. It got dark fairly quickly. It was a very slow journey because the road was obviously cluttered up with other regiments, other people, who were moving to the docks. And I remember one occasion when we stopped by some bungalows by the side of the road and I was rather surprised that nobody but nobody came out to look at us. They were obviously still occupied but I suppose people in that area were so used to people making dummy runs to the docks.

Sergeant James Bellows
1st Battalion, Royal Hampshire Regiment
Away we go in a three-ton lorry down to Southampton and we stopped by Queen's Park, a little park right by the docks. There was a workman passing us and he started passing various remarks. One of them, jokingly, was, 'Another fucking training? When are you going to get on with the bloody job?' Various

Amphibious DUKWs of a Royal Army Service Corps beach group company lined up ready for loading, early June 1944.

Sherman tanks and amphibious DUKWs of 13th/18th Royal Hussars, Gosport.

remarks was passed backwards and forwards but there wasn't one man who said, 'We're just going to get on with the job.'

Private Frederick Perkins
5th Battalion, Royal Berkshire Regiment, attached to 3rd Canadian Division
The buzz got round: 'It's on.' We were marched down right through the city centre in three ranks fully equipped. Camouflage netting, all our equipment, the ammunition, we had to carry. I was a Bren gunner myself. Our disposal point for loading was the 101 Dock, which was called the New Dock, Southampton. That dock must have gone three-mile back and it was nothing but landing craft tied to the jetty, seven or eight deep all the way along. A vast and unimaginable sight to see all these landing craft and we had to walk from one landing craft to the other to the other to the other to load.

Marine Edward 'Tommy' Treacher
45 (Royal Marine) Commando
We had a game of football with 3 Commando whilst we were waiting to get on the landing craft. We dropped our gear and said, 'Come on boys, we'll have a game of football.' Nobody seemed afraid. D-Day, they was looking forward to it. You'd never believe it. The morale in No 1 SS [Special Service] Brigade was so high it was absolutely brilliant. Nobody thought about getting killed.

Major George Chambers
8th Battalion, Durham Light Infantry
I remember standing on the quay waiting to board. We were going over on American landing craft infantry, LCIs, and who should come along but Winston Churchill, Ernie Bevin, Field Marshal Smuts and I can't remember who else; Churchill with his great big cigar. He passed by with tears running down his cheeks. 'God bless you, boys, God bless you, boys.' And he walked on, smoking a cigar. Which didn't altogether improve our morale. We thought, 'My God, what are we up to? What are we in for?'

Landing craft massed along the quayside at Southampton.

Lieutenant Herbert Jalland
8th Battalion, Durham Light Infantry
I remember being open-mouthed at some of the equipment that was being assembled. I remember seeing part of Pluto, which looked like an enormous bobbin, floating about in Southampton Water. We didn't know what that was. We saw pieces of Mulberry, some with cranes, some without. Again, we'd no idea what they were. We saw the Scorpions and the flails.

Sub Lieutenant Herbert Male
LCT first lieutenant
Tanks had to be backed into the ship: down the beach, up the ramp, backed in two abreast. Then we had to chain them down and scotch them up: big scotches, so they wouldn't move if the sea got rough, so they wouldn't slide around on the deck. We scotched them with great bulwarks of wood under the tank tracks and we bottle-screwed each one down. We took in twelve on D-Day.

Lance Corporal John Blake
288th Company, Royal Army Service Corps (RASC)
We moved down to Tilbury and was put on an American Liberty ship. This meant lifting the trucks on. We just sat in the trucks and they lifted us up and put us down in the hold. We drove on to this wire netting stuff that had a hook at each end and they just hooked it on to one of the cranes on the ship and, whoosh, we was on, in no time at all.

Private Lionel Roebuck
2nd Battalion, East Yorkshire Regiment
Looking down on to the quayside, a couple of red caps came along marching some prisoners. They were obviously 'Absent Without Leave' chaps who had been picked up and held in the clink right up until the last day but they weren't going to be allowed to miss out on the event of the morrow. They'd all had their hair cropped and looked a bit miserable.

Completed Phoenix caissons floating off Selsey.

A Pluto Conundrum, loaded with pipeline, ready to be towed across the Channel.

Sergeant James Bellows
1st Battalion, Royal Hampshire Regiment
The adjutant came up and said, 'I've got some news for you.' 'Sir?' I said. 'What's that?' 'I've got a prisoner for you.' 'Do what?' I said. And he brought him out. He was a Channel Islander. He'd joined up after me; his number was one after me; we'd done our basic training together; we were signallers together; I took him into action in Sicily as a matter of fact. But directly he got back to England he'd done a runner. Got caught; got away, done a runner again.

He'd been up before the CO just before he'd done this last run, and the CO said, 'Now, look. You know what we're going to do. One of the first places to be liberated will be the Channel Islands and all your family are there. Surely you want to take a part in liberating the Channel Islands?' He told the CO what he could do with the Channel Islands and he tipped the table up and done a runner and got away with it; but he'd got captured the next day and the adjutant had brought him down to me. So there I had my prisoner complete with handcuffs.

Then, later on, another man appeared, dressed in civilian clothes. 'Oh,' he said, 'I ain't half glad I found you, sergeant. I've been looking everywhere. They told me you was here.' He was an Irishman. He'd been on leave to southern Ireland, compassionate leave. I believe his mother had died or something. He said, 'I was afraid that if I didn't get back in time and missed this, my mates would've said I was trying to get out of it.' He was as pleased as punch to be back. I had to fix him up with a uniform, arms and equipment, ready for the next morning.

Private Frederick Perkins
5th Battalion, Royal Berkshire Regiment, attached to 3rd Canadian Division
We had this vast amount of equipment. As a beach group we didn't land in the assault with small battle order, we had field marching order, which was a big pack, small pack, everything. A blanket tied in a groundsheet and then tied round the top of the big pack, going right round the pack, and all our clothes, all our spare clothing, socks, pants and a greatcoat, all that was wrapped in the gas cap and pushed down inside the big pack. That became buoyant, then. It acted like a life jacket for us, really. We all had Mae Wests as well. Loading was extremely difficult with all this equipment because one got jostled.

Corporal Frank Cosgrove
45 (Royal Marine) Commando
In my rucksack at the bottom I had four two-inch mortar bombs, explosive, two smoke bombs and I carried six Mills bombs. I had, I think it was, near enough two hundred rounds for the tommy gun and they would also fit the American automatic that I had. I had two smoke bombs; they were dangerous, they'd got phosphorus in them, and I was worried about getting a bullet near them. Then every man in the unit from the colonel down carried two hundred rounds of rifle ammunition in a cloth bandolier. So it was a pretty good load. I would think about seventy to eighty pounds in the rucksack. Then everybody carried a few personal bits and pieces, which helped to put the weight up again. There was no spare tunics or trousers, obviously. Everybody's boots were checked. You had to have thirteen studs in each boot with a steel toe piece and a steel heel.

Lieutenant Herbert Jalland
8th Battalion, Durham Light Infantry
Some of us, including myself, had to carry a bicycle, the idea being that we'd rush off down the road as soon as we landed. I also had a spare battery and some extra Bren gun magazines to generally help out so that we'd have sufficient ammunition when we got on the other side. We were given a good supply of condoms with which to waterproof things like grenades; I think all officers had two grenades. Watches, compasses, they all went into condoms. Separate ones. We had a very heavy load to carry and, in addition to that, the final part, they gave us huge waders which went over our boots and up under our armpits, over the equipment, over everything, the idea being to keep us dry going ashore. I remember that in common with certainly a number of other officers and probably quite a few of the men I was in fact wearing my pyjamas under my battledress, the reason being that it prevented chafing.

Ordinary Seaman Thomas Bartlett
Radar operator, HMS Bulolo (converted liner and Royal Navy Flag Ship)
I always remember it. I stood on the top deck of our ship looking at all these soldiers boarding and, as I watched, I saw quite a little man, very young, and he was struggling up the gangplank with this great pack on his back. It was nearly making him drop to his knees going up the gangplank. I suppose

79

somebody might have thought the same about me, but I thought, 'The poor little devil, he's not fit for this.' But he was; he went. And you see these blokes and it goes through your head, 'I wonder how many of those will make it back,' and you know damned well that some of them won't.

Sub Lieutenant Terry White
Landing Ship Tank (LST) crew
We also took on board a lot of medical staff. Lots of doctors, army medical staff and naval medical staff. It all seemed a bit pessimistic when you looked at this lot coming aboard, but it was a necessary thing, I suppose.

Driver Robert Lunn
101st General Transport Company, RASC
The sergeant gets up on the side of my DUKW and says, 'What you got on, fellas?' I said, 'Shells'. He said, 'What kind of shells?' I said, 'I don't know what kind of shells. All we're doing is delivering them.' They lifted the canvases up and they looked at them and said, 'Well, we don't want you in here.' He calls an officer over and says, 'We've got some funnies over here,' and the officer got up on the side of the DUKW and said, 'Oh, yes. We don't want you here, you'll have to go into a special bay.' So they took us out of the transhipment area, up a lane, into a field. A gang of Pioneer Corps came along and we took our canvases up and got them unloaded and I said to one of them, 'Why is it so special to bring us from the transhipping area to here?' He said, 'Well, don't you know what's in these shells?' I said, 'It must be something important?' And he said 'Very important. It's a special type of shell and we won't use it unless we're forced to.' Then Owen said, 'I think I've guessed what they are and I sincerely hope they're not going to use it. I think it's gas. They're prepared in case Jerry uses gas.'

DELAY AND DECISION

Lieutenant Commander Lawrence Hogben
New Zealand officer, Royal Navy meteorological team
I was one of Eisenhower's six weather forecasters. I worked underground in the Admiralty Office, near Admiralty Arch, on the weather forecasts. That remained our centre for the whole D-Day operation.

Men of the Green Howards embark for Normandy.

We were told that the invasion was coming early on in 1944 but we were not given an exact date. I'm not sure if the exact date had even been decided. We were also told that two of us would represent the Admiralty in the six-man team which would make the actual forecast, the others in the team being two Americans and two nominated by the Met Office. Our sources of information were the hundreds of weather observations made by the Allies and, in addition, all the observations made by the Germans, which Bletchley Park decoded for us very rapidly and enabled us to put on our maps. There was also the occasional flight into the Atlantic and the occasional weather ship out on the Atlantic – not very many.

May was a pleasant, easy month and we made eighteen successful theoretical invasion forecasts because the weather was so good and, as a result, the generals had considerable confidence in what we were doing. Then, at the end of May, it was clear to everybody that the good times influenced by an Azores anti-cyclone had ended and that things were going to get rough. By 1 June, of course, the military and ourselves were all getting very itchy because we knew then that the date was 5 June and we were being asked on the first for five-day forecasts, which we couldn't make. All we knew was the weather was breaking up and it was liable to be a bit rough at the beginning of June.

June 5 was settled as the date because of all the different requirements that the military and the navy had. They wanted three to four days with rather calm weather and winds not more than force three to four. We told them it was 31–1 against getting that sort of weather; they knew that they'd have to be satisfied with something less. What they did insist on, however, was that the tide should be right, so that the tide would be at half-tide when twilight arrived and the mine-clearers could get to work on the beaches and at full tide the troops would come in in their landing craft. In addition, there had to be a nearly full moon for the parachutists. Then again there had to be not too much cloud so that the bombers could do their work. All that added up to 5 June but the sixth was an alternative if the worst came to the worst. If the invasion didn't happen on the fifth or the sixth then the invasion would go on the nineteenth when the tides and moon and so on would be similar. In that case, of course, there would be more chance of the Germans finding out what we were up to.

From the first until the third we were forecasting that there was going to be a break-up of the weather but we didn't know how bad it would be or how long it would last. The Americans took the view that the Azores anti-cyclone was magically going to make things possible. They continued to take this view until the evening of the third. This was the crunch forecast because the night of the third was crunch night. We had to forecast for the fifth, which was Ike's chosen day for invasion.

Group Captain James Stagg
Chief meteorological adviser
I had to go before General Eisenhower and his commanders, who met for nothing else, twice a day during those fateful days, the first, second, third of June, down in Southwick House behind Portsmouth.

As the time went on, the seriousness, the ominousness, of the whole situation got worse until by Saturday night, 3 June, it became obvious that there would certainly be a storm in the Channel area on the Sunday night and Monday. Next morning, early on Sunday, 4 June, General Eisenhower confirmed the decision that he had made the previous evening and suspended the whole operation.

Here was the whole business completely suspended, the naval craft all returning to what bases they could get into in England and no suggestion on our charts that the weather situation would or could improve for many days ahead. That day, Sunday, was a day of dreadful tension. The whole operation was hung up.

Midshipman John Cahil
HMS Mauritius (Royal Navy cruiser)
I, with a number of my shipmates, went to Holy Communion before breakfast. An unusually big congregation: men kneeling under under-slung hammocks. And at a particularly serious moment of the service, I remember, the broadcast was made throughout the ship by the boatswain's mate: 'The operation has been postponed.' Whereupon the majority of the congregation got up and went to breakfast.

Petty Officer Reginald Samuel Francis Coaker
HMS Urania (Royal Navy destroyer)
I can remember the motorboat going up and passing us and the chappy waving his arms and shouting through a megaphone that it had been postponed. I can remember that as plainly as anything.

Wren Messenger Margaret Seeley
Women's Royal Naval Service, HMS Squid (Royal Navy shore station, Southampton)
The ships were full of these men. They'd all embarked and there they were sitting in Southampton Water and the Solent for twenty-four hours and one way of keeping them occupied was to send two Wrens down in this ML [motor launch] to wave at them for forty minutes. Of course we had the most wonderful time on this trip and the highlight was having tea on the Admiral's flagship, HMS *Bulolo*, where we actually had white bread. One never had white bread during the war except on board ship.

Lieutenant David Wood
2nd Battalion, Oxfordshire and Buckinghamshire Light Infantry
We were all briefed and kitted up and ready to go and then the whole operation was postponed. This was a severe shock to our morale, temporarily. And I, who don't normally drink much, and another couple of officers bought two bottles of whisky which we demolished that night in our small tent.

Brigadier James Hill
Commanding Officer, 3rd Parachute Brigade
It was a godsend for commanders. It gave you time to relax and rest when you had nothing to do.

Private Sidney Capon
9th Battalion, Parachute Regiment
Next morning it was a beautiful day and I thought to myself, 'Oh, good God. It would have all been over by now.'

Lieutenant Commander Lawrence Hogben
New Zealand Officer, Royal Navy meteorological team
So we had to go through it all again and our nerves, already jangling, had to suffer another twenty-four hours of the same thing. On the fourth, forecasting for the sixth, we looked at all the observations again carefully and fearfully. We made our forecast maps and then we all issued our individual forecasts. On this occasion there was another obstacle to a perfect agreement. The

Americans, clinging to their anti-cyclone, said, 'Everything will be fine and dandy.' While we agreed that marginally it was possible, the Met Office were a bit doubtful. Ike asked Montgomery what he thought and he said, 'Go.' He asked Admiral Ramsay what he thought and he said, 'We can accept these conditions.' He asked Mallory, the air force man, who was a bit doubtful but accepted. And Ike said, 'Well, let's go.'

Colonel Thomas Collins
Director of Movements, War Office
I was the Director of Movements, Continental Operations. What we had to do was deal with the marshalling and embarkation, getting the troops into craft loads, getting them briefed and so on. It was such an enormous undertaking: millions of men and thousands and thousands of vehicles. And I can well remember going to the conference at Eisenhower's and Monty's headquarters and they finally decided, 'No, if the men are going to be sick, it's just too bad. We can't turn everybody back off the ships.' And I can remember coming away thinking, 'Thank Heavens we've not got to do that.' It could have been awful. You can imagine the whole army going into reverse in England. It would have been almost impossible.

Sergeant Major Russell King
2nd Battalion, Royal Warwickshire Regiment
We weren't back in the training camp for more than a few hours and then we went back on the ship again, which was a bit off-putting. We were on and off, on and off, and people got a bit disconcerted. They thought it was just a bloody big flap, like. Typical army.

Captain Guy Radmore
Brigade Signals Officer, 5th Parachute Brigade
The following night, of course, we went. If it had been postponed a second time I think we should have been absolutely shattered.

THE CROSSING

Major David Warren
1st Battalion, Royal Hampshire Regiment
I think we up-anchored at about five o'clock in the afternoon in the Solent and we sailed out past The Needles. Not a bad evening, not too rough, good visibility, and you could see other ships moving in the same direction as us, see the minesweepers that led the convoy ahead. And I remember standing on deck and admiring the scenery. It seemed unrealistic that we were going to go to war in the morning.

Sergeant James Bellows
1st Battalion, Royal Hampshire Regiment
We pulled off straight away and got out in the midstream and this sailor said, 'We're in a bloody hurry today, aren't we? Where are we going this time? Hayling Island?' Of course we were amazed that he didn't know. We said 'No, France.' And he said – and he used that favourite word of ours – 'Now don't fuck about, mate. Where are we going?' And we said, 'France!' We'd already been paid in French francs and one of the lads showed him.

Sergeant Joe Stringer
48 (Royal Marine) Commando
When we moved off on the evening of 5 June we passed through the rest of the craft all lined up in Southampton harbour and on the Solent and we were told by our CO, 'Get on deck with your green berets on. Let them see you. Give them encouragement.' We sailed through to cheers and what have you.

Piper Bill Millin
HQ 1st Special Service Brigade
Lovat had me up at the front of the landing craft playing the pipes, piping the flotilla down. And as we drew level with the Isle of Wight and all these ships, a terrific roar went up, because they'd put me over the loudhailer system, and all kinds of people were throwing their hats in the air.

Engine Room Artificer Ronald Jesse
HMS Belfast (Royal Navy cruiser)

We were able to line the decks and wave and cheer to all the soldiers. The soldiers in their landing craft were all waving back. We were overhauling dozens of them as we went along the south coast; they were all coming out of their little harbours and taking up their allotted stations.

Telegraphist Harry Siggins
HMS Ajax (Royal Navy cruiser)

Everywhere you looked there were ships: battleships, merchant ships, landing craft of all descriptions, hundreds and hundreds of ships, seagoing tugs, trawlers. If there ever were a word, it was 'armada'. I don't know what the Spanish Armada was like; it must've been a fearful sight.

Private Reginald Barnes
4 Commando

I would like to mention that it was most exhilarating, sailing through the greatest armada the world has ever seen. And I never loved England so truly as at that moment.

Lieutenant Gerald Edward Ashcroft
LCT commander

By the time we cleared the Isle of Wight, the sea really began to build up. We had a very heavy pounding, we were shipping water over the tanks, had our pumps running full pelt all the time. And as the seas came up, so the army's stomachs came up also. We felt really sorry for the troops on board. Our only worry was that we would be putting them ashore when they'd reached a state where a few minutes before they'd been afraid to die and by the time they got on the beach they'd be glad to die.

Private Leslie Perry
1st Battalion, Suffolk Regiment

As you clear the breakwater there's conflicting currents and as they came together that's when the landing craft started to toss and turn. Being flat-bottomed they were just bobbing about like corks. That is when I started being sick. The officer was the first one to the rail and I followed him and I

87

The view from a Royal Navy aircraft of invasion vessels assembling off the Isle of Wight, 5 June.

was sick all the way over. I was sitting on top of the stairs munching biscuits and sipping water because when you're retching and haven't got anything to bring up it tears you to pieces.

Lieutenant Eric Ashcroft
1st Battalion, South Lancashire Regiment

The chaps that were sick, their vomit bags were pushed over the side. And one chap was signalling frantically, you know: 'Don't throw the bag over!' Apparently his teeth were in the bag. And that seemed to break the tension of things: this chap wasn't worried about landing on the beaches; it was more that his teeth were in the bag.

Sergeant Robert Palmer
Sexton (self-propelled gun) commander, 147th Field Regiment (Essex Yeomanry), Royal Artillery

In my honest opinion, it was rougher then than it had been the night before. And, oh, so many people were ill on the boat. My friends were all sick. One of my friends I remember in particular said, 'I don't care what we face, Bob, just as long as we can get off this bloody boat.' He kept being sick and sick and sick. It was horrible. I don't get seasick ever, so I was one of the lucky ones. Almost everyone on board our craft was seasick, including most of the sailors.

Sapper Thomas Finigan
85th Field Company, Royal Engineers

We had a lot of Canadians on board ship who were cleaning their arms and also sharpening their knives. You've got to realise that a lot of Canadians were brothers of chaps who had been killed at Dieppe and they were all looking forward to this landing. They really wanted to avenge what had happened at Dieppe.

Private Frederick Perkins
5th Battalion, Royal Berkshire Regiment, attached to 3rd Canadian Division

We were told on the way over that the landing was in the morning, that this was the real thing. We knew that anyway because we'd gone so far: we were more than halfway across the Channel when we were told. So we were on our way and we thought, 'Good, let's get the job done. Let's get on terra firma.' We were so ill. 'Let's get onshore.'

Bound for Normandy, vehicles and men aboard an LST in the Channel.

A landing craft en route for Normandy carrying Sherman tanks and other vehicles of 13th/18th Royal Hussars.

Corporal Frank Cosgrove
45 (Royal Marine) Commando

Nerves take a part then. We was pretty quiet for a bit. Different people act differently. Four of us played cards. Hours and hours we played cards and you're pretty cramped in an LCT, there's not much room to move around. I think we nearly wore the cards out.

Sergeant Kenneth Lakeman
Royal Corps of Signals

Andrews was a great big fellow: six feet tall, fifteen, sixteen stone, but he had this jumpiness about him and he was wandering around this limited space of this LST and there were huge packing cases and boxes there with serial numbers on them, like X/34321. And he prised one of these open and he changed colour. They were white crosses. 'God,' he said, 'I don't mind going to my death but to take my own cross...' He was visibly upset. Being in charge I rollicked him for this because it was upsetting for the rest of the crew. And my driver-mechanic, a wonderful guy called Fred Mincher, he would take the mickey sometimes, and he said, 'Well, of course, Andy, it's probably got your name and number on it.' And that nearly started a fight, so I had to calm that down. That's the sort of edginess around at that time and you can understand it.

Sergeant Desmond O'Neill
Cameraman, Army Film and Photographic Unit

I was half-terrified and half-enthusiastic. You know, 'This is what we've been trained for,' and I thought it was going to be exciting. I was also cagey enough to know that there was a good chance of having my head knocked off.

Trooper Ronald Mole
Sherman tank gunner/wireless operator, 4th/7th Royal Dragoon Guards

I was as innocent as a newborn babe. Never had any experiences before. I was perfectly innocent and quite honestly it didn't register.

Major Allan Younger
Commanding Officer, 26th Assault Squadron, Royal Engineers

I think we'd done so many training exercises by then that it was difficult almost to realise that this was the real thing. It was just a case of, 'Oh, well, we've done all this before. Come on, let's get it done. We've got better tanks this time, let's get it done.' I think on future occasions when I had to do assaults across the Rhine I got far more worked up than on this one.

Major David Warren
1st Battalion, Royal Hampshire Regiment
I think we were perhaps slightly influenced by the fact that we had done two in the Mediterranean. I think we felt very confident that having done it twice we could do it a third time. But I think we were all rather prepared for things not to be as simple as we hoped them to be because we had come through it twice reasonably well and the third time one always feels something might go wrong. But what we all felt, and this was the most astonishing thing about the Normandy landings, was that everyone was one hundred per cent confident that whatever happened to me or to anyone else or perhaps to the Hampshires it would be successful. There was no question of thinking it might not be. And I think everyone was quite glad to get on with it because it was like the green light for the end of the war, or so it seemed at the time.

Corporal George Richardson
6th Battalion, Durham Light Infantry
The men who'd gone through the Middle East, we were very experienced in war by then and we thought, 'Well, we've already done one invasion, on Sicily, and it was fairly easy. This one's not going to be easy. The Atlantic Wall's supposed to be impregnable.' We fully expected the first few waves of us to be mown down. We never expected to make it inland. I never did. I didn't expect to come through it.

Major Richard Gosling
147th Field Regiment (Essex Yeomanry), Royal Artillery
The parson gave us communion, he gave us wafers, but that wasn't a great success. We all went up, those of us who were confirmed, to take communion but there was a hell of a gale and suddenly the wafers all blew overboard into the sea. The poor parson, he said, 'Bloody hell, lucky fishes,' and had to go down into the galley and get some loaves of bread, chop them up into bits and start all over again.

Captain Arthur Rouse
1st Battalion, South Lancashire Regiment

Colonel Burbury spoke to all the men and told them very briefly what was expected of them. Then he turned to me and said, 'You say something now,' and he whispered, '*Give them a bit of uplift.*' I thought, 'My God, Henry V had more warning than this.' But Shakespeare came to the rescue, of course. I said, 'Tomorrow afternoon the BBC will tell your parents and your wives and so on that you have landed and they all know you're an assault battalion, they all know you'll have gone in first.' I didn't give them the full business of 'Gentlemen in England now abed'.

Lance Corporal Alan Carter
6th Battalion, Green Howards

Kirkpatrick said to the sergeants, 'Synchronise your watches.' And my sergeant said to him, 'That watch'll be mine tomorrow night.' You wouldn't have dared said that to another officer. Kirkpatrick just laughed.

Able Seaman Kenneth Oakley
Beachmaster's bodyguard

The senior army officer had all the group gathered on the upper deck and said, 'You will be taking part in this massive invasion. Many of you will be in the first assault. Many of you will be killed. But don't worry, the second assault wave will pass over you and, if that fails, a third will pass over you also, until we have gained a foothold on that beach.' And with those thoughts ringing in my head, I went to sleep.

Trooper Joseph Ellis
Churchill Crocodile tank driver, 141st Regiment, Royal Armoured Corps

We were supposed to sleep in hammocks. I'd never slept in a hammock in my life and I tried to get in and fell out t'other side and tried to get in and fell out t'other side so I thought, 'Well, bugger it, I'll get in the tank,' and I fell asleep in the tank. Dropped the seat right back. It wasn't made for people to sleep in them but if there was nobody else in, you could do.

Gathered on board their landing craft, men of 4 Commando receive final instructions from their commanding officer, Lieutenant Colonel Robert Dawson.

Lieutenant Ian Wilson
73rd Field Company, Royal Engineers

Our landing craft and several others were towing a thing called a Hedgerow. This was a small assault infantry landing craft which was packed with spigot mortars and the idea, so we were told, was that it ran up on the beach and fired its spigot mortars to add to the general bombardment that was going on at the enemy. We were also told that if it fired its spigot mortars without being beached it blew the bottom of the craft out. But I don't know, this is all hearsay, because in fact the last we saw of our particular Hedgerow was upside down in the middle of the Channel round about three in the morning before the towrope parted. What happened to the crew, I don't know.

Sapper William Dunn
AVRE driver, 26th Assault Squadron, Royal Engineers

The main order we got as we were sailing, and this came over the loudspeaker, was, 'You don't stop for anything. If any ship falls foul you don't stop to pick them up. If anybody falls overboard you don't stop to pick them up.' And some of these little landing craft did overturn as we were going and our skipper was pretty good, he slowed down to try and pick some of the lads up. This MTB came along and they weren't very happy with us and told us we had to get back into line and leave them, other MTBs would come along and pick these lads up, to make sure the timing would be exact.

Stoker Albert Rogers
LBV crew

It was pitch black and I'd just got relieved to have a jimmy riddle over the side and a smoke and I noticed a seaman get washed over the side. I seen him go and I went in after him, grabbing hold of a lump of what we called 'hanging line' for safety, 'cause I had a duffel coat on, sea boots, trousers, overalls; and I had a steel helmet on but I flung that off because they're more trouble than they're worth in water.

I grabbed hold of him and hung on to him; they shouted out 'Stop engines!' He was so terrified. Don't forget he had a duffel coat on and that. I'm trying to push him up. A couple of the crew came up and started to get hold of him. They got him on board and that's when the second-class stoker came up to help and as he was pulling him up his feet went from underneath him and he went in so I had to grab hold of him. When we eventually got underway we was on our own, we'd fallen behind.

Ordinary Seaman Don Reynolds
HMS Virago (Royal Navy destroyer)
A ship's siren blasted. There'd been an attack, I think it was a U-boat attack, and one of our destroyers, the *Svenner*, a Norwegian one, was lost. We did a quick reshuffle so that if any U-boat or anything had got us lined up we were all working at different angles.

Petty Officer Lawrence Alfred Moorcroft
HMS Urania (Royal Navy destroyer), off Gold Beach
We arrived in the early hours of the morning of 6 June and we actually went up through candlelight to our desired anchor position. There were tins with holes cut and with a candle in that the front men had put with little anchors, weights, keeping them in position. They were in an alleyway. Ships went in and where they widened out you counted the number of candles so you moved left or right, port or starboard, to your anchoring position.

Petty Officer Reginald Samuel Francis Coaker
HMS Urania (Royal Navy destroyer), off Gold Beach
Things got strangely quiet on the bridge. Something odd, this. Because on a bridge of a destroyer in wartime you've got this perpetual 'Ping! Ping!' going on the whole time, the Asdic thing, and of course there's the usual chatter of 'Port tens!' and 'Steady!' and all this. But when the first signs of dawn are starting to appear, you're approaching an enemy coast and you get a dark outline of the enemy coast, voices somehow seem to drop on the bridge; voices almost take on a whisper. 'Don't speak too loudly, otherwise they might hear us coming.' That sort of thing.

Commander Felix Lloyd-Davies
HMS Glasgow (Royal Navy cruiser), off Omaha Beach
We arrived off the approaches to Normandy and *Glasgow* was then told to take the head of the line of the force going into Omaha Beach. As we steamed down the line the padre said to me, 'Shouldn't we say a prayer?' and so I said,

'Why not say Nelson's Prayer?' because it was exactly right for this day. So he started to read Nelson's Prayer and as we passed the *Texas* all their ship's company took off their helmets, they were at their guns, as they heard us reading the Prayer, going in.*

FINAL TOUCHES

Flight Lieutenant Arthur Poore
Lancaster bomber pilot, 617 Squadron, RAF

In the very early hours of D-Day, the squadron – we had assiduously practised this for many weeks before – flew in line abreast, about two thousand feet up, over the narrow part of the Channel between Kent and the Pas de Calais dropping this tin-foil strip, code-named window, and doing exact turns to fly in a reciprocal direction back towards England and turn again and fly maybe half a mile back towards the French coast and then turn again and back. Meanwhile, fast motor torpedo boats were doing the same thing down on the surface of the sea. This had the effect on the German radar of an invasion force about to invade the Pas de Calais area. In other words: a spoof invasion.

Flying Officer Malcolm Hamilton
Lancaster bomber pilot, 617 Squadron, RAF

The navigator had to work out the exact course, we did it with stopwatches, and we'd go down towards Calais and each time we'd go eight seconds further than the last time and then you'd go round and back up your course, dropping window. Then you'd turn round and come down and each time you extended the leg a little bit further. The weather was filthy, it was drizzling with rain, there were high winds, so the navigator had to work very hard to keep you on course.

---

* In October 1805, on the eve of the Battle of Trafalgar, Vice-Admiral Horatio Nelson wrote in his diary:

May the great God, whom I worship, grant to my country and for the benefit of Europe in general, a great and glorious victory: and may no misconduct, in any one, tarnish it: and may humanity after victory be the predominant feature in the British fleet.
For myself individually, I commit my life to Him who made me and may His blessing light upon my endeavours for serving my country faithfully.
To Him I resign myself and the just cause which is entrusted to me to defend.
Amen. Amen. Amen.

Flying Officer Thomas Bennett
Lancaster bomber navigator, 617 Squadron, RAF

The crews had all been doubled up because it was assumed to be a four-hour operation, but when the operation order came through it had been decided that eight aircraft would go off in the initial phase and would be relieved after two hours by the second eight. And of course this handover business had never been practised in the training period at all. We had no idea that this was going to spring on us and that caused a bit of a hiatus at the beginning. We had to give the second wave start times on the English coast and they would fly down and pick up the aircraft they were relieving and do their last circuit with them. The aircraft that was windowing would be at three thousand feet; the relieving aircraft would come along at three thousand five hundred, pick them up and do their last circuit with them. The first aircraft would then fly off back to base and in the turn the second aircraft would drop to three thousand feet and pick up the sequence. But this had to be done within a tolerance of ninety seconds, otherwise the whole of that segment of the convoy would disappear from the radar screens and of course that would mean the Germans would immediately suspect the veracity of this thing. So this was something that concerned us very greatly but in the event the handover, the takeover, went off beautifully.

Warrant Officer George Oliver
Australian Stirling bomber pilot, 196 Squadron, RAF

There were a lot of precautions taken to try and fool the Germans as to whether it was the main thing or whether it was just a one-nighter, just a bit of a raid. One of them was somewhere quite well away from the landing place, up north, and they dropped a lot of dummy paratroopers. These dummy paratroops had gimmicks all over, which exploded so it sounded like gunfire. That was one deception plan to give the Germans something to think about.

Ordinary Seaman Sidney Taylor
HMS Seagull (Royal Navy minesweeper)

We arrived on the other side at 9pm on the fifth. Our job was to sweep back and forth along from Le Havre and when the enemy's radar came on we could jam it: we were there to sweep a passage for the *Warspite* and all the American battle wagons and things to stand off and shell. When we got there it was absolutely pitch black, we could just discern the shoreline, and a searchlight came on. And as soon as it did, I don't know where it came from, but a fighter, a Spitfire I suppose, shot the light out and we just carried on sweeping back and forth.

Flight Sergeant Jack Nissenthall
Radar specialist, RAF

Two hundred ships were each equipped with two to three kilowatts of Mandrel jammers which were used on that one night and of course that's what got us in on D-Day. When Eisenhower said, 'Go,' everybody onboard their ships, wherever they were, threw this big master switch. It was really a Mandrel jammer, which we'd told nobody about. When you threw this switch and you were in Salcombe or wherever you were going to come from, it didn't affect the German radar at all. But as you approached the coast of France, all the German radar operators would see is some hash on that bearing, which could be a faulty tube, a faulty valve, and it would get worse and worse. And they'd be tired and fed up and waiting to go off duty and it would be getting worse and worse and finally they'd say, 'Oh, to hell with it. Let's not touch it tonight. Let's wait until the mechanic comes on duty and he'll replace the tube and everything will be all right.' But by the time morning came all the capital ships were in position, some of them three or four or five miles offshore with their big guns. They were all lined up there.

Airborne Assault

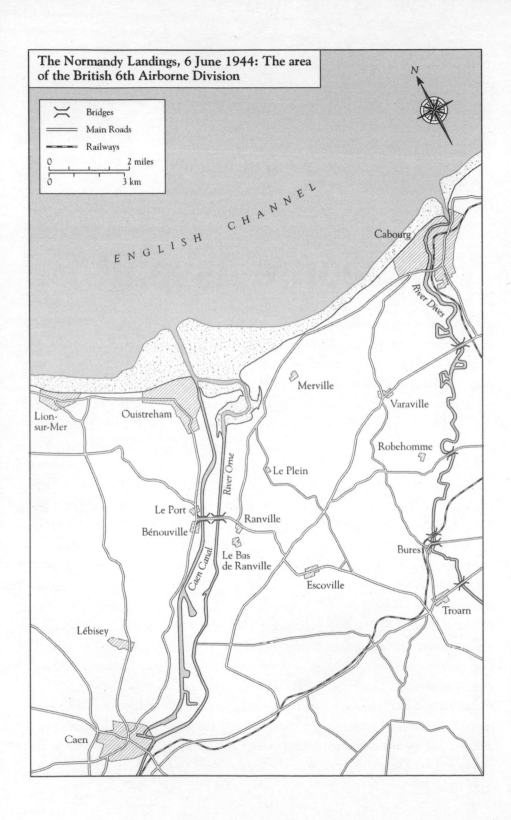

The Normandy Landings, 6 June 1944: The area of the British 6th Airborne Division

Bridges
Main Roads
Railways

0   2 miles
0   3 km

N

ENGLISH CHANNEL

Cabourg

River Dives

Merville

Varaville

Lion-
sur-Mer

Ouistreham

Robehomme

River Orne

Le Plein

Le Port

Ranville

Bénouville

Bures

Caen Canal

Le Bas
de Ranville

Escoville

Troarn

Lébisey

Caen

There was flashes all over the place, there was tracer coming up
and I think 'Get out the plane!' was the main thought.
That's it: 'Get out!'

On the evening of 5 June 1944, thousands of British and American airborne troops assembled and took off from airfields across southern England and flew south, across the Channel, to open the Allied invasion of Normandy. Their aim was to secure the east and west flanks of the fifty-mile stretch of coastline due to be assaulted after dawn from the sea. Two American divisions – the 82nd and the 101st – were to land in the west. Major General Richard Gale's British 6th Airborne Division was assigned the task of securing the eastern flank.

Selected for a daring spearhead role – what became known as the Pegasus Bridge coup de main mission – was a small glider-borne force of 180 British soldiers under the command of Major John Howard of the Oxfordshire and Buckinghamshire Light Infantry. The first company-strength Allied unit to land in Normandy, it had orders to capture two adjacent bridges over the Caen Canal and River Orne – parallel watercourses running north to the sea – and then hold on against German counter-attacks. Securing these crossing points promised to hamper German attempts to strike at the expected beachheads from the east and, if the seaborne troops could get ashore and push inland, facilitate future Allied advances.

Minutes after Howard's force landed, and as the American airborne assault opened simultaneously in the west, thousands of men from two British parachute brigades – comprising five battalions of the Parachute Regiment, a Canadian parachute battalion and a host of support troops, from medics and engineers to naval liaison teams – began landing by parachute and glider on a series of pre-planned zones. High winds and enemy ack-ack – anti-aircraft fire – caused problems, however, and the drop was badly scattered. Many men found themselves miles adrift. Several drowned after dropping into a wide area that the Germans had deliberately flooded as a counter-invasion measure. Everywhere, as it began to go about its allotted tasks, the 6th Airborne found itself under-strength.

Captain John Sim
12th Battalion, Parachute Regiment

The evening came, the evening of 5 June, when we got into our lorries and were transported to the airfield. We collected our chutes and the lorries took us around the perimeter, miles away into the country where our aircraft had been dispersed. The aircraft that we, the battalion, were going to jump out of was the Stirling, which had been coughed up by Bomber Command for us to use. We were right out in the countryside, a peaceful June evening, lovely and calm. We just sat and talked for a while amongst ourselves and then the padre came whipping up in his jeep and we had a little prayer. He wished us well and then he dashed off again to another aircraft.

Major Kenneth Darling
12th Battalion, Parachute Regiment

We had a marvellous padre, Joe Jenkins, a Welshman. He had a great sense of humour, he knew his job from A to Z, every man in the battalion knew him and he knew every man. On the morning of 5 June we had a sort of drumhead service, which became our normal practice later on in our various battles, with the battalion sitting on the grass around him in a big circle, and he conducted a short and very moving service.

What I would like to recall is an extraordinary scene. At the end of the service, after he'd given the blessing, he casually mentioned that he had a pile of small pocket bibles, which were about two to three inches long, I suppose, very small, which had been produced for the army. And he said, 'If any man would like to pick up one before you go away, you are welcome to do so.' There then occurred the most extraordinary scene. The men surged towards where he was standing and scrambled for these bibles. If he'd said, 'There's a pile of hundred pound notes there,' I don't think you'd have seen a greater keenness to get to them. It was quite extraordinary. But I think it did exemplify how human beings probably have, we all probably have, a certain degree or fund of faith, but there are times when that faith needs kindling and Joe Jenkins had done just that that morning. The sad part was of course that within a week or so many of the men who were present had been killed. But it's a scene I shall never forget.

Captain Guy Radmore
Brigade Signals Officer, 5th Parachute Brigade

We had a very impressive service given by our padre, Parry, who was the son of the Bishop of Liverpool. He was the padre for the 7th Battalion. He was an absolutely super chap and he was killed, actually, in the first hours of D-Day. I always remember how we'd all blacked our faces and you could just see the white of his dog collar sticking up above his tunic.

Private Gordon Newton
9th Battalion, Parachute Regiment

There was an air of excitement, coupled with anxiety, as a lieutenant read out a statement from Eisenhower, telling us we were all fighting for freedom, making history and all this stuff. We were very subdued. There was no clapping or anything. We were all pretty tensed up.

Lieutenant Hubert Pond
9th Battalion, Parachute Regiment

I think at that sort of age – I was, what, twenty, I suppose – fear doesn't really come into it. You get a tremendous excitement and you wonder what it's going to be like. None of us had any experience of battle at all. We'd seen crummy films in black and white, we'd seen shells exploding and we'd seen *All Quiet on the Western Front* and so on. But it really did not sink into our young brains. It was an excitement and an adventure, something we'd never done before, and I suppose you could say that everybody looked forward to it. The danger and that sort of thing didn't really come into it and I think that applied to most people.

Each soldier was issued with a parachutist's knife, a rifle and bayonet, two 36 fragmentation grenades, two 77 grenades, which I think were smoke grenades, and everybody had a bandolier of fifty rounds of ammunition. If he

British paratroopers apply camouflage cream at Harwell airfield, Oxfordshire, on the afternoon of 5 June.

thought he could carry more, he was allowed to carry more. We also had a Hawkins grenade, two Bren gun magazines and concentrated rations for two days and we were allowed spare underpants and spare vests and socks and that sort of thing, a waterproof gas cape, one morphine syringe, six benzedrine tablets to try and keep us awake and we had our field and shell dressings. So we were fairly well loaded. The first thing I did was to get rid of my revolver and take a Sten gun because I thought a revolver was a pretty pointless thing to have when everybody else was firing much heavier ammunition and more accurately too.

Sapper Wilfred Robert Jones
3rd Parachute Squadron, Royal Engineers
I was the mortar bloke for the troop. I was jumping No 6 with a rifle and a two-inch mortar. In addition, I was carrying 110 rounds of .303, two pounds of PE, which is plastic explosive, two 36 grenades, one Gammon bomb and two magazines for the Bren, some two-inch mortar bombs, a change of clothing and twenty No 27 detonators and two ration packs.

Private Gordon Newton
9th Battalion, Parachute Regiment
We were issued with 117-pound lifebuoy flame-throwers which we carried on our backs: the big boys carried these. A dreadful weapon it was. It had a container which could hold two types of fluid. One was a flash fluid, which gave a flash of fire and then retracted. The other one, which we were going to use, was a fluid laced with petroleum jelly, which was sticky. It didn't come out in a flash, a flame, it came out in squirts. The idea was to approach your target and wet them with dry squirts and then set off a live squirt to set fire to everything that had been squirted. Dreadful things.

Private John Weathers
12th Battalion, Parachute Regiment
Every man had a parachute on his back of course, a helmet, personal weapons; I had a radio as well in a kit bag fixed to my leg. As part of our training we'd had to get used to jumping with a kit bag because prior to that they had used these canisters with everybody's equipment in. A lot of it used to get lost of course on being dropped, the canisters with all the gear, so they introduced

these kit bags so that every man took his own wireless set or bit of his mortar or whatever.

Private Anthony Leake
8th Battalion, Parachute Regiment

When you've got your chute on with all your ammunition and everything else, you're carrying about a hundred pounds' weight of kit. The chute itself weighed about twenty-three pounds.

The kit bag was a big padded army kit bag and you could put things in it like the barrel of a machine gun or parts of a two-inch mortar, heavy equipment, and you jumped with this on your leg. There was a recess in this bag and you put your leg in it and it had two quick release straps, which you pulled out, and a cord attached with one end to your parachute harness, the other end to the kit bag. The cord was about twenty feet long. The idea was, as soon as your chute opened, you released your kit bag and so the kit bag landed before you did. Not only that, you would have an easier landing yourself, because not only were you not carrying so much weight but also the kit bag had the effect of slowing you down at the last minute while you landed.

Not everybody had kit bags. The light machine guns and rifles with which we were equipped were put in what they called a rifle valise, which was a thick felt sleeved thing like a big sock, and you shoved it in that and that had a cord attached like the kit bag. Also, unless you were carrying a Bren gun, which was about twenty-three pounds – a rifle weighed about nine pounds – you had to carry a pick or a shovel as well, a full size one, strapped to it.

Private Victor Newcomb
Medical Orderly, 224 Parachute Field Ambulance

Bandages and dressings and bottles of antiseptic, things of this kind were thrust into every pocket and pouch around our uniform. In addition to this, some of us were expected to carry into action a stretcher. The stretcher was a specially designed collapsible stretcher but nonetheless it stood, when collapsed, something like five foot high. You jumped out of the aircraft clutching it to you and then released it or dropped it as soon as the parachute had opened, so it was floating down independently of you.

Private John Weathers
12th Battalion, Parachute Regiment

We had our chutes with us and we were all herded together. We could see all these planes lined up down the runways. It was getting towards dusk by then; it was about nine o'clock in the evening. There was a lot of hanging about and waiting and finally the word came through for us to get aboard, so we all trooped off looking like I don't know what.

Warrant Officer George Oliver
Australian Stirling bomber pilot, 196 Squadron, RAF

We had to go out and start up our aircraft. When we walked up to our old Stirling, there it was, with these three white stripes about a foot wide painted on each wing and on the fuselage. The logistics of that really made an impression on me because we didn't know anything about it, but every aircraft that was going to take an actual part in the D-Day landings was painted like this. Of course it was for our own protection because aircraft that didn't have these white stripes on it would be subject to attack.

We checked our aircraft over. I ran the engines up, made sure they were OK, the bomb bays had been loaded with the supplies we were going to take. And then we just had to wait till we got the order to come down and pick up our gear and be taken out in the evening. I had a few butterflies in my tummy at the time, a mixture of apprehension and excitement, but there was no way I could sit still and mooch around. I walked back to my hut, which was quite a long walk – they had a PA system so wherever you were you could be called in easy enough – and I had a shower and a shave, polished my shoes, all for something to do, really.

We were going to drop these airborne boys from eight hundred feet so we weren't going to run into cold weather, it was windy and wet, very windy and wet, but it wasn't cold, so I thought, 'Ah, I'm not going to wear any flying gear tonight.' You'd got to wear your helmet because it's got the earphones in it and in any case it's good protection in a fire, and I always wore gloves and goggles. I mightn't have had the goggles on but they were hanging round my neck, and that was the same thought: protection from fire. But I didn't wear any gear apart from that.

In the evening we got the call to go and pick up our parachutes and get out to the aircraft. We were out there probably an hour before take-off and we had to check our aircraft and run our engines up again and make sure everything was right. And there were all these airborne soldiers standing there, just by our aircraft. They all had black on their faces and leaves in their helmets and they had grenades hanging off them and machine guns strapped on their shoulders, all that sort of thing. They really did look fearsome and I remember thinking, 'I'm glad they're on our side, these blokes.'

The officer in charge came over to me – I was twenty-two years old and looked pretty young even at that age, I think – and said, 'Are you the pilot of this aircraft?' I said, 'Yes, sir, I'm the pilot of this aircraft.' He said, 'Have you been over before?' I said, 'Yes, I've been over a few times before.' He said, 'Ah, that's good, that's good.' Then he looked me up and down and he said, 'Good God, man, you look as though you're going to a bloody dance!'

So that started off the rapport we had with the troops. We were all strangers but we had this instant rapport that we were in it together. And then he gave me a little five-franc note. All the stick, seventeen lads from the 5th Parachute Brigade of the 6th Airborne Division, they'd all signed this and he gave it to me as a little gift. I've treasured that all my life.

Pilot Officer Ron Minchin
Australian Stirling bomber pilot, 196 Squadron, RAF
Talking to the guys, they were pretty steamed up. There was a lot of urinating around the aircraft: the aircraft didn't smell too good. It was interesting to see how they were approaching things. Some were very quiet. Like myself, probably. Some were outgoing and loud and wanted, I suppose, to get rid of the pressure and tension that existed in them. I felt a youngster, in a way, because there were some more mature men amongst them. The way they spoke and approached language was quite different to the way that we did. Some of them were a bit more basic; their language wasn't exactly what my ear was attuned to. But then again I was only a kid and our own ground staff was just as bad.

Sergeant Brian Spencer
Glider Pilot Regiment
Ken wrote on the front of our glider – they all had names – '*Quo Vadis?*' The padre, who was coming past, said, 'Very appropriate, Hannon.' But with my elementary education I had to wander up the line until I found an old friend

Horsa gliders wait to be loaded for D-Day.

of mine and I said, 'Hey, Bob, what does "*Quo Vadis?*" mean?' He said, 'A free translation would be, "Whither goest thou?"'

Captain John Sim
12th Battalion, Parachute Regiment

We emplaned under the belly of the aircraft through the hole. The hole wasn't a circular hole in the Stirling, it was a coffin-shaped hole, oblong; and in the Stirling one was able to stand up, which was rather nice, but there were no seats. Seventeen entered the aircraft, in reverse order of our jumping out. I was to jump No 1 so I was the last in. Then the door was closed and we sat on the floor with our backs to the fuselage. It was quite dark inside the aircraft, there were only about six little red lights along the fuselage, and there was nothing else to do except sit. We couldn't talk to each other because the engines started up, roared away, and we taxied around.

Warrant Officer George Oliver
Australian Stirling bomber pilot, 196 Squadron, RAF

We knew it was D-Day and it was so important. If it failed we knew that either the war might be greatly prolonged or we mightn't even win it. That's the way it looked to us, or to me anyhow, and I really felt we were going into the unknown and I can remember thinking to myself, 'I wonder what it's going to be like and I wonder if we'll come back from it.' At any rate, that's how I felt before I got on the aircraft. But once I got in and started the engines I didn't think any more about those sort of things.

Major Goronwy Rees
21st Army Group planning staff

One had this terrible feeling of, 'Now, what is actually going to happen on D-Day?' I went to the headquarters of the 101st American Parachute Division at Newbury, they were taking off from Newbury racecourse, and you suddenly saw these men being flown across the Channel really into conditions that nobody knew. And then we sat and waited to hear what the results were going to be. After that, of course, it was in the hands of the fighting soldiers. It wasn't our job any more.

Four stick commanders of 22nd Independent Parachute Company, British Sixth Airborne Division, synchronising watches prior to take-off from RAF Harwell, Oxfordshire. Among the very first Allied troops to land, this Pathfinder unit parachuted into Normandy in advance of the rest of the division to mark out dropping and landing zones. Left to right: Lieutenants Robert de Latour, Donald Wells, John Vischer and Bob Midwood. De Latour, a Canadian, was killed in action on 20 June.

Coup de Main

Major John Howard
Commander, D Company, 2nd Battalion, Oxfordshire and
Buckinghamshire Light Infantry

My company was lucky to be selected for what turned out to be a wonderful operation. It was a coup de main operation, glider borne, to capture two bridges in Normandy soon after midnight before the seaborne landings on 6 June. For this operation I was given two extra platoons and thirty Royal Engineers, a force of 180, each glider containing one platoon of around twenty-five infantry and five Royal Engineers.

It would be a night landing and they chose gliders to do the job as distinct from parachutists in order to get complete surprise. Parachutists take a long time to get together and form a platoon and company to attack an objective, whereas gliders will land thirty men on the spot, provided the glider pilots do their job properly. But I was quite satisfied on that account in that I knew that we had the very best glider pilots that the Glider Pilot Regiment could produce.

Lieutenant Richard 'Sandy' Smith
14 Platoon, B Company, 2nd Battalion, Oxfordshire and
Buckinghamshire Light Infantry

We were told it was going to be an attack on two bridges and three gliders would have a go at one and three at the other. We were going to go in the night before and hold them for as long as possible until major reinforcements arrived, and that would form the left flank of the invasion and we would keep away what armour and other German forces there were on that side. As these two were the only bridges between the coast and Caen, which is a distance of eleven miles, it was pretty obvious that if we held those two bridges we could prevent the Germans from attacking the left flank of the major invasion. Hence its importance.

One of the advantages we had was the fact that the operation would be a surprise, that we had the best glider pilots available and that they could land us exactly where they wanted to. And of course our ignorance of the hazards of the whole operation: we had no idea how risky it was because we had no experience of that sort of thing, so you can really say ignorance is bliss. I think some of the more experienced planners didn't really regard our operation as likely to be scot-free of casualties. Indeed, I think we were called 'The Forlorn Hope' at one time. But it seemed to us a perfectly feasible thing to land on an enemy coast before D-Day, hold the two bridges. And the fact that there were eighty Germans on our bridge and a smaller number on the other, just five hundred yards apart, didn't seem to deter us, although our own strength of three gliders on the main bridge was somewhat less than the Germans holding it.

We carried the normal airborne equipment, which meant you had an anti-tank PIAT as your sole defence against tanks. We carried two-inch mortars and Bren guns and the odd grenade, phosphorus and 36, Sten guns and the ordinary Enfield rifle. So it was pretty obvious to even the unimaginative that if we didn't get relief fairly quickly from the Paras, who were going to drop in the vicinity, and subsequently from the commandos, who were coming from the coast six miles away, we were going to be in real trouble. The 21st Panzers were only a matter of half an hour away, stationed just the other side of Caen. Also the coastal forces had their own weaponry, plus tanks.

Private Harry Clarke
24 Platoon, D Company, 2nd Battalion, Oxfordshire and Buckinghamshire Light Infantry

On the morning of 5 June the wind had dropped, it was still raining slightly but not too badly, and it was just after midday, I think, that we were informed that it was on for that night. And so once again we put the fuses back in the grenades and got all our equipment and gear ready for the operation that night. We had a sleep in the afternoon and I can recall being woken up by Corporal Godbold, probably about six in the evening. 'Come on Nobby,' he said. 'Getcha gear together and we'll have a meal and we're gonna be off.' It would be about eight o'clock, half-past eight, when the lorries drove into the camp and we staggered aboard. We were absolutely loaded. God knows how we climbed up the four-foot into the lorry.

We were quickly driven to Tarrant Rushton airfield where the lorries drove straight out to the gliders. The airfield itself was absolutely teeming with people and everyone seemed to know where we were going, and this did concern me. There were cries of 'Good luck!' and 'Godspeed!' all the way across and I was absolutely convinced that everyone on the aerodrome knew where we going or certainly that the invasion was on.

We were driven straight to the runway. We discarded our equipment and wandered round the other gliders chatting to friends. In my particular glider, the glider pilot was Staff Sergeant Oliver Boland, the co-pilot was Staff Sergeant Hobbs, and I recall saying to Ollie Boland at this point, 'Do you think we'll make it all right?' And he said, 'You've got no worries. I can land on a sixpence.' He was very, very confident. He was concerned about the amount of equipment and stuff we were carrying because he was worried about overloading but he said the Halifax would pull us off the ground anyway. And we sat around talking and I think it was round about ten-ish when some kind RAF chap came over with a big dixie of tea and on tasting it I was delighted to detect that there was a good measure of rum in it. This helped considerably again. We didn't expect such luxuries at the last moment. It was great that.

Staff Sergeant Geoff Barkway
Glider Pilot Regiment
I don't think you had time to be fearful because there's never enough time to get ready for these things. At the last minute: 'Wouldn't it be better if we did this?' 'Wouldn't it be better if we did that?' 'Let's move that here.' 'You carry this in your glider. We'll carry that in ours.' 'Is there anything we've forgotten?' I remember various people came round and wished us good luck. Lots of putting names on the gliders: 'Adolf here we come' and that sort of business. Everybody was in pretty high spirits.

Private William Gray
25 Platoon, D Company, 2nd Battalion, Oxfordshire and Buckinghamshire Light Infantry
Everyone was so excited, wanted to get cracking and to get on with it.

Lieutenant David Wood
24 Platoon, D Company, 2nd Battalion, Oxfordshire and Buckinghamshire Light Infantry
I think we were all raring to go. I'd had the same platoon for over two years and only about three men in it had changed and we'd already had a great disappointment at the time of the Sicily invasion when we all went on embarkation leave but weren't actually chosen to go. We were keyed up, we were ready, we really didn't think we could do any more training and we

116

wanted to get on with it and get into action for the first time. Although we knew D-Day was coming we thought that if we didn't get into action soon we'd never fire a bullet in anger.

Private Harry Clarke
24 Platoon, D Company, 2nd Battalion, Oxfordshire and Buckinghamshire Light Infantry

About half past ten we were ordered to board the Horsas. This again was a feat in itself because we had to climb up a ladder and we were so overloaded that it was a job to stagger in. I got in and I sat about four seats down, four places down, on the starboard side. David Wood sat by the door, about four places along, on the other side.

We sat in the glider talking. There was still no sign of nervousness. A slight tenseness because none of us had ever done a night flight in a glider before, it had always been daylight flights. And about ten to eleven, I would think it was, the planes started revving up, trying out their engines: they were Halifax bombers.

At about that time John Howard also came round the gliders, wished us luck, thanked us for our past help and cooperation, and you could detect the emotion in the chap's voice, you know. It was a very emotional moment for all of us. I felt sorry for him and I looked across at David Wood and I could see that David looked a bit tense because he'd got a hell of a lot on his mind that night. He was only a boy, like the rest of us. We were all in the twenty-one age group; there were one or two slightly older. Anyway, the doors were shut and we were sat there just waiting then.

Private William Gray
25 Platoon, D Company, 2nd Battalion, Oxfordshire and Buckinghamshire Light Infantry

Somebody, probably John Howard, said, 'We're off,' and the old Halifax, you could hear the engines, roared away. And up went the glider behind the Halifax.

Private Harry Clarke
24 Platoon, D Company, 2nd Battalion, Oxfordshire and Buckinghamshire Light Infantry

Suddenly we became airborne. We could barely see, it was quite dark, there were a few cigarettes going and there was obviously a tenseness and nervousness because there wasn't the usual idle chatter. Nobody was singing and there was almost silence in the glider. But within about ten minutes the usual round of conversation started, people began to sing and the tenseness evaporated, and it became just another glider flight.

Corporal Edward Tappenden
HQ wireless operator, D Company, 2nd Battalion, Oxfordshire and Buckinghamshire Light Infantry

We were singing all the old London songs, because most of the lads were cockney boys and Londoners. They were singing 'Abie, Abie, my boy' and all sorts of things until we got over France. Then the major ordered quiet and everything went quiet and everyone was on their toes, waiting.

Private Harry Clark
24 Platoon, D Company, 2nd Battalion, Oxfordshire and Buckinghamshire Light Infantry

We heard the glider pilot shout, 'Casting off!' and suddenly the roar of the aeroplane engine receded and we were in a silent world. It was like being trapped in a floating coffin in mid-space. Immediately the glider cast off, the singing, the talk, the conversation stopped. People realised what we were heading for. There was no going back now. We'd reached the point where we could only go forward.

Major John Howard
Commander, D Company, 2nd Battalion, Oxfordshire and Buckinghamshire Light Infantry

When we levelled out a bit at a thousand feet we opened the doors of the glider. One of them was straight in front of me. Sitting on my left was Lieutenant Brotheridge, my leading platoon commander, and he undid his safety belt, I held his equipment one side and his platoon sergeant the other side and he leant forward very precariously and opened the door which lifted up into the roof. At the same time this was happening the back door was opened the same way by some of the men at the back.

When Den Brotheridge slumped back into his seat and put his safety belt on again I looked out at the fields of France and it had an amazing tranquillising effect on me and on those near to me who could see. There you

Major John Howard, Oxfordshire and Buckinghamshire Light Infantry, who commanded the coup de main raid to capture the Caen Canal and River Orne bridges in the early hours of D-Day.

had the magnificent stock, horses and cattle, grazing very, very quietly. It was so quiet; it was like being on an exercise in England. And the tranquillising effect went right throughout the glider because we were all quite silent by that time.

But there wasn't much time to think about that because the glider suddenly did a right-hand turn, because we'd gone a way inland towards Caen, and then another right-hand turn, so that we were coming into the landing zone from the south, losing height all the way. And as we did that turn I could see the River Orne and the Caen Canal, reflected in the half-moon, running down towards Caen. And we came to what we knew was going to be the toughest moment of the lot: the crash land.

THE BENOUVILLE / CAEN CANAL BRIDGE (PEGASUS BRIDGE)

Private Francis Bourlet
25 Platoon, D Company, 2nd Battalion, Oxfordshire and
Buckinghamshire Light Infantry
The glider pilot shouted out, 'We're making our approach!' So we immediately linked all our arms together, which was the usual procedure, lifted our feet up off the floor and just waited for the landing. Well, we'd expected to land about eighty to ninety miles an hour. I now know it was well over a hundred miles an hour. We hit the deck and, lo and behold, before we knew where we were, we was airborne again, the wheels had come off the glider, and we came down with a terrific thud on the metal skid underneath the glider. The chute was thrown out of the back door, this turned out to be absolutely useless, it caught in the undergrowth and snapped off, and we was in a shower of sparks – this was where the metal skid was running over the flints in the earth. And we come to a shuddering stop.

Major John Howard
Commander, D Company, 2nd Battalion, Oxfordshire and
Buckinghamshire Light Infantry
Suddenly everything went dark and I felt my head had been knocked rather badly and my own feelings were, 'God, I'm blind. We've been training and waiting for this all this time and now, when the moment comes, I'm going to

be bloody useless.' But all that had happened was my head had bumped the top of the glider and my battle-bowler had come down over my eyes.

Once I'd realised that, of course, I eased up the helmet and the first thing I saw was that the door had disappeared. It had completely telescoped. I could hear the glider pilots on my right moaning in their cockpit, it would seem to have been smashed, but I was conscious that everybody in the glider was moving. I could hear the click of the safety belts being undone and I knew that men were getting out of the glider and people were pushing in front of me to get through the broken door.

I let Den Brotheridge and his platoon get out first because if they were indeed the first platoon down their job was absolutely one of speed. The leading section was to go up and put the pillbox out of action by throwing a smoke bomb on the road as they came up from the landing zone and, through the smoke, throw short-fuse grenades through the gun slits of the pillbox and then continue with the rest of the platoon across the bridge. This had all been planned. Every platoon was ready to do that job in case they were the first platoon to get to the bridge that night.

Private William Gray
25 Platoon, D Company, 2nd Battalion, Oxfordshire and
Buckinghamshire Light Infantry
Den Brotheridge, our platoon commander, quickly got the door open and said, 'Gun out,' which was me. Out I jumped, stumbled on the grass because of the weight I had on me, and set the Bren up facing the bridge and the rest of the lads jumped out. Den Brotheridge got in front of me and looked round to make sure that everybody was out and said, 'Come on, lads.' We were about thirty yards from the bridge and we dashed towards it.

Major John Howard
Commander, D Company, 2nd Battalion, Oxfordshire and
Buckinghamshire Light Infantry
I heard them pattering up the little tracks to the bridge from the landing zone and I emerged from the glider, broke my way through all the debris, the wood, which had smashed all around it, and I suppose that really was the most exhilarating moment of my life. Because I stood there and I could see the tower of the bridge about fifty yards from where I was standing. The nose of

This photograph, taken in July 1944, shows the three Horsa gliders that landed Major John Howard's coup de main force in the early hours of D-Day to capture the Caen Canal bridge (Pegasus Bridge) at Benouville. The bridge itself is just through the trees, sixty yards from the furthest glider.

the glider was right through the German wire-fence, where, back in the UK, I'd almost facetiously asked the glider pilot to put it so we would not have to use the Bangalore torpedoes, which every glider had brought with them for the purpose of breaking through the wire. And above all, and this was the tremendous thing, there was no firing at all. In other words, we had complete surprise: we really caught old Jerry with his pants down. But there was no time to wonder about that. I followed the platoon up the track; I saw the smoke bomb explode, the phosphorus bomb; I heard the 'Thud, thud, thud' in the pillbox as the grenades exploded and I knew we'd get no trouble from there.

Private Francis Bourlet
25 Platoon, D Company, 2nd Battalion, Oxfordshire and Buckinghamshire Light Infantry
The pillbox was very, very simple. We, the rest of the section, kept back. Jack, that's Corporal Bailey, and Parr went on just ahead of us and Bailey put the grenade actually into the slot of the pillbox. By this time the first section was already halfway across the bridge. We immediately ran round the back of the pillbox, which we knew contained troops. There was a large dugout, I went down one end of the dugout and O'Donnell went down the other and, lo and behold, we caught them in bed. There was approximately eight workers – these, I understand, were digging the anti-glider poles – and three Germans. We rounded them up and put them into the pillbox.

Lance Corporal Thomas Packwood
25 Platoon, D Company, 2nd Battalion, Oxfordshire and Buckinghamshire Light Infantry
My section's job was to go over on the right-hand side of the bridge, which we did. Halfway over the bridge I realised that Bill Gray should be in front of me so I stepped aside. I said, 'Come on Bill, you should be in front of me,' because you don't want a bloke firing from the hip with a Bren gun if you're in front of him. So we rushed over the bridge and he let fly.

Private William Gray
25 Platoon, D Company, 2nd Battalion, Oxfordshire and
Buckinghamshire Light Infantry
I saw a German on the right-hand side and let rip at him and down he went. I
still kept firing going over the bridge and on the other side was another
German and he went down too.

Private Denis Edwards
25 Platoon, D Company, 2nd Battalion, Oxfordshire and
Buckinghamshire Light Infantry
There were only, I think, two or three Germans up and about at that time on
the other side of the bridge. One of them fired a Very light up into the night
sky when we charged across the bridge, because he didn't know what the heck
was happening, and suddenly found himself facing all these guys with
blackened faces charging across at him. Another one fired the machine gun
that they had mounted there which unfortunately hit Danny [Den]
Brotheridge, our platoon commander. He got a bullet through his neck and he
died soon afterwards, which was very sad.

Private Wally Parr
25 Platoon, D Company, 2nd Battalion, Oxfordshire and
Buckinghamshire Light Infantry
There were two dugouts there with doors. I dashed to the first one, put my
rifle to the side of it, whipped out a 36 grenade. Charlie was there with a Bren
gun. I slung open the door, pulled the pin, slung it in, shut the door and
waited. There was a terrific explosion. I shouted to Charlie, 'Get in!' He went
to the doorway with his machine gun and sprayed it. I went to the second one
and repeated the same operation. As we came back I went to pick up my rifle
leaning against the door and I heard a voice groaning and moaning inside. I
stopped Charlie straight. The door was still wide open. I pulled out a 77
phosphorus grenade, if the shrapnel didn't get them the phosphorus would,
and I just took off the top, a green thing, gave it a couple of whirls, undone it
and threw it in. It went off a treat.

Private Denis Edwards
25 Platoon, D Company, 2nd Battalion, Oxfordshire and Buckinghamshire Light Infantry

We were throwing grenades around, I threw one or two and we were firing rifles literally up into the sky just to make a noise. The grenades I threw I aimed at the far side of the Caen canal bank and they fell into the canal. Probably the only thing they killed were a few fish but they went off with quite a good bang. And the Germans literally ran. They scattered.

Major John Howard
Commander, D Company, 2nd Battalion, Oxfordshire and Buckinghamshire Light Infantry

It was a tremendous sight to see all the tracer bullets firing in all directions. There seemed to be three different colours, red, yellow and white, with the enemy firing at us and my men firing at them as they went over the bridge. And while all this was happening I suddenly heard two more crashes behind me in the landing zone and I could hardly believe that two more platoons had got there, but it could only have been that. And in next to no time, it seemed to me, David Wood came running up with his platoon. And after a bit of a pause No 3 glider came up, Sandy Smith with his platoon. He seemed to be limping very badly.

Lieutenant David Wood
24 Platoon, D Company, 2nd Battalion, Oxfordshire and Buckinghamshire Light Infantry

Quite suddenly and unexpectedly the pilots said, 'Christ, there's the bridge,' and they put the nose of the glider down very steeply. The next thing I knew was that there were sparks coming from the skids underneath, they didn't have wheels, and I thought these sparks were actually enemy fire but they were in fact the skids striking the ground. And then there was an almighty crash and I was thrown out through the side of the glider, landed on the ground, still clutching my canvas bucket of grenades. I had my Sten gun with its bayonet still fixed but wasn't in any way hurt.

The rest of the platoon got out of the glider. Some were like me thrown out and some got out through the doors. I collected them together, we knew exactly what we were supposed to do, although we didn't know at that moment whether we were the first glider to land or the second or the third, because three were destined to land at our particular bridge. I took the platoon forward to where I knew the bridge was and the road running up to it and there, crouching in the ditch, was my company commander, who said, quite simply, 'David, No 2.' And I knew that No 2's job was to cross the road and sort out the enemy on the other side in the inner defences of the bridge.

Private Harry Clarke
24 Platoon, D Company, 2nd Battalion, Oxfordshire and
Buckinghamshire Light Infantry
David Wood said, 'Forward,' and with all his boyish enthusiasm, he was a great leader, he went gallantly into action and we all tore in like a pack of hounds after him. Suddenly I was brought to an abrupt halt, I was snagged on a load of barbed wire, and to this day I bear the scar on me right knee where a huge barb took a lump of flesh out. Actually I cursed rather loudly and I can still recall David Wood saying to me, 'Shut up, Clarke' – and this was in the middle of an attack.

Anyway, we ran forward and there were at least two machine guns firing from the position we were about to attack. Charles Godbold and I were together and as we neared the trenches we could see from the flash there was a gun firing and Charlie said, 'We'd better sling a grenade.' I said, 'We'd better not sling a 36, let's sling a couple of these stun grenades, otherwise we'll kill our own blokes.' So we flung two stun grenades and we saw two people rise out of the trench and run towards the bank of the canal. Charlie let loose a long burst from his Sten gun but I think they got away: we found no bodies there the next day. And within probably about five minutes, a few skirmishes, there was a bit of firing, it all went quiet. We'd captured our objective. We moved up to the riverbank, my section, and we passed a pillbox, there was smoke coming out of it, and all was quiet on our side. There was a machine gun firing on the other side and a few bangs so they were obviously still engaged on the west bank of the canal.

Lieutenant Richard 'Sandy' Smith
14 Platoon, B Company, 2nd Battalion, Oxfordshire and
Buckinghamshire Light Infantry
My glider crashed rather badly in what you might call static water and smashed its whole front up. I was myself flung through the cockpit of the

glider and ejected on to the ground, only to be over-run by the glider when it slithered to a halt, and I had my knee rather badly damaged as a result of that because the wing or the undercarriage ran over me. I had a Lance Corporal Madge and I remember groping in the dark covered with mud and water and shock and he said, 'What are we waiting for, sir?' I tried to find my weapon and couldn't and found somebody else's Sten gun and ran towards the bridge. Or rather hobbled. Of my platoon, only about seven or eight were able to get out of that crash. Although they were not badly hurt they were very, very shocked and bruised. One man was killed.

I found a Spandau firing right down the centre of the bridge, so I swept left, down the catwalk running along the side of the bridge, to avoid this machine gun, and arrived at the other end to find Brotheridge dying. And then in the flurry I remember a German throwing a stick grenade at me and I saw the explosion, felt the explosion. My right wrist was hit. I was extremely lucky because the grenade exploded very close to me and hit various parts of my clothing but not my body, although there were holes in my smock. And that was the first German I actually shot. Having thrown his grenade, he tried to scramble over the back of one of the walls adjoining the café and I actually shot him with my Sten gun as he went over.

Major John Howard
Commander, D Company, 2nd Battalion, Oxfordshire and
Buckinghamshire Light Infantry
So I had three platoons down on the ground in exactly the same places where all the briefings had hoped they would be. But by this time I was suddenly wondering what was happening on the other bridge, which was only a quarter of a mile away, and I couldn't see any signs of firing over there. There were no radio messages but that didn't surprise me because the radios in those days were pretty frail. I mean, in crash landings we didn't expect them to survive. But another part of my orders was that because of the radios being a bit uncertain a runner from each platoon would report to my company headquarters by the canal bridge, from the river bridge particularly, but no runners had arrived either. I was beginning to consider whether I would have to send a platoon or half a platoon over to the river bridge to try to capture that but then all the luck turned. The captain of the Royal Engineers, Captain Jock Neilson, reported to me that there were no explosives under the

canal bridge: we found the explosives in a hut down the bank later on next morning. So that was the first good bit of news. And then we picked up, to our surprise, a radio message that 17 Platoon under Dennis Fox had captured the river bridge almost without firing a shot – the enemy had run away because of all the commotion – and 23 Platoon under Todd Sweeney had reached them. So there were two platoons over there and that was indeed very good news.

THE RANVILLE / ORNE RIVER BRIDGE

Corporal Wilfred Robert Howard
23 Platoon, D Company, 2nd Battalion, Oxfordshire and
Buckinghamshire Light Infantry
Our primary objective, 23 Platoon, was to support the glider in front of us, Freddie Fox's glider, and rush over the Orne Bridge through Freddie Fox's platoon and take up position on the other side.

Freddie Fox's glider landed in fair shape. My glider, we landed about three hundred yards short of the objective, landed perfectly, no problem with the landing, and Todd Sweeney was out and we did the usual thing we did when we jumped out of a glider: all round defence. In other words, a circle all round the glider. Todd Sweeney sat in the centre and the first thing he did was to call an O group, which was an order group; that meant he called together the corporals and the sergeants and issued his orders. The next thing he had to do was find out where he was and he and the glider pilot in fact pinpointed the spot very well, actually, and off we trotted down to a hedgerow.

We probably travelled down this hedgerow 200, 250 yards, before we came out on the road which actually led to the bridge. We dashed on to the bridge, not shouting too loudly, but making plain to the other platoon on or near the bridge that we were in fact British: as we ran along the bridge we all shouted out, 'Easy! Easy! Easy!' That was our call sign. The call sign of the platoon on the bridge I think was 'Fox' and they shouted out 'Fox!' so that we recognised one another. Remember it was pitch black, we really couldn't see too far, so we had these call signs.

So we dashed through the ranks of Freddie Fox's platoon, who were either lying on the bridge or were on the other side of the bridge in their gun position, and we then attacked our objectives. I came upon this little farmhouse, it seemed to be more of a farmer's cottage than a farmhouse, and banged on the door, big wooden door, and it eventually opened. Then we used our ersatz French to the little old lady and the little old man who came to the door. '*Où est le Boche?*' They just didn't want to know. Not interested. They didn't know whether we were Germans or whether we were Polish; we could have been Czechs, we could have been Hungarians, we could have been anything. We just motioned to them to go indoors and there was very little we could do. It was a very small place and one of my men went in and just rooted around to make certain there were no Germans in there.

Then we repaired to our positions. We didn't trouble to dig in. There didn't seem to be much point in digging in at this stage because my blokes were expert at finding well-concealed positions and if there did happen to be any fold in the ground where they could hide themselves they would do that. I took up a position in a little dip by the side of this farm cottage and I had with me Buck Read, one of my men, and we decided we were going to have a smoke.

Sapper Cyril Larkin
249 Field Company, 591 Parachute Squadron, Royal Engineers

I ran across the bridge, got off the bridge and down on to the riverbank, and I could hear people running away, the defenders running off. So I went down underneath the bridge and there was a well-worn path down the grass bank and I thought, 'Well, this has been used quite a lot.' Then I looked up into the girders of the bridge and I could see a scaffold board that ran all the way through the bridge. There was some moon but there was a lot of cloud so you had an off-and-on moon that night. And right under the middle of the bridge was a dark object.

With this dark object in the middle of the bridge, it was evident to me that work was in progress. We had been informed by the French underground movement that the bridges were quite likely to be ready for exploding and that dark object I thought was probably was a barge and they were working with the explosives off the barge. And then in the moonlight I thought, 'No, it isn't that.' There seemed to be some brickwork somewhere.

Claude, that's my twin brother, had come down as well and I positioned him near the bridge. I said, 'I'm going to check along these scaffold boards and see what's on the other side. To me, that's where the explosives will be, in the

The River Orne bridge, assaulted in the early hours of D-Day by men of John Howard's coup de main force.

middle of the bridge. Keep your finger on the trigger and if you've got to use your rifle don't be frightened to. But remember I'm just ahead of you so obviously don't put a shot up my tail end.'

So I had to crawl with my rifle and a backpack along this scaffold board and I got to the middle and there was a huge brick construction and it contained inside huge cog wheels. Obviously, in past time, it had opened the bridge. I had a torch with me, we all carried them as engineers, and I shone the torch around and I found there was no explosive. I felt a bit vulnerable actually, I thought somebody seeing torchlight underneath the bridge could put a shot into me, but anyway I had to do it and there was no explosive.

So having done that I thought, 'We've got to get out of here now,' so we decided then to climb back on to the road south of the bridge. And as we got on to the road, away in the distance an air-raid siren sounded, just like we had here back in the UK. And that was another laughable incident really: we were here already and they didn't know.

Major John Howard
Commander, D Company, 2nd Battalion, Oxfordshire and Buckinghamshire Light Infantry

As soon as I knew there were no explosives under the other bridge as well then we started sending out what has turned out to be a famous success signal, 'Ham and Jam'. 'Ham' for the canal bridge and 'Jam' for the river bridge captured intact. There were other code words, which meant they weren't captured or they were captured but blown up, but 'Ham' and 'Jam' were the important words as far as we were concerned. And that's the situation some fifteen or so minutes after landing.

HOLDING ON

Lieutenant David Wood
24 Platoon, D Company, 2nd Battalion, Oxfordshire and Buckinghamshire Light Infantry

The whole thing was over very quickly. I heard the magic words 'Ham and Jam' on my 38 set radio carried by my batman; and, as we were consolidating, my company commander came up on the radio and said I was to report to him on the road for further orders. So, taking my batman with me and the platoon sergeant, Sergeant Leather, I started to make my way back when I was hit in the leg by what turned out to be a burst of three rounds of Schmeisser machine pistol and fell to the ground quite unable to do anything. I was extremely frightened. I thought that at any minute the chap who'd fired at me was going to come along and finish me off, so I shouted, loudly. I didn't know at the time that both my batman and my platoon sergeant had been shot at the same time. But quite quickly a couple of men in the platoon came up and they did what they could for my leg, put a rifle splint on it and gave me some morphine, and by then I was effectively out of the action.

Lieutenant Richard 'Sandy' Smith
14 Platoon, B Company, 2nd Battalion, Oxfordshire and Buckinghamshire Light Infantry

I took over Brotheridge's platoon and put them in a defensive position round the far end of the bridge, the one nearest the village of Le Port, and gathered what was left of my platoon and put them in together with Brotheridge's platoon. Then I went back to the other side of the bridge, only to be told that David Wood's platoon were leaderless because he'd been shot through the legs. I reported back to John Howard and said Wood was wounded and Brotheridge was dead or dying and I'd been knocked about a bit and he told me to go back and organise the defence at the far end of the bridge, which I did. After a while the Germans had recovered from the initial shock and surprise and they were coming down from the village of Le Port, a matter of two or three hundred yards, and started to infiltrate through the backs of houses and gardens towards the bridge, and they started making it obvious that they were going to do something.

So there I was, as the only officer on his feet, with these three platoons. I felt rather exposed so I went back to Howard, who was stationed between the two bridges, and I said to him, 'Look, I wouldn't mind another platoon. If there's no trouble on the other bridge, could you please send me one of those two platoons?' Denis Fox arrived, much to my relief, marching up through the bridge and I told him to go up to the village of Le Port, where there's a small crossroads, and to hold that so at least we'd have some idea of what the Germans were trying to do. I remember him saying to me, 'I haven't got an anti-tank PIAT,' because he'd left it in his glider in a hurry, and I said, 'Well, take mine,' which we had extricated from our crashed glider. And I remember him saying, 'Well, thanks for nothing.' He took this PIAT and handed it over to Sergeant Thornton and took up a position near the crossroads at Le Port.

Major John Howard
Commander, D Company, 2nd Battalion, Oxfordshire and Buckinghamshire Light Infantry

We knew the Germans were billeted in villages and always had somebody standing ready to counter-attack the bridges. They were known to have small tanks and lorries and be ready to get to the bridges, I was told, within an hour of our landing.

The first movement was a motorcycle and what turned out to be a German staff car, rushing down the road from Ranville towards the river bridge. It crossed the bridge and then was shot up as planned and in that car was the German commander of the bridges, a Major Schmidt. The car came to a halt just between the bridges and the German commander, in perfect English, was shouting that he wanted to be shot. He said that he'd lost his honour, no doubt meaning that his bridges had been captured. The doctor happened to be nearby, Doc John Vaughan, and he gave him a couple of shots of morphine and put him to sleep.

But it was while this was going on we heard the ominous sound we most dreaded and that was the sound of tanks, and, sure enough, round about half-past one, two tanks were heard slowly coming down the road. The only anti-tank weapons we had were PIATs and we didn't have much faith in them. Even under ideal conditions they had a maximum range of fifty yards. They threw a three-and-a-half pound bomb and, if it didn't hit directly whatever it was firing at, it had a nasty habit of not exploding and there wouldn't have been much time to reload, of course, with a tank under fifty yards away. We didn't like using them at night anyway. But the tanks came rumbling along.

Lieutenant Richard 'Sandy' Smith
14 Platoon, B Company, 2nd Battalion, Oxfordshire and Buckinghamshire Light Infantry

I heard, to my horror, the rattle of tank tracks coming down the road from the Le Port direction. And I remember feeling very, very hopeless because there we were without an anti-tank weapon, except for the one we'd given to

Dennis, with my platoon only about seven or eight strong and Brotheridge's twenty-odd people. I thought, 'Well, this is going to be it,' and I vividly remember the troops looking at me to see whether I was reacting in any way to the arrival of this tank. And I remember my order: 'Look to your front.' What else I could have said I don't know. I gave that order because they wanted some form of reassurance, though I must confess that I didn't really feel very reassured myself. Anyway, a minute or two later the rumbling of this tank was heard to be getting louder and louder and then there was a sharp explosion as Sergeant Thornton, as I subsequently discovered, had fired at it at point-blank range.

Private Denis Edwards
25 Platoon, D Company, 2nd Battalion, Oxfordshire and
Buckinghamshire Light Infantry
Wagger Thornton let these tanks get really up close to him and then he let fly. We never thought those PIAT bombs would ever do much damage to a proper tank but this flaming tank literally blew up, exploded. The whole thing went up. It was well loaded with ammunition, I don't know what sort of ammunition, but within moments of Wagger firing there were great spurts of green and orange and yellow as all the ammunition inside was exploding, making a hell of a din. And the other tank behind did a quick revving of engines and disappeared, backed off up the road, and we never heard from them again.

Lieutenant Richard 'Sandy' Smith
14 Platoon, B Company, 2nd Battalion, Oxfordshire and
Buckinghamshire Light Infantry
It blew up, fortunately, right on the crossroads, blocking the entrance to the bridge either way, killing most of the crew, and one poor soul was flung out and his legs had almost disappeared and he subsequently died. I had to pass him every time I went up to see how Dennis Fox was getting on and I remember Dennis saying to me 'Look, why don't you shoot that fellow, because he's disturbing my men.' And I just couldn't shoot him.

The Germans then started infiltrating down the backs of the gardens away from the crossroads to try and come into us from either side, from the canal, down through the towpaths on either side. So we withdrew ourselves to a much closer defensive position around the head of the bridge and I tried to give the impression that we were much stronger than we were by moving Bren gun sections from one position to another and firing off tracer into the dark. It seemed to have some effect. It kept the Germans away from us and we didn't really have any what you might call hand-to-hand scrapping. It was really more them trying to find out what the hell was going on.

The Sixth Glider

Sergeant Raymond Rayner
22 Platoon, D Company, 2nd Battalion, Oxfordshire and
Buckinghamshire Light Infantry

My glider was supposed to land on the River Orne bridge. No 6 landed on the bridge where I was supposed to land, on the River Orne Bridge, and then No 5 glider came. But where's No 4? Where were we?

We were cast off in the wrong place, so we landed on a bridge that we actually took but wasn't our objective. It was eight miles away from our objective. Actually, when we came in, they were firing at us worse than what the other bridge had, where we should have landed. There were tracer bullets nearly hitting us as we came in, tracer bullets as we landed. Now, we actually took that bridge, but we had to split our platoon to take the east side and the west side of the bridge, to defend it. And as we crossed that bridge the wireless operator was running aside of me with his wireless on and he was hit straight through the head, he fell down dead, straight away. I was running beside of him and I looked at him and I tried his pulse. He was dead all right. We had to leave him there, we tried to get the wireless off him but we couldn't. He was the first man killed on D-Day. They say Danny Brotheridge was the first man killed but that man, Everett, he was the first man killed. Danny Brotheridge died of wounds two hours afterwards.

But that wasn't the end of the story. As soon as we landed we knew we was at the wrong bridge, we knew every blade of grass that was on those other bridges, so we had to send out Lieutenant Tony Hooper, who was my platoon commander, to find out where we were. Captain Priday was second-in-command of the operation, he was in my glider, and Priday told Hooper to go and do a reconnaissance to find out exactly where we were.

Now, Hooper went out, he got captured in a wood where he was trying to find out where we were and the Germans brought him back to their headquarters just over from this bridge; they were firing on us from there. And two Germans were bringing him back over the bridge, one of them with a Schmeisser in his back, one escorting him, and Tony kept talking to them aloud. Course, he knew we were there; he talked to them very loudly so we'd know where he was – it was pitch black as you can imagine. So, myself and Captain Priday, both of us shouted, 'Jump, Tony!' He jumped in a ditch away from the Germans, left the Germans exposed on the road, ten yards away from us, we couldn't let them get any further, and as he jumped we fired and they fell down dead. But as they fell down dead one pulled his trigger, which he'd had in Tony Hooper's back, and sprayed us. He hit me through the arm.

Course, our job wasn't to hold that bridge at all. Captain Priday said, 'We've got to get back to the others as fast as we possibly can.' There were about thirteen of us out of the platoon. The others were on the other side of the bridge and we didn't wait for them to come back over, they couldn't get back over, and three of them got captured. Later, they were in this house being interrogated by the Germans and one of them got a bit stroppy with the Germans and the others heard a gunshot. They'd killed him. The people from the village buried him and he's the only soldier in that cemetery today.

THE ARRIVAL OF THE SIXTH AIRBORNE

Captain David Tibbs
Regimental Medical Officer, 13th Battalion, Parachute Regiment
The plane took off and one's pulse rate went up a little bit when you realised this was it. It was a Dakota, a twin-engined plane, with an open door on its side where we were going to jump so it was fairly noisy and there wasn't much opportunity for conversation. But most people were trying to rib each other a bit. Some chaps were a bit silent and looked a little bit green but really a general attitude of cheerfulness was kept up without any problems. I was tense and excited as I think anyone would be on this sort of occasion. It was my job as the officer in charge of the twenty men within the plane to keep up morale and not show any doubts but I think we all felt much the same.

Corporal Bob Sullivan
3rd Parachute Squadron, Royal Engineers

There was banter, there always is. Chaps took it different ways. Some dozed, there was a bit of a sing-song, but I think most people were wrapped up in their thoughts about what was going to come.

Captain David Tibbs
Regimental Medical Officer, 13th Battalion, Parachute Regiment

There was a blackout all over England so it was difficult to gauge where we were but we could judge when we were over the sea. I was sitting near the door of the plane so I could see down but really it was just blackness with the occasional burning embers of carbon from the engines coming back, which rather surprised me. At first I thought they were ack-ack shells coming up but they were little glowing embers off the aircraft engines.

Lieutenant Colonel Terence Otway
Commanding Officer, 9th Battalion, Parachute Regiment

I actually stood in the door of my aircraft when we flew over the Solent and it was a most fantastic sight. It was bright enough to see quite a lot of detail. I could see all the ships in the Solent. They seemed to be in a ring round the Isle of Wight and they seemed to be already streaming towards the French coast.

Staff Sergeant John Potts
Glider Pilot Regiment

As far as the eye could see there were ships and battleships and I remember saying to Bill, 'I'm glad I'm not going to be on the receiving end of that tomorrow.' It really was an awesome sight. Only the people who flew across the Channel that night ever had this view.

Sergeant Arthur Batten
Stirling bomber rear-gunner, 190 Squadron, RAF

Once we'd got about a mile across the Channel, I looked back. I've never forgotten it. I sat in my turret, I was looking for enemy aircraft, and the only thing I could see, 180 degrees either side of my turret, looking back to England, was twinkling wing-lights on the following aircraft. Right across, as far as I could scan, twinkling lights. A sight never, ever to be seen again.

Private Sidney Capon
9th Battalion, Parachute Regiment

None of us is going to die. We're all brave men. We're not going to die. 'Twenty minutes to go, lads! Equipment check!' Each man would check the equipment of the man in front of him, his chute, etc., and each chute would be on to the strongpoint. It didn't seem long, those twenty minutes. Then, 'We're approaching the coast!' And as we approached the coast of France the German ack-ack came up at us. You could see the amber glows.

Staff Sergeant John Potts
Glider Pilot Regiment

I could see quite clearly the estuary of the River Orne, the river we were making for, and the flak was much, much greater than we'd ever anticipated. In fact as we approached the estuary of this river we were really rocking and rolling because the vibrations from the flak were sending the glider upwards and down. It was rough. In fact we were hit twice. Once, way back, almost on the tail section. We heard it. But another shot came right between Bill and myself and right through the top of the cockpit. And as it did there was a strike of tracer on my side, I was in the starboard seat, and you could see the wooden fabric of the glider was burning between the mainplane and the fuselage.

Corporal Bob Sullivan
3rd Parachute Squadron, Royal Engineers

We were bouncing all over the sky. When we crossed the coast the plane dropped some anti-personnel bombs and this led the plane to surge upwards and a number of lads fell to their knees. What with the plane veering and bouncing around, really it was pandemonium. There was flashes all over the place, there was tracer coming up and I think 'Get out the plane!' was the main thought. That's it: 'Get out!'

Captain John Sim
12th Battalion, Parachute Regiment

We all moved up closer. I was astride the door, looking down, and I hoped to see some of the task force, some of the armada, but I didn't see any ships at all, just the speckly wave tops of the sea below me. Suddenly I saw the parallel lines of waves coming ashore on the dark yellow beach and then a cliff and woods and copses and hedgerows, only about eight hundred feet below me.

Warrant Officer George Oliver
Australian Stirling bomber pilot, 196 Squadron, RAF
The bomb-aimer, down in the bomb-aiming compartment, he had a good view of the ground and he guided us in. I had to fly the aircraft at the exact airspeed and keep my height so I was fully occupied doing that. The bomb-aimer was giving us directions. He'd say, 'Left, left,' and I'd veer a little bit to the left and he'd say, 'Steady.' Then he might say, 'Right,' and I'd go a bit to the right and then he'd say, 'Steady. Steady. Steady. Steady. Steady.' Green light. I was concentrating so much. I remember shouting, 'Good luck, fellas!' but I don't think they heard me.

Private Ron Dixon
12th Battalion, Parachute Regiment
First was the company commander, Major Stephens. He said – I can see it now – 'Flak coming up at us!' and you could see it outside, banging. Then it was green light on, 'Go!' and he was out and I was next.

Sapper Wilfred Robert Jones
3rd Parachute Squadron, Royal Engineers
What we thought were pretty lights – later we discovered they were tracers – were coming up from the ground. Some people got hit. A bloke called Matheson, from York, he didn't survive the jump. When he was found he was still in his parachute harness. We'd been in the boys' service together. He'd been training to be a blacksmith.

Private Philip Crofts
7th Battalion, Parachute Regiment
B Company carried rubber dinghies with two paddles in a kit bag on their leg. The kit bag was so heavy: not only did you have a rubber dinghy and paddles in there, you had your weapon and your small pack all on top. And when the

time came to jump, about all we could do was move the leg into the hole and fall out after it. As soon as I fell out of the plane, my chute opened, the ack-ack was coming up, I pulled the quick release and the kit bag was so heavy that it just broke away and all I could see was a white-painted kit bag vanishing below me.

Private Anthony Leake
8th Battalion, Parachute Regiment
The first man, an officer, jumped. His batman, who was No 2, fell down in the doorway so there was a delay while they got him to his feet and pushed him out. I was No 16. Number 15, he turned round in the doorway and said, 'I'm not hooked up!' I said, 'You are,' and I pushed him out. Hooked up or not we couldn't wait any longer. It sounds a bit hard but I knew he'd be hooked up because it had all been checked and double-checked, but somehow he got into this panic.

Private James Baty
9th Battalion, Parachute Regiment
We had a dog and a dog handler, Jack Corteil, and he was to go No 1 and I was to go No 2. The dog was trained; he had his own parachute and he had a little red light on the back as a guiding light for the dog handler and he was trained to stand still as soon as he hit the ground. Of course, he loved jumping. But when we came over Normandy with all the flak coming up – no door on, you could see it all coming up – he wouldn't jump. Course, it took Jack Corteil and myself all our time to throw him out and nobody else could go because everybody was all hooked up. The dog went out and Jack Corteil went out as the handler. And as I was in the door to go out the plane banked and went off at a different tangent, it threw me right back to the other side of the fuselage. Course, couldn't get up. The RAF dispatcher and the next chap behind me managed to lift me up and get me to the door and I jumped.

Jack Corteil, incidentally, was only nineteen. His mother was English and his father was French and he was a bit of a wag. He came from London and he loved the countryside and when he was in Bulford he used to nip off and do a bit of poaching. And he was caught one day so naturally was up on a charge and that's how he got the job of handler.

He was marched up to the company commander, Major Allen Parry – who, incidentally, was a real gentleman and a nice man, he always put his men before himself – and he said, 'Corteil, what the devil have you been up to?' He said, 'Sorry, sir.' 'Right, there's the charge sheet. Would you like to accept my punishment?' He said, 'Yes, sir.' 'We are going to have a dog, an Alsatian, and you can be the handler. It's at present down at Bulford field' – that's about a mile away from the barracks – 'go down there and report to the head kennel man and he'll give you the dog and all the bumf.' So he went down there and from that day he loved that dog. He said it meant more to him than a fiancée. It was a beautiful animal and he called it Glen and he trained it and they were inseparable.

I got to know the dog and he got to know me because I was used as a sort of hideaway with different scents and that and the dog had to come and find me. I think, actually, it became a game for the dog, and I enjoyed it because he was a beautiful animal. He loved jumping on exercises, on training jumps; he loved it. He was a marvellous dog, really. Everybody loved him. Naturally he was the pet of the battalion. I don't know whether dogs are colour blind or not but he knew anybody with a red beret on. But nobody was allowed to feed him or pet him. You weren't allowed to go 'Good dog' or 'Lovely fella' or anything like that. He wasn't allowed to get too friendly with anybody. You didn't want him to lose his potential, to get too soft or too friendly.

Later I did hear that Brigadier Hill had landed in the same DZ as the dog and dog handler and for their reward they were bombed by the RAF and the dog handler and dog were killed. It was sad. A young lad really enjoying his job got killed at nineteen.

Warrant Officer George Oliver
Australian Stirling bomber pilot, 196 Squadron, RAF

There were hundreds of aircraft around. You couldn't always miss the slipstreams and the aircraft was heavy because it had all these soldiers in it. And we had to fly at a definite height because if you flew any old height the people above would be dropping their parachutists on top of you and if you were too high you'd drop yours in amongst the aircraft below. So we all tried to keep the same height but it wasn't that easy in those days because our barometric pressure altimeters weren't a precision instrument like they've got today. You couldn't see that far but you could see the dim outlines of the aircraft and this kind of thing. How we didn't have any collisions is beyond me. But as I was turning around after the drop there was flak around and I noticed a Stirling on fire, plunging down.

Pilot Officer Ron Minchin
Australian Stirling bomber pilot, 196 Squadron, RAF

Some of the guys were not as good pilots as others and they weren't controlling the aircraft at the right height. So suddenly you'd find paratroopers that were nearly above you and we had a hell of a time trying to miss paratroopers in the air that were dropped too high. In fact some of the guys brought back shrouds embedded in their wings, near the engine, meaning that they'd killed a paratrooper.

I was horrified to find, after we had done the drop, that I was suddenly having to accelerate like mad to get above a group of chaps. Fortunately they were shown up by an aircraft blowing up – if the aircraft hadn't blown up we'd have never seen them and we'd have gone right into them – but we only just missed them. They would have seen us, these four great rings, the red rings of the engine, coming towards them. It must have been horrifying.

Private William John Le Cheminant
7th Battalion, Parachute Regiment

I saw a plane cut a parachute and the occupant in half. It went right through his parachute and dragged him to the wingtip and snapped him off. The chap went down and landed and burst into flames because he was carrying phosphorus grenades.

Captain David Tibbs
Regimental Medical Officer, 13th Battalion, Parachute Regiment

I was jumping No 1, standing at the door of the aircraft, when suddenly I saw to my horror another plane heading absolutely for us. The visibility was not very good so it must have been very close, it was a four-engined Stirling, which was one of the planes also involved in parachute dropping and glider tugging, and what it was doing there I don't know, but we were clearly going to hit. At that point our pilot heeled right over to take evasive action and this plane did and by some miracle we did not hit each other. I glanced back at the men in the plane behind me and they had all been thrown to the floor, heavily laden men with parachutes all sprawling on the floor, and one realised

Warrant Officer George Oliver. A Stirling pilot with 196 Squadron, RAF, he was one of many Australian airmen to take part in D-Day.

the difficulty they would have in getting out of the plane. The plane righted itself and immediately the green light came on warning us to jump. There was nothing I could do, I couldn't help the men behind me, so I jumped. But one didn't realise fully at the time the consequence of this. These men couldn't get upright with their heavy loads, they had to crawl to the door of the aircraft. And so, instead of jumping out one a second, because the aircraft was covering the ground at sixty yards a second they were spread out over a mile or two because they would be dropping every ten seconds, struggling to get out of the aircraft. So, as a consequence, many of these men we didn't see again. Only about five turned up on the dropping zone with me. Some were captured; others we didn't ever hear what had happened to them; others made their way back.

Private Sidney Capon
9th Battalion, Parachute Regiment
I had a beautiful landing, the best ever landing I've ever had. I landed in a field right near a hedgerow with a road running parallel and a dwelling opposite. I wasn't interested in the dwelling. You was always taught: 'There's only one objective. No private battles.' I released my chute. I felt most dejected: there was nobody around. I saw the plane go round, along and away and all of a sudden another parachute came down about two or three yards from me. We took the cover of the hedgerow, then we met another chap, and off we went, three of us now, and carried on another hundred yards and we met Lieutenant Dowling from B Company. He had about six people with him and he was trying to find his bearings and was slaying these stinging nettles. A lorry came along with some Germans on it but we laid and we hid in the hedgerow, not forgetting: 'No private warfare.'

Company Sergeant Major Barney Ross
9th Battalion, Parachute Regiment
I fell right on to the dropping zone. There was a little hut in the middle of the dropping zone and I dropped within twenty yards of that. Not many got to the dropping zone. The first person I saw when I landed was a medical officer. We were quacking away at each other: we had these little quacker things so that you knew who it was if someone was coming along; you could find out whether they were a Jerry or not. Don't forget it was pitch black at night. I

actually thought I was the only one in France at one time 'cause I didn't see anybody and you're expecting a whole mass of blokes to be all around.

Sergeant Bill French
7th Battalion, Parachute Regiment

I got myself together and I picked up one of my mates and we eventually found another one and the three of us got together. And we hadn't been on the ground ten minutes and Jerry opened fire on us. We heard a tank go along the road and he must have seen us as he opened fire, but none of us was hit. Then we found a sunken road and got into it and I met another lad from Bradford, Reg Ball, and he came with us. Then we saw somebody walking up the sunken road towards us. We asked him for the password and he said, 'Bloody hell, I've forgotten it.' That was our platoon commander.

Captain David Tibbs
Regimental Medical Officer, 13th Battalion, Parachute Regiment

There was a system of passwords and you had to give the appropriate reply. You might say 'B' and they would say 'Bulldog' in return. There was some confusion over this because each day had a different password; and of course the day before we had been geared up for the attack and now some people were still using the password for that day. In fact, I met, during the hours of darkness, one rather distressed journalist, because several journalists dropped with us, who'd got two Sten bullets in his neck. Fortunately he wasn't too badly hurt; they were just lodged under the skin. He had apparently given the wrong password or been misunderstood and been shot by our own men.

Sergeant William Higgs
Glider Pilot Regiment

Along came a Frenchman on a bike with a long loaf under his arm and he stopped immediately he saw us because we had those funny hats like the Germans and wings on our breasts. We looked like Germans. He pulled out his identity card to show us and I said, '*Je suis Anglais.*' He said, '*Anglais?*' I said, '*Vous allez.*' He went down the lane to a farm. All of a sudden we heard him shout out and we saw all the cows moving in. He was sensing trouble and getting his cows in.

Lieutenant Colonel Terence Otway
Commanding Officer, 9th Battalion, Parachute Regiment
We met two rather stout German soldiers on bicycles, who we stopped. When we told them we were British troops they said they were rather sick and tired of the SS dressing up in British uniforms and doing exercises and could they please get back to barracks. We did convince them we were British troops, we took their rifles and threw them into the marshy water and we told them to get on their bikes, literally, and get the hell out of it, which they did, rather thankfully. I often wonder what happened to them.

Lance Corporal Ron Phelps
9th Battalion, Parachute Regiment
All of a sudden I heard the sound of marching feet and I thought, 'Cor, that must be Germans.' I dived behind cover and I watched our medics go by, marching in threes down this road, just like as if it was an exercise, to set up a field hospital. And I thought to myself, 'Perhaps it's not a war. Perhaps it's an exercise.' I couldn't understand how they could march along there. I suppose there was about twenty or thirty marching along in threes as if without a care in the world.

Captain Guy Radmore
Brigade Signals Officer, 5th Parachute Brigade
When we were milling around in the dark I heard a vehicle and told some chaps to get their grenades out – I thought it was an armoured car – and it was two parachute sailors* in a vehicle. I stopped them and I said, 'Get out. What are you doing?' They said, 'Well, in the Navy no one taught us how to march so we bumped off these Germans and we're going to motor to the rendezvous.' I said, 'You're going to walk from now on.' The terrible arrogance of the senior service! But I thought it was absolutely marvellous. These chaps, so matter-of-fact.

Captain John Sim
12th Battalion, Parachute Regiment
Having got out of my harness I reckoned that I'd been dropped on the right spot and I shouted for any men who happened to be landing around me and could hear me. I gathered up a little group of four and together with my compass we marched off westwards towards the rendezvous. The 7th Battalion

---

* Parachute sailors: Royal Navy personnel who dropped with the Airborne forces to provide a wireless link with the naval bombardment force offshore.

had a bugle to rendezvous their lads in the copse on the edge of the dropping zone. The 13th Battalion had a hunting horn. But we, the 12th, had a red light. I got on to a little hillock on the dropping zone and flashed my torch around the area, hoping that our men would see the light and come towards me and then I'd despatch them to the battalion rendezvous in the quarry. Very few people came in during the hour that I was there.

Captain Guy Radmore
Brigade Signals Officer, 5th Parachute Brigade

I met up with the intelligence officer and said, 'Where are we?' and he said, 'I've no idea.' We came to a signpost – by now we'd got a few soldiers round us – and I said, 'Well, let's cheat.' He swarmed up on to my shoulders and we shone a torch at the signpost.

Major Kenneth Darling
12th Battalion, Parachute Regiment

Having been in England for the last few years we weren't accustomed to signposts, because, certainly in southern England, they had all been removed. The stupidly efficient Germans had made every preparation to resist our arrival but they had forgotten to take down all the bloody signposts as we'd done in England four years earlier.

Private Victor Newcomb
Medical Orderly, 224 Parachute Field Ambulance

I found myself hanging in a tree, not very far above the ground. I released myself from my parachute and just dropped the extra few feet to find that I was up to my ankles in bog. The accuracy of the drop didn't match the confidence of the briefing that we had got earlier. I was somewhere that I couldn't identify at all except by the presence of a large number of croaking frogs. I knew it was marshland. Therefore I knew fairly well that it was well to the south of where we had expected to be dropped.

I released myself from my harness. I rescued the bag of medical equipment that I had been carrying and moved to where I could hear low voices in another part of this rather swampy area and found two or three other members of other groups. Not the group that had been dropped with me; I seemed to have drifted slightly away from them.

We formed a small group and then found our way to the nearest road and to the nearest farmhouse where we were able with maps and so forth to identify exactly where we were with the local farmers. Our reception was a somewhat joyous one. They were only too anxious to tell us everything that they could about where we were and where there might have been members of the German army. They offered us a little bit of hospitality but I don't think we were in the mood for either eating or drinking.

Private James Baty
9th Battalion, Parachute Regiment
I landed in water, much to my fright. The Germans had flooded a vast area and it was all sticky mud underneath. I was wet, soaking wet. My boots and my legs were more muddy than anything else. I seemed to have landed on a patch of ground in the water where there was a rise and naturally I just felt with my feet all the way along until I got out of the water. But I was very, very lucky: there was no-end odd drowned. If they didn't release their chutes in time or if they were loaded with gear, they went straight down.

Brigadier James Hill
Commanding Officer, 3rd Parachute Brigade
I dropped a quarter of a mile from Cabourg where the Dives enters the sea and close to the River Dives in four feet of water. I had a four-hour struggle to reach dry land near our own dropping zone. During that period, to my annoyance, I found myself making tea: being a good soldier I always had teabags sewn in my battledress and, of course, dropping in four feet of water, I left a stream of cold tea behind me. And when I was still in the water I heard shots and I thought, 'By God, here we are, we're getting into battle at once.' When I investigated, it was one member of my bodyguard shooting the other one in the leg by mistake, thinking he was a German.

I collected forty-two soaking wet stragglers, who included two parachute-sailors and an Alsatian parachuting dog. And as I walked with these forty-two chaps it was getting light and we were in a very narrow track with no ditches and there was water on the other side of the hedge. Suddenly I heard a horrible noise. Because I'd seen fighting before I knew what it was: it was pattern bombing by low-flying aircraft. So I shouted to the chaps to get down, we all flung ourselves down, I flung myself on the 9th Battalion mortar platoon commander, and there we were, right in the middle of this pattern bombing and I thought to myself, 'This is it,' and I knew I'd been hit.

All you were aware of was dust and the smell of death. It was horrible. Then I looked to my left and in the middle of the path I saw a leg and I thought, 'By God, that's my leg.' And I had another look at it and I realised it wasn't because it had a brown boot on it, and I had a strict rule that no one was to wear brown boots, which were American parachute boots. But I was lying on Lieutenant Peters, who was dead, and it was his leg. I'd had much of my left backside removed but otherwise I was OK.

I staggered to my feet and I could only see one other person who was able to get up and that was my defence platoon commander. So, the first problem of a commander: what do I do? I was surrounded by dead and dying chaps. Do I look after them or do I get on with business? And of course the answer was, you have to get on with business. So with my defence platoon commander I went round all the bodies that were dead and took their morphine off them and we handed the morphine to the living, so they at least had that little bit of comfort, and then there was nothing for it but to leave them. And I shall never forget, and it will haunt me to my dying day, that as the two of us moved on they all gave us a cheer and wished us luck. And I don't think any of them lived to tell the tale.

Corporal Michael Corboy
9th Battalion, Parachute Regiment
I was about twenty miles adrift: I'd been dropped the far side of the Dives instead of the east bank of the Orne. I came down into a little orchard and got out of my parachute, it was hanging in a tree, and then I had my first sight of this huge hedgerow, it's called *bocage*, and I clambered over that and then I saw, silhouetted on the skyline, two guys. I went up to them and said, 'Haven't you ever been told about skylining?' and they said, 'Well, we're not in any danger from you, mate. You've still got your rifle in your leg bag.'

During the night I picked up about six more guys and eventually we came out into daylight. There was a river there and there was a glider that had crashed into the side of the river and the men were extracting a jeep and a trailer and things. We went past them. We carried on down the road to a little village, Dozulé, and went round that and then we came in touch with a sergeant with about another half-dozen. And this sergeant, his name was Bullock, he decided that we'd go back to Dozulé.

It was a straight road through the village and we'd got about a hundred yards down, all the natives were coming out and bringing us cider and milk and apples, and then suddenly a German car came through the middle of the village. Of course we opened up and blew all its windows out and two German soldiers got out and gave themselves up. While this was going on a man came running out of a house and dragged some bundle out of a parked car and ran back. I went over to the house to find out what it was and it was a little child, about four years old, and I thought what a brave thing that was to do with all the firing going on.

Staff Sergeant John Potts
Glider Pilot Regiment

We had five to six-and-a-half minutes' flying time depending on the wind before we should have come across the landing zone. Now, the special paratroopers who had dropped before us, their leader, a lieutenant, a Scottish rugby international, his last words to us were, 'There will be lights there for you. If there aren't any lights, we'll be dead.' Well, there were no lights, nothing; we couldn't see anything at all.

The six minutes went on to ten and the ten went on to at least twelve and there was a degree of worry in the cockpit. The bodies in the back were not aware of this but we'd overshot a tremendous amount. In fact we were trying to decide what was the best thing to do. Our communication with the tug was so erratic, static-wise – it just wasn't working – and then we ran into another belt of flak. There shouldn't have been any there at all but it was certainly coming up from the port side of the aircraft and it was heavy, very heavy.

Now, within seconds of this flak, we suddenly found we were in free flight. What had happened, I don't know. The rope may have been hit, the tug may have been hit, I don't know. And I don't know whether there's a patron saint of glider pilots but, if there is, he or she was working overtime because on Bill's side, the port side, he spotted a field. The field was obviously big enough for us to get into, so I took the aircraft to starboard and then turned it back in line with the field. The next minute we were hit again. I was wounded. The last shots fired in the air exploded over the top of me and my face was black on the outside and red raw on the inside.

There was a crunching sound before we hit the deck – I knew instantly we'd gone into trees – and then we were down and it was as good a landing as I've ever seen in a Horsa, right bang in the middle of that field. But the fact that we'd done it should have alarmed us as there were no anti-glider poles in the field and that was significant, because Rommel had seeded all the other fields and here we were landing in one that hadn't got them. There wasn't panic but there was a very quick exit: we'd got twelve bods on board, three sections of four.

The first thing to do was to get the fire out, which we did, and the next thing was, 'What do we do now? Where are we? There's nobody else here.' We didn't have to answer those questions. German troops at night move in a rather strange way: instead of observing silence, they're a noisy lot, particularly as they all carried a gas-mask in a metal container that swings on the back of the belt. You can hear them coming. And we could hear them. So everybody finds themselves a position and a weapon and I can recall thinking to myself, 'They think a bomber has come down here. Are they are going to get a surprise.' And they most certainly did, because the blokes we'd brought hadn't come all this way just to look at the scenery, they'd come to let off their weapons, which they did.

So the Germans then realised that it wasn't a bomber and they did exactly as they always do, they took their riflemen and machine-gunners back a little and they used mortars. The German mortar is the one great dread of World War Two because you know it's coming, you can hear it over your head, it has what I refer to as a 'wobbling' sound. You can hear this wobbling above you and you know it's coming but there's nothing you can do about it except press yourself into the ground and try to cover your vital parts. Now, the first one was on the other side of the glider, away from me. I reckoned the next one would certainly come in my direction so I tried to move as far away as I could, but that was it.

The next thing I remember, I'm coming out of unconsciousness and I'm lying on a bench and, staring down at me, there's a person of enemy persuasion, a German, just gazing at me. And I realise that I'm in a church and there are one or two other people stretched out on benches and one or two of them were in grey uniform. I don't really know what happened; all I know is my head is bad, I can hardly see except through one eye and my face is swollen. I'm dragged outside reluctantly to be photographed and then before an officer and interrogated. I knew nothing, I said nothing; I didn't know anything at all. And as night fell we were bunged into a truck. The truck stopped in the middle of Rouen, I know that because we were within forty or fifty yards of the statue of Jeanne d'Arc, and before dawn I'm in the prison at Amiens.

Private Philip Crofts
7th Battalion, Parachute Regiment
War is all chaos and a drop is one magnificent bit of chaos that somehow comes right at the end.

THE 5TH PARACHUTE BRIGADE

Each of the two brigades of General Gale's Sixth Airborne Division had its individual tasks. Centred on Ranville village, a kilometre east of where Howard was holding his canal and river bridges, Brigadier Nigel Poett's 5th Parachute Brigade was to occupy ground either side of Howard's bridges and prepare the brigade's dropping zones for the arrival of further gliders. By dawn, Poett's men had reinforced Howard and successfully secured Ranville and the landing zones. German troops, however, were fighting hard to break through.

REINFORCING THE OX AND BUCKS

Lieutenant Richard Todd
7th Battalion, Parachute Regiment
I had quite a good landing. Can't remember if it was a stand-up landing but I wasn't winded and didn't thump down particularly and was only too glad to get rid of my harness. Then I saw a smudge on the horizon. It didn't appear to be more than two or three hundred yards from me, it was a wood of some sort, and I thought, 'I'll get to that first of all and work out my bearings from there'. There was rather a lot of unpleasant activity, a lot of tracer bullets were criss-crossing the DZ, the dropping zone, and it wasn't very healthy hanging around and that's why I made for that wood. And then I thought, 'Christ, I've done the wrong thing,' because I heard voices and I thought I'd walked into a

German strongpoint or something. Then I recognised English and there were eight or ten other paratroopers there, including my CO, Geoffrey Pine-Coffin.

Lieutenant Colonel Geoffrey Pine-Coffin
Commanding Officer, 7th Battalion, Parachute Regiment

All one could see were other parachutists blundering about as lost as oneself. The Germans were there, too, firing tracer ammunition. Officers and others collected parties and began to search systematically but it was a question of the blind leading the blind. It was an hour and a half before I found the rendezvous for my party and we were the first there even then. My rallying signal was a bugle and luckily my bugler was with me, and Private Lambert sounded off continuously and we waited and hoped.

They came in as fast as they could but it seemed desperately slow and there was practically none of the heavy gear with them. No sound came from the bridges. I decided to move off when I reached half-strength but this took so long that I gave the order earlier. No mortars, machine guns or wireless had arrived so we would just have to do without them. The coup de main party's success signal went up just as we moved off and put new life into us. Half the job had been done: the bridges had been captured.

Private Philip Crofts
7th Battalion, Parachute Regiment

We ran like hell. Believe me, we did run. I mean, we were eighteen-, nineteen-year-old boys, young men, and we ran for these bridges. Only 150 men were ready to go.

Private Bill Gray
2nd Battalion, Oxfordshire and Buckinghamshire Light Infantry

We heard running feet behind us. It was the 7th Para Battalion or their advance guard. They'd reached us. There was a bit of rejoicing when they saw that we'd taken the bridge because, if we hadn't taken it, they were going to have to have a go. They just went past, patting us on our helmets, saying, 'Good lads, well done,' and away they went, to a little village called Benouville.

Private Harry Clarke
2nd Battalion, Oxfordshire and Buckinghamshire Light Infantry
There were some jocular remarks from our chaps, like, 'Where the hell have you been?' I can recall those quite well. But it was all done in a happy sort of fashion because we were extremely glad to see them. We were getting a few counter-attacks coming in at that time.

Private Philip Crofts
7th Battalion, Parachute Regiment
We ran over the first bridge, the river bridge, then we ran over the second bridge, the canal bridge, and immediately went off the road and went across ground to Le Port.

As we were leaving the road something happened and it's always amused me. We were crossing some Dannert wire and somebody said, 'Halt!' and our sergeant, Vic Bettle, said, 'Who is it?' He most likely thought, as I did, that these were Ox and Bucks just wanting to see who we were, and old Vic gave him a mouthful of Fs and Bs and the next word came: '*Halten!*' So we fired into where the voices came from and just swept through them into Le Port. This was one, half-past one, at night, pitch black, you really couldn't see anything, and we ran into Le Port and held Le Port until the morning.

That was a most confused night, really. There were attacks everywhere. We was in an upstairs part of a house, on the first floor, and the Germans were passing by on the pavements down below and old Scotty was putting a little bit of mirror out of the window and when they come he was firing at them. It went on like this for another three, four, five hours, this spasmodic fighting all the time. We had no machine guns or mortars, they had all got lost on the drop; it was all small arms and Gammon bombs. Gammon bombs are basically plastic HE tied up in a stocking holder with a detonator on the top: very effective.

Private William John Le Cheminant
7th Battalion, Parachute Regiment
We were behind a wall in an orchard. We were quite isolated, there was only about a dozen of us. We lost an officer and one chap shot in the temple there – there was a sniper around – and, when it got daylight, about ten yards behind

us was a stick of five German stick grenades tied together. The Germans must have thrown them over the wall that night but they'd never exploded.

Lance Corporal Thomas Packwood
2nd Battalion, Oxfordshire and Buckinghamshire Light Infantry
John Howard sent a section up to Le Port to help 7 Para out because they were getting a bit bogged down. We took up positions in houses, there was quite a bit of street-fighting going on between the Germans and 7 Para, and we were just occupying different houses to deny them to the enemy. Unbeknown to us, the Germans broke in to a first-aid room. There were some wounded 7 Para parachutists in there and the Germans shot the lot of them, including the padre. They're all buried in Benouville churchyard.

Private Harry Clarke
2nd Battalion, Oxfordshire and Buckinghamshire Light Infantry
Certainly 7 Para must have been having a sticky time because by now the crescendo of firing was rising, it was getting very noisy, and we weren't fully aware of what exactly was happening out there. We were in our own little unit clustered round the bridge but we had the feeling all the time that something nasty was happening. And as first light got underway, about half-past four, five o'clock, we suddenly found that we were pinned down by very heavy and very accurate sniper-firing.

Private Francis Bourlet
2nd Battalion, Oxfordshire and Buckinghamshire Light Infantry
When it got first light, that's when things began to happen. Hell of a lot of sniping. You couldn't move about, nobody could, we were pretty well pinned down by snipers. They were firing at us from the direction of the chateau but we couldn't place them at all, we couldn't find them, but they practically pinned down any movement we was making on the bridge. We was putting berets up on shovels and getting holes in them and things like that.

Lieutenant Richard 'Sandy' Smith
2nd Battalion, Oxfordshire and Buckinghamshire Light Infantry
I remember lying in a ditch in this little gully-way between the two bridges having my wrist bandaged by one of our first aid people, and a sniper bullet

came cracking over my right shoulder. It hit this fellow in the chest – he was actually bending over me – and knocked him clear into the road. The bullet went straight through him. I remember him lying in the middle of the road and I expected the next bullet from the sniper to come and get me on the back of the neck because I couldn't get any lower. That wasn't a very pleasant moment.

Private Francis Bourlet
2nd Battalion, Oxfordshire and Buckinghamshire Light Infantry
The snipers was firing at us from the water tower and from the chateau which we didn't know at the time was a maternity home. We looked round and we found three armour-piercing shells, we loaded this German PaK gun, aimed it, fired it at the water tower, put a hole completely through the water tower. Fired another one at a very large tree in front of the chateau which we thought the snipers might be up; being armour-piercing that just whistled straight through the tree, didn't do anything at all. Fired a third shell at the water tower again and missed, when John Howard shouted out to us, 'Stop firing that bloody gun!' Trouble was, after we'd pierced the water tower, a woman appeared on the balcony of the chateau waving a white flag and Howard forbid us to fire on this building again. We couldn't use it any more anyway because all the shells that were stacked there were calibrated to be used in kilometres and God knows what, which we didn't understand. We didn't understand metric whatsoever.

Major John Howard
2nd Battalion, Oxfordshire and Buckinghamshire Light Infantry
We opened up the Café Gondrée alongside the bridge. I knew in my intelligence that the patron, whose name was Georges Gondrée, spoke perfect English; also that his wife was of German origin and understood the Germans who used the café for drinks and that a lot of information had been obtained and passed on to the French Resistance. So we opened up the café as a first-aid post and the first thing Georges Gondrée did, bless him, he went down into his garden and dug up nearly a hundred bottles of champagne that he'd buried away in the garden. The sick and the wounded were having quite a good time, there was a lot of cork-popping going on and all my men in reserve at the other side of the canal at the time all wanted to report sick. But

Georges Gondrée and his family – his wife and two young daughters – did a marvellous job that day.

Corporal Wilfred Robert Howard
2nd Battalion, Oxfordshire and Buckinghamshire Light Infantry

I went down to see John Howard who seemed to be over the moon and he invited me to drink some bottled water which they'd found down there. John Howard offered me blasted mineral water when all the rest of them were drinking champagne, which I thought was a bit of a shame.

Lieutenant Richard Todd
7th Battalion, Parachute Regiment

I was to look for an outlying platoon of ours, which had been told to take up a position on the road to the beach-landing area and we hadn't heard anything from them. I gathered the best part of a dozen chaps and we set off between the road and the river to a quarry where this platoon was to be. We found them intact except for one chap. He was lying, shot, in a field just beside the platoon's position and he was a young chap I recognised, a very young boy, about eighteen.

Coming back from that platoon's position, that was when I saw a couple of luggers or boats or lighters on the canal moving slowly. I worked out in my mind that they were going the wrong way because the current was going towards the sea and they were coming from the sea. So when I got back to the battalion headquarters, which was a few holes in the ground, I said to the CO that I'd seen these things and was a bit suspicious of them and I had a feeling that they were actually under control. Could we put a few shots into them to find out? He said, 'Yeah, go and have a go,' which we did, and so did a group of John Howard's chaps, who were ensconced in the old German positions round the bridge.

Sapper Cyril Larkin
249 Field Company, 591 Parachute Squadron, Royal Engineers

Still early in the morning, a German river patrol boat appeared. I jumped into my slit trench and fired at the wheelhouse. It was quite a windy morning and I had my rifle down on the soil and with the strong wind I fired just one shot and then the wind blew a lot of grit all over my rifle and I couldn't pull my rifle bolt back. I had to push the butt down on to the bottom of the trench and kick the bolt back with my heel to draw out the spare cartridge. That was the only shot I fired. But other people were firing as well, some of the Ox and Bucks lads, some of our engineers.

Private Harry Clarke
2nd Battalion, Oxfordshire and Buckinghamshire Light Infantry
Corporal Godbold said to me, 'Grab the PIAT, Nobby,' and the three of us went down and took up a position behind a grassy knoll and set the PIAT up. Corporal Godbold took over the PIAT, we loaded it, and when the boat was about fifty yards off he let off a round and – much to my amazement, because they weren't the best of things to fire – he hit the boat slightly behind the wheelhouse. The boat immediately turned and drifted into the bank just a few yards from where we were.

I moved forward and two Royal Engineers appeared as well and I personally took off two prisoners from the boat. One was, I believe, a Polish bloke, but the commander of the boat, a tall, blondish chap, he looked German. He wasn't very happy about it and I believe he said so in as many words in German. I butted him on the shoulder with my rifle and he shut up.

I took the two prisoners to Major Howard who had his command post by then on the eastern side of the bridge by a pillbox and he said, 'Take them off to the cage down at brigade headquarters at Ranville.' So I started off with these two prisoners, fearing at the time that the snipers were still very active and it wasn't a very nice thing to be walking along that road with two slowly moving German prisoners.

As we were about to cross the River Orne bridge I noticed a paratrooper lying by the side of the road and he was obviously in agony. I went up to him and it looked as though he'd been shot through the spine and this is another thing I shall remember till the day I die. He asked me to shoot him, put him out of his agony, which I just couldn't do. I said, 'Lay there, old chap, and I'll get you some aid. As soon as I get down to brigade headquarters I'll get someone up here to look after you.'

As we got on to the bridge we came under intense sniper fire and I said to the two Germans, 'Run!' and I prodded them both with my outstretched rifle to indicate that they should run, by which time they'd guessed why. So they ran like the devil till we got to the far end of the bridge where we got down into a dip by the side of the road and we were OK there. From there we just carried on down to Ranville village and 5th Para Brigade headquarters. I arrived there, delivered the two prisoners to a compound, I believe there was a sergeant of the Military Police controlling it, and I recall saying to him, 'Where can I scrounge a mug of tea?' Much to my surprise he pointed and said, 'Over there's a dixie,' so I had a welcome cup of tea.

SECURING RANVILLE

Captain John Sim
12th Battalion, Parachute Regiment

We were going to establish a defensive position facing Caen with C Company on the right, with its right flank on the River Orne, B Company on the left and A Company in reserve in Le Bas de Ranville. When we left our rendezvous we were extremely alarmed because C Company had only thirty men and we were very short in numbers but the CO said we couldn't stay there much longer, we had to get cracking. But when we reached our defensive position south of Le Bas de Ranville, to our delight we found a hell of a lot of our chaps there already established and digging in like mad. Such was our briefing in England that every soldier knew exactly where he was going to dig his hole and his arcs of fire, it was so clear on the aerial photographs, and the bulk of the battalion was there already, digging in. They had been scattered in their drop beyond the dropping zone and with all this kit that they had to carry they weren't going to flog all the way back to the rendezvous on the dropping zone and then flog back again to the defensive locality, so they took a short cut and got themselves established.

Corporal Harald Cammack
12th Battalion, Parachute Regiment

We'd had to go about a mile and a half to Ranville and once we got there we dug our trenches as quickly as possible and took up defensive positions around the area. It was high ground, because we knew that as soon as dawn broke we would be expecting some movement from the enemy, which did occur, and the high ground was vital to be held for the seaborne troops coming in. If that high ground had not been held the Germans would most probably have inflicted devastating casualties on the seaborne coming in.

Captain John Sim
12th Battalion, Parachute Regiment

Before I went off to my own position I was told by Major Stephens to clear a group of four houses about fifty yards away to see whether there were any enemy in those houses, because that was where battalion headquarters were going to establish themselves. So I gathered a sergeant who happened to be standing nearby and two soldiers and, in the dark, it was now about two o'clock in the morning, I went up a little lane to the first of the four houses and I knocked at the door of the first house. After some time the door was opened and a middle-aged lady in her day clothes, not in her nightie, looked at me, very frightened, because we were all camouflaged up with darkened faces and scrim-nets on our helmets and we must have looked a terrifying sight. I looked past her and there was her husband, standing by the foot of the stairs, and a couple of kids. They were all in their day clothes, which was rather a strange thing at two o'clock in the morning.

I then started to speak to her. I wasn't very good at French, I was hopeless at French at school, but anyway I had a go and this is how it went. I saluted her and said, '*Bonjour Madame, nous sommes soldats anglais. Nous arrivons ici par avion: parachutistes. L'heure de la liberation est arrivée. Où sont les soldats allemands? Ils restent ici?*' I thought I was brilliant getting through that but she looked blankly at me and still frightened, so I thrust a pamphlet into her hand. We were issued with little pamphlets in French to tell the civilians that this was not a raid, this was D-Day, and that the battles would rage around them and they would be safer if they stayed in their cellars. Then I started again. '*Madame, nous sommes soldats d'Angleterre. Où sont les soldats allemands?*' She still looked blankly at me. Then I spoke to my sergeant behind me. 'Can you speak this wretched language, sergeant?' And I spoke to my other two soldiers as well and of course they couldn't.

So after this little conversation I started a third time and suddenly she burst into tears and embraced me and said, 'You're British soldiers, aren't you?' So I said, 'Yes, I've been trying to get this through to you for the last three minutes or so. Why didn't you let on sooner that you can speak English?' She said, 'I *am* English. I was born in Manchester, I married a French farmer and we settled out here before the war. I had to make sure that you were genuine, that you were not German soldiers masquerading as British commandos and parachutists and testing us out, because they've been doing quite a lot of that around here recently. But it wasn't until I heard your frightful schoolboy French and your backchat to your Yorkshire sergeant that I realised that the Germans couldn't have possibly acted this part.'

Lieutenant John Watson
13th Battalion, Parachute Regiment

13th Battalion's objective was to take Ranville, which we did successfully. It was actually completely cleared by 0230 and in fact we were the first battalion to liberate the first village during the assault into Normandy. My particular task with A Company was to proceed to the rendezvous and then get back on to the DZ with a team of engineers with explosives. Our task was then to blow these poles and lift them side to side into what we called 'a herring bone situation' and clear a run for the first wave of gliders coming in that night in the early hours of the morning. We also had to dig slit trenches for ourselves because once we'd completed our task we had to wait for the first wave of Horsas to come in. The experience I had was of the frightful noise of crashing wood and skidding gliders, caused through the wings of the gliders smashing through the outer poles which we hadn't blown. I think this was the most frightening thing of my life.

Sergeant Brian Spencer
Glider Pilot Regiment

We were very lucky. I was second pilot to a man called Ken Hannon and he turned the glider around in a U-turn and the field was full of these anti-glider posts but we went through and we never touched a thing.

We'd been told, 'When you land, first thing you do, get your flying helmet off, put your steel helmet on and away.' Well, when we stopped rolling I got my steel helmet out and a voice at me elbow said, 'Would you like a cup of tea, Sarge?' and when I looked up it was one of the chaps we'd taken and he had a Thermos flask. And I'm drinking this tea and looking sideways and, on the road, not more than fifty to a hundred yards away, there's some fella firing up in the air with a heavy machine gun and I thought, 'Well, he's not one of ours.' It was after that the other gliders came in and the glider behind me came in with his nose wheel off, I remember, and another glider flew into him straight from the side and then, of course, I began to see the first dead bodies I'd ever seen.

We carried a jeep and a trailer and we had to drop the tail to get the jeep out so I went round the back of the glider to see about this and two chaps came up to me. They were in airborne smocks but hanging loose, no belts on, I remember, and we were stood in corn right up to our thighs and one of them said to me, 'What's the password?' I said, 'Punch,' expecting the reply, 'Judy.' But they both closed up on me and one of them got a fighting knife into the side of me stomach and I thought, 'Oh God.' We'd taken an old major – well, I say old, he must have been a fella of thirty-five to forty – and he came round the back with a pistol: 'What's going on?' They said, 'What's the password?' He said, 'V.' They said, 'For Victory.' I said, 'Hey, just a minute. If you meet any of our fellas, they'll give you "Punch" and "Judy".' The major said, 'No, that's tomorrow's password.' So we'd been given the wrong password at the kick-off.

He went blind, did Ken Hannon, my first pilot, when we landed. He went back to these gliders that had crashed to see if he could do anything and this old major came back and said to me, 'Your friend's gone blind.' Well, I thought something had gone off in his face, something like that, so I went down. Ken was there with his eyes stuck out like chapel hat pegs and he said to me, 'It's strain. It happened once before.' So when we set off down to the chateau I was walking along with my rifle under one arm and steering Ken with the other arm. But as dawn began to break, when we got down to the road, he began to get his sight back and he was OK after that.

Captain David Tibbs
Regimental Medical Officer, 13th Battalion, Parachute Regiment

My mission was to collect my men together and start rounding up any injured or wounded on the dropping zone and, when daylight came, to do a systematic search of the dropping zone, so, after I landed, I walked steadily in the direction of Ranville. In the distance I could hear the thump and crackle of the attack going on at the bridges over the river and canal about a mile away but apart from that it was extraordinarily quiet and I trudged along in the darkness for about a mile until I reached Ranville. I bumped into a few other men but considering that about two thousand men had dropped into this area at much the same time as myself it was extraordinary how few other people one met. Everyone was just making for their particular rendezvous points and various units were assembling, ready for their particular tasks.

I think 68 gliders landed in quick succession on the dropping zone. One or two crash-landed but the great majority landed safely. This was very important because they were bringing a number of weapons we needed, such as anti-tank guns, both six-pounders and seventeen-pounders. The Germans didn't realise that we were able to bring down seventeen-pounder anti-tank guns, which were state of the art technology then and very much necessary for us. Also some light artillery came and a number of other heavy supplies of that sort. I went to one or two gliders where there had been crashes. One or two people had been killed. I retrieved some of the injured there. One of my chaps had been very resourceful and had got a gas-driven wagon belonging to the French and that was very helpful in lifting out these people and taking them back to Le Bas de Ranville, where the medical centre was being established.

When daybreak came, I had five men with me. This was rather upsetting because I'd hoped to have twenty, but we started a systematic search now that it was day. One unexpected thing was that most of the dropping zone was wheat, about two to three feet high, so that a man lying badly injured on the ground was very difficult to see because he was just buried in wheat, but we did our best to cover the ground. Many of the injured we had to collect were men with fractured femurs. It was quite interesting how this had occurred: they had all dropped with their kit bags still attached to their legs.

A number of men portrayed their presence when they realised we weren't far away by waving anything they could find up in the air. We would see a hand waving and realise there was somebody there and we would immediately go over and rescue him. My main memory of this was the sheer physical exertion of carrying these men by stretcher. Two of us carrying a stretcher, perhaps carrying him up to mile over the ground, is very hard work indeed, and that is where we missed the full squad of twenty men.

The gliders and lots of helmets were still lying on the dropping zone and lots of gas masks had been discarded, so it was covered in litter. But apart from that, during the morning of D-Day, this particular dropping zone was almost deserted. All the troops, British and German, were keeping well out of sight in houses and woods and so on and I was left comparatively unmolested. I was wearing, and so were my men, Red Cross armlets, so we were fairly easily distinguished as medical people, and although a few shots and a certain amount of mortars were fired in our direction we were left to get on with our task without too much disturbance.

THE 3RD PARACHUTE BRIGADE

The role of Brigadier James Hill's 3rd Parachute Brigade, which included a battalion of Canadian parachutists and teams of specialist engineers, was twofold. One job, east of the Orne, was to frustrate enemy movement towards Howard's bridges and thereon to the invasion beaches by destroying five bridges over the River Dives and by occupying an important ridge of high ground. This was achieved.

The second task, which was assigned to Lieutenant Colonel Terence Otway's 9th Battalion, was to silence the heavily fortified coastal battery at Merville, about a mile inland from the easternmost invasion beach. The D-Day planners believed the battery to be capable of causing havoc among the seaborne landing forces. Depleted by parachutists and gliders going astray and suffering heavy casualties in the assault, Otway's force was unable to neutralise the battery completely, but the attack did prevent the guns firing that day.

THE DIVES BRIDGES

Private Anthony Leake
8th Battalion, Parachute Regiment
The 8th Battalion were due to be the troops to be dropped the furthest inland of the Sixth Airborne Division and when we landed we were the furthest inland of all the British assault forces. Our dropping zone was seven or eight miles due south of the coast.

I got to the RV and there were very few people there. I'm not quite sure on these figures, but probably there were only about a hundred 8th Battalion soldiers there and there should have been about 750 because there should have been 650 of the 8th Battalion and going on for about a hundred of the 3rd Para Squadron, Royal Engineers. But Alastair Pearson, our commanding officer, was there. He was in a filthy mood because his batman had dropped a loaded Sten gun which went off and shot Alastair in the hand. The bullet had lodged in his hand and he was there with his arm in a sling.

So we thought, 'God, everything's lost. There should be a lot more men here and we should move off very soon.' But we waited and a few stragglers came in and eventually we did move off. We had to, the sky was beginning to lighten a little bit and we wanted to get to our objectives while it was still dark. When we moved off there were only about 140 men out of all that 750 but we'd all got great faith in Alastair Pearson. We knew he'd been in desperate situations before and thought somehow he'd get us out of this.

So we moved off from Touffreville, east, towards the village of Bures, on the River Dives, where there were two bridges to be blown. We stopped by the side of the forest and at 5.20 it was first light and they sent me off with some others, maybe ten of us went down, to do a recce on the bridges, see if there was anybody there, German or anything. No Germans there at all, very, very quiet, and when we got there we found that some Royal Engineers who'd been dropped on the wrong DZ had gone straight from Ranville to Bures. So we covered them, sort of guarding them, whilst they put their charges on the bridges and they blew up these two bridges. We'd been lucky so far but the wrath of the Germans could descend on us any time so we melted back into the woods.

Corporal Bob Sullivan
3rd Parachute Squadron, Royal Engineers

We actually jumped with weapons and ammunition and some explosives within our smocks. I had about two pounds of PHE plus the detonators. Then we had our grenades, rifle ammunition, Bren gun ammunition. But as soon as we got on the ground the first thing was to find the containers and to unload the containers and pick up the explosive charges they were carrying, and this we did, and then we formed a group and marched off.

My small group, which consisted of a stick of ten men, an officer, myself and eight others, continued our way towards our objective which was to blow a bridge at a place called Robehomme – a road bridge across the River Dives. Well, we marched along the roads until it started to get light and then as dawn started to break we had to take to the hedgerows. That was very hard going because we were spending a lot of time following the hedgerow to keep out of sight and ploughing through water, gradually making our way to the objective.

A small group had landed ahead of us, a small group of Canadians, including one of our sergeants, and they had in fact blown the bridge, which was a small lattice girder structure – they'd made a clean cut to drop it into the river. Then we set to and blew some craters to completely destroy the approach to the bridge. We stayed there until some Germans came up on the opposite side of the road to where we were and we had a bit of a gunfight. They had some mortars, which gave us a little bit of a pasting, and then we retired.

Sapper Wesley Worgan
3rd Parachute Squadron, Royal Engineers
As I was approaching my bridge there was firing going off all over. I came along the path, there was a big embankment going down, and I could see about four hundred yards. It was a road bridge over the river and I could see there were five Jerries there holding this bridge, so, being the chief Bren-gunner, I let fly a burst and I got all five, which I often dream about.

Sapper Wilfred Robert Jones
3rd Parachute Squadron, Royal Engineers
We were on the wrong DZ. The RAF had dropped us in the wrong place, I don't know why, and we had a long way to walk to get to the bridge. We then met up with other members of the squadron, and the OC, Major Roseveare, set off in a jeep to blow a road bridge over the River Dives. We set off after him on foot and when we arrived at the bridge after a few hold-ups, a little bit of shooting and what have you, we found that the OC and his party had blown a gap. We then laid our supply of General Wades – shaped charges – over a pier and blew those making a larger gap. We then demolished a dam which was upstream. I had a job to sink a boat, like a skiff, which was tied up to the dam. I filled up the Gammon bomb with my two pounds of PE and threw it and it landed in the skiff and it blew it to smithereens.

Sergeant Sidney Nuttall
3rd Airlanding Anti-Tank Battery, Royal Artillery
Royal Engineers were supposed to have landed on Dropping Zone K with 8 Para. They had missed it and had landed on the big dropping zone. They had no transport so they loaded on to my jeep and trailer with their explosives and I was sent to make for a place called Troarn.

We came out on the main road, came under fire, we had to cut across country, cut through an orchard – a jeep'll go anywhere and it was in the right direction – and we eventually hit another road and we bumped into some of 8 Para. We was told that 8 Para had blown their bridges up to the north, the

Canadians had blown the bridges at the far north but there was one bridge they hadn't been able to blow because they had no REs to blow it. These were the people I was bringing in.

We got to the place, Troarn, and there was only one street, the main street, and the Germans was fighting a fierce rearguard action to stop us from getting through their village to blow the bridge. 8 Para were quite small in number, they had been dropped up and down the place as had almost everybody, and they were having difficulty trying to take this village to get down to the bridge. The officer of 8 Para there said he'd put every bit of firepower he could down this main street and I had to drive this jeep down with these Para engineers to take the explosive down to the bridge.

It worked. They fired the two-inch mortars, all the machine guns, and we went down. A couple of the REs were wounded getting through. Once we got clear of the village we had a straight run then down to the bridge, dropped the engineers, and I went up to the far end to give them some covering fire if people came down the road. They got into position, they shouted at me to come back, they blew the bridge. Once the bridge was blown, the Germans that was in Troarn seemed to disappear into the countryside.

THE MERVILLE BATTERY

Lieutenant Colonel Terence Otway
Commanding Officer, 9th Battalion, Parachute Regiment
Our plan was to drop on the dropping zone side and to attack at 4.30am and have three glider-loads of troops land inside the battery, stopping themselves by knocking their wings off the casements and taking the garrison entirely by surprise. The last part of the gliders' journey would be lit up by mortar flares laid by us.

I'd planned four attack parties for the casements, one for each casement, and therefore four gaps in the wire to be blown up by what were called Bangalore torpedoes. And I had two diversion parties: one to go to the main gate and kick up a hell of a row and one to go to the left and kick up a hell of a row, to divert the garrison. There was an anti-tank ditch on the seaward side of the battery, I presume they expected tanks to come in across the beach there, and I wasn't sure whether that ditch would be extended round to our side so I'd had special lightweight bridges made.

Lieutenant Colonel Terence Otway, Commanding Officer of the 9th Battalion Parachute Regiment. On the morning of D-Day, Otway's men had the task of assaulting the Merville Battery.

I also took with me, in gliders, some anti-tank guns to blow down the rear steel doors of the casements should they be shut: there was no point in attacking the battery and trying to get through a steel door. I also took Royal Engineers to blow the guns up and I took Royal Navy telegraphers because I was told that if we had not succeeded by five or five-thirty HMS *Arethusa* would bombard the battery, and these men, who dropped with us, were to direct the fire. So that, in outline, was the plan.

I arrived at the rendezvous about one o'clock, maybe earlier, to be met by my batman – and here I am not exaggerating – who said, 'Shall we have our brandy now, sir?' He was an ex-valet and he literally held out to me a flask of brandy he had taken – my flask of whisky had been smashed on landing. I then found that out of the total group strength of around 750, that's to say the 650-odd of the battalion plus the artillerymen for the anti-tank guns, the medical men who dropped with us, the sailors, the engineers, I only had a hundred of all ranks, including myself.

Lieutenant Alan Jefferson
9th Battalion, Parachute Regiment

I got along to the RV and saw Colonel Otway looking very peculiar indeed. The reason was that there was hardly anybody there. I was the junior subaltern of C Company and when he saw me he said, 'You're commanding C Company. Well, don't stand there. Get on, go and see your company.' My company was about five men. Gradually it dawned on us that something had gone frantically wrong. The plan that Colonel Otway had devised for this operation was exceedingly complex, so complex that it was like a multiple chain that depended on each individual link, and the links were all disappearing one by one before our eyes, at this stage.

I had to go back and report to him every quarter of an hour how many men there were. Two of my men were in a dreadful state, one had lost his rifle and the other had lost his helmet and his rifle, and we'd been told – it was more of a threat than an intention – that any man losing his rifle would be court-martialled. A silly threat, because you can't have court-martials in battle, but it was sufficient to upset these two chaps very much. So I tried to cheer them up by saying that we'd soon be able to find some German rifles for them and it would be all right. Then, at last, Lieutenant Parfitt arrived. He was just senior to me and I very proudly said, 'Here's your company. You can take it over now, you're senior to me,' and he goggled. We'd got about ten men by then, I suppose. It was really lamentable.

Colonel Otway waited as long as he dared before moving off. Greenway and his mine-lifting party had already gone on but with no mine detectors and no tape. They were meant to have arrived in gliders on our dropping zone immediately after we'd come down but there had been no gliders there. Three-inch mortars hadn't arrived either and one three-inch mortar was going to be vital because it was going to be placed outside the wire which would illuminate the area very quickly so that the three gliders bound for the battery would see where to land. One machine gun, a Vickers, had arrived, fortunately. But worst of all there were no Royal Engineers with special explosives with which to destroy the guns. We hadn't got much in the way of explosives, every two men carried parts of a Gammon bomb, a bag with explosive mainly for use against tanks, but that wasn't much really.

Lieutenant Colonel Terence Otway
Commanding Officer, 9th Battalion, Parachute Regiment
Unbeknown to everybody else I'd kept a quarter of an hour on the timing up my sleeve as a cushion and in that time another fifty came in. But I was then faced with the decision: 'I'm supposed to attack this battery with a battalion of six hundred-odd men, excluding the ones coming in on the gliders, and I've only got 150.' I had no wireless sets. I had one machine gun and I had ten Bangalore torpedoes out of forty to blow the gaps with. I had no bridges in case we had to cross the anti-tank ditches. So far as I was aware, I had no anti-tank guns, no sailors, one doctor and very few medical people. So the question was, do I go on with 150? Or do I pack it in?

Private Sidney Capon
9th Battalion, Parachute Regiment
I would not have liked to be in Otway's shoes to have had to make decisions then. Later on, I said to him, 'What made you decide to advance?' He said, 'It wasn't me, it was Wilson, my batman. I'd said, "I don't know what I'm going to do, Wilson," and he'd said, "There's only thing, sir." And that was it. That gave me the incentive to carry on.'

Lieutenant Colonel Terence Otway
Commanding Officer, 9th Battalion, Parachute Regiment
So we moved off at 2.15, following the path which we knew so well so from photographs. We heard a German anti-aircraft battery firing, I suppose, not more than a hundred yards from us on our left and some of the soldiers wanted to go for that and I wouldn't let anybody do that, that wasn't our job, and we let them get on with it.

A farm halfway to the battery was the rendezvous to where Major Smith was due to come back from his job with the reconnaissance party, which he did. He told me that they had had no mine detectors and no tape for marking paths through the minefield. But he also said Paul Greenway and another man had cut the wires, had crawled through the minefield, neutralising the mines with their fingers, and had then sat on their backsides and dragged their heels on the ground, making a path through the minefield. Quite extraordinary. But I was faced now with two gaps instead of four to put in four parties against the encasements and I had to completely re-plan. I simply cut my encasement assault parties right down to the maximum one could get out of 150 soldiers and would put in two parties through each gap.

We then moved on towards the battery and we found that the RAF had mostly missed it. There were a hundred Lancasters in support of my operation, each carrying a thousand-pound bomb, and they had missed the battery but they had successfully bombed our route without knowing it, so we had to go in and out of these huge craters. And when we were about halfway between the farmhouse and the battery we heard a noise of troops moving and we guessed it was a German patrol. They didn't seem to be making any effort to conceal themselves and we all lay down and they passed so close to us we could have reached out and caught them by the ankles, but they didn't see us or hear us. And we moved on.

Lieutenant Alan Jefferson
9th Battalion, Parachute Regiment
The moon was coming and going behind clouds and we had our first sight of the casements, looking like toads squatting there, somehow nasty, and we came to the outside wire. The bombing of the battery had not disturbed the casements at all but it had made enormous craters, so you had enormous depths and heights of earth, and it had been raining and it was greyish and

Overhead photograph, taken shortly before D-Day, of the Merville gun battery pockmarked by aerial bombing. Subsequent heavy bombing in the early hours of 6 June also failed to penetrate the battery.

wet and nasty and sticky. I got my little party together and gave them a little pep talk. 'We're here, we've trained for it, we're ready for it. If we don't do it, imagine what will happen to your wives and daughters,' and so on.

We were waiting for the gliders and then we saw the first glider. It came from the north-west and did a kind of circle and whistled as it went over and disappeared. In front of us was an ack-ack gun on a concrete block, it hadn't spoken, and then a few moments later another glider came – this was Hugh Pond's – and this gun opened up, a little clip of five rounds, and five balls of fire shot up. The glider seemed to pause, looking, searching, and then another five got nearer and then the next five and one hit it. There was a flash and the tail of the glider was on fire.

Lieutenant Hubert Pond
9th Battalion, Parachute Regiment
The first shots exploded outside the glider and all we heard were distant thumps, which didn't really worry us. We knew what they were but it didn't bother us. But then we were actually hit by four or five small anti-aircraft shells, one of which, unfortunately, set fire to the flame-thrower. So in the last minute, the last few seconds, the glider was on fire and one of the unfortunate chaps was of course on fire. We swooped in, we did see the battery – both Sergeant Kerr and I shouted at the same time, 'There's the battery!' – but then immediately a very large barbed wire entanglement loomed up in front. Sergeant Kerr pulled up the rudder, we shot over the fence and the glider crash-landed in an orchard about fifty yards outside the battery. There was a facility for breaking the glider in half with explosives – it was lined with explosives in the middle and you pulled a wire and set it off – but there was no need because the crash-landing had broken the glider in half and the wings were off. By this time this poor chap must have been dead with the flames and we all rushed out of the gap in the glider as quickly as we could. It was all confusion.

Private Sidney Capon
9th Battalion, Parachute Regiment
The third glider never arrived. That landed back in England, the towrope broke. So there were no gliders and it now came that we had to attack the guns. Otway turned round and said we'd got to attack now. 'Get ready, men,' he says. Then, 'Get in! Get in!'

Lieutenant Alan Jefferson
9th Battalion, Parachute Regiment

The Bangalores went up, there were two enormous explosions, and we ran through shouting and yelling, which is what we always did in training. It did us good and we hoped it frightened the enemy as well. I hadn't got far before something hit my leg and I went down, I was like a sheep on its back, and I watched my men going in and I thought, 'My goodness, the training has worked.' There was a sergeant now leading them and they didn't stop and they were firing and there was an MG42 firing from an embrasure by the side of No 1 gun.

Private Sidney Capon
9th Battalion, Parachute Regiment

There were about seven men, instead of thirty-two, to attack No 1 gun. Jefferson fell down wounded. We carried on zigzagging and I shouted, as I did in training, 'Bastards! Bastards! Bastards!' and I heard shouts and explosions from my left, No 2 gun, and shouts of 'Mines!' It was very, very quick. Don't forget, you're rushing in. I never saw Mike Dowling again. He was killed.

Company Sergeant Major Barney Ross
9th Battalion, Parachute Regiment

It was very difficult: (a) it was dark and (b) there were so many machine guns and everything else firing. We went in on No 3 gun and you could only see tiny slits in it. It was really solid concrete and they were all covered with grass and everything so you couldn't really see where you were for a minute, especially in the dark. But we did see all the air vents sticking up and we just threw grenades down them and by the time we got round to the front of the gun the guys had had enough, they were coming out the iron doors. So we just took them all prisoner and then started to go back out of the battery again. By the time our emplacement was cleared, the people from No 4 gun had got some prisoners as well. They were only too pleased to give up, some of them. 'Kamerad! Kamerad! Kamerad!' with their hands up. We just pushed them all along. I think we'd have liked to have shot the bloody lot but we didn't.

Private Sidney Capon
9th Battalion, Parachute Regiment
We reached the rear of No 1 gun, still on our feet, four of us. We threw two grenades into the lobby and there were noises from inside the casement and the Germans pushed themselves out the rear and I remember one or two of them shouting, 'Russki! Russki!' and I thought, 'What the hell are they on about, "*Russki! Russki!*"?' But by all accounts they were Russians made to fight for the Germans. The last chappy was a big chap, he wore glasses, and he was in a terrible state. He was on his hands and knees.

Lieutenant Colonel Terence Otway
Commanding Officer, 9th Battalion, Parachute Regiment
By five o'clock we had completely occupied the battery. We had taken all the casements, we had taken twenty-two prisoners and there were a lot of German casualties, killed and wounded, in the casements, and I was able to send a success signal. I had no radio to send a success signal but I lit a yellow signal flare and an RAF plane went over, saw it, and waggled its wings. And my signals officer, unbeknown to me, had got a carrier pigeon with him, brought it all the way from England in his airborne smock, and he tied a victory message around its leg and sent it off.

Then the problem was to get out. I went round the casements and I told all the troops to get out but we didn't know how to get through the minefield so I told the prisoners to show me the way. They refused. So I said, 'Well, OK, we're going to make you walk forward and if you don't show us the way through the mines we're just going to start shooting the ground and you're going to lose your feet and maybe the mines will go up too.' So they showed us the way and we got out.

I went and sat by the calvary near the battery and I told everybody to take up defensive positions such as we were able to do. Because, out of the 150 men that we went in with, all ranks, there were only 75 of us left standing on our feet. The others had been killed or wounded.

Lieutenant Hubert Pond
9th Battalion, Parachute Regiment
I remember the colonel was sitting on the steps of this calvary, writing or talking to the IO or something, and scattered around were troops looking

pretty worn and torn. There were a lot of wounded on stretchers and there were stretcher-bearers moving around. They all claimed that the attack was a great success but they had had to get a move on, because, without a success signal from us, the cruiser *Arethusa* was going to fire on the battery with its six-inch guns.

I think the attack put the battery out for a certain amount of time but in point of fact that battery was never completely put out of operation. I think the plan was as near perfect as could be, but never, ever, ever has any battle gone according to plan. You just cannot foresee the chaos that is going to ensue. The 9th Battalion were the people trained to get in there and do the job and they did the best they could. They'd lost most of their equipment. They tried to wreck the guns; they weren't engineers, they did not wreck the guns. They broke a few things. They hadn't been trained to remove the sights; they hadn't been trained to do anything. They threw grenades into the bunkers and through every air vent but they didn't have time to go down and see if there were many left. They knew that the cruiser was going to open fire and if they didn't move off they were all going to be killed, so they went.

Luckily the guns were very small guns. They were not the 150-millimetres which everybody had said, they were only very, very ancient 75-millimetre guns of Czech manufacture, so although the guns did continue to fire they were not very effective because their calibre was so small. In fact the Germans did not give up that battery until they were told to withdraw when Montgomery's 21st Army Group started to advance. So although it has been made a battle honour of the regiment, and it was a glorious thing and I think for a lot of men a tremendously brave thing to do, it didn't really have the outcome on the battle that we thought it would.

Company Sergeant Major Barney Ross
9th Battalion, Parachute Regiment

We felt we'd done a grand job. But afterwards you think, 'My God, what's happened to all the guys?' and you start looking round to see who's left. Like in all regiments, you have a certain circle of fairly close people you know fairly well, and so it was in the 9th Battalion that that circle was really the old Essex Regiment, where we'd been together for two years, three years, up to that time. There might have been hundreds of people that you didn't even know, not personally, put it that way; but then there's another hundred or so that you did know quite personally, especially a lot of the NCOs, because we were all young NCOs together. And then you thought, 'My God, where's he gone?' And that's the only time it really hit you, to think, 'I was bloody lucky to get out of that.' Something you don't think about when you're going in.

Seaborne Assault

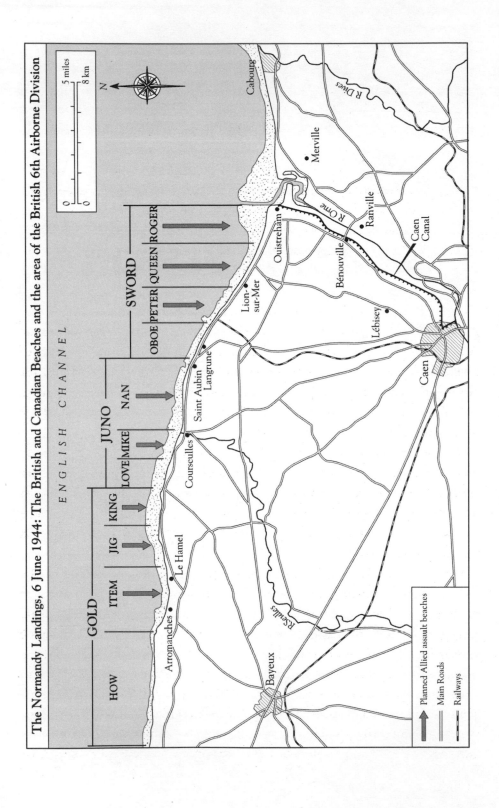

The Normandy Landings, 6 June 1944: The British and Canadian Beaches and the area of the British 6th Airborne Division

ENGLISH CHANNEL

N

5 miles
8 km
0

HOW

GOLD

ITEM

JIG

KING

Arromanches

Le Hamel

LOVE MIKE

JUNO

NAN

Courseulles

Saint Aubin

Langrune

OBOE PETER QUEEN ROGER

SWORD

Lion-sur-Mer

Ouistreham

R Orne

Bénouville

Caen Canal

Ranville

Merville

Cabourg

R Dives

Lébisey

Caen

Bayeux

R Seulles

Planned Allied assault beaches

Main Roads

Railways

I was shocked by the number of bodies, dead bodies, living bodies,
and all the blood in the water giving the appearance they were
drowning in their own blood for the want of moving.
The whole place was littered like it.

On the fifth of June 1944, seven thousand vessels, including more than twelve hundred warships, had assembled off the south coast of England. At nine in the evening they had set sail, in two task forces, for Normandy. Ships from eight navies and many merchant fleets were part of the armada and on board were more than 130,000 troops earmarked for the assault.

The Allied plan was to begin landing these men on five Normandy beaches shortly after dawn the next morning. The Americans were allocated the two westernmost beaches, code-named Omaha and Utah. To the east, the British were to assault Sword and Gold while the Canadians would land at Juno. The fleet dropped anchor opposite the invasion beaches in the early hours of 6 June.

Prior to the assault, a massive aerial and naval bombardment of the enemy's coastal defences took place. First, thousands of heavy bombers of the Royal Air Force and United States Army Air Force bombed ten coastal batteries; further air attacks, involving hundreds more aircraft, on enemy movements, fortifications and lines of communication would continue throughout the day. Then, as dawn broke and the landing craft began to circle and make their way in, the naval bombardment began. Each beach had a designated bombardment force of ships and these proceeded to engage targets all along the coast, from strongpoints and batteries perched above the beaches to troop concentrations far inland. Meanwhile, specialist landing craft equipped with rockets and guns engaged obstacle fields and enemy positions along and above the shoreline.

BOMBING AND BOMBARDMENT

Air Vice Marshal Donald Bennett
Australian commanding officer, Pathfinder Force, RAF
There were about ten batteries and we had to silence all of them to prevent them sinking the invasion fleet. We had to give a guarantee to the naval representatives on the planning committee that this would not happen – in other words, that we would effectively deal with the coastal batteries. And we were not allowed to touch them more than six hours before the invasion, just to make life easy. I gave that guarantee and my guarantee was only conditional on one thing: that if the weather was good enough for the navy then it was good enough to get the coastal batteries.

Pilot Officer Herbert Kirtland
Halifax bomber wireless operator, 76 Squadron, RAF
They explained to us that fifty Halifaxes and Lancasters were being assigned to each of these coastal batteries and we all looked at each other. This was a different kind of briefing to what we'd ever had before. The CO couldn't say, 'This is the invasion,' but there was a definite buzz, it was something different.

Pilot Officer Roy Edmondson
Canadian Halifax bomber pilot, 433 Squadron, RCAF
We were to go near Caen, in France, and we could have gone straight there but we didn't, we were diverted out to the North Sea, then came around to the English Channel and then turned south again. Well, as we were going through that area, the navigator came up and said, 'There's something peculiar with our H2S,' and then he came back a bit later and said, 'There's thousands of ships down below.' He'd picked up the invasion fleet. We weren't told anything about the invasion being on that night.

B-24 Liberators of the United States Eighth Air Force flying over part of the Allied invasion fleet gathered off the Normandy coast. These B-24s were part of the vast force of aircraft dispatched to bomb enemy positions, fortifications and lines of communication in the early hours of D-Day morning.

Flight Sergeant Rex Oldland
Lancaster bomber flight engineer, 405 Squadron, RCAF

A filthy night, too. It was rainy and cloud was low. We were flying in cloud all the time, bumping around like a fly in a trap.

Flight Sergeant John Taylor
Lancaster bomber navigator, 50 Squadron, RAF

Our target was the naval gun emplacements at the tip of the Cherbourg peninsula. It was just approaching dawn on the sixth, we couldn't see much because it was dark, but as the sky lightened we flew in and bombed and we wiped out that gun emplacement. And as we turned round there were breaks in the cloud, the sky had been pretty overcast, and we saw all these hundreds and hundreds of landing craft making their way to the beaches, and then we knew for sure that it was the invasion.

Petty Officer Edward Rose
HMS Diadem (Royal Navy cruiser), off the Normandy coast

What I remember well about that night was the bombing of the RAF. The planes were continually going over and coming back and I looked at the French coastline and it was all one mass of flame right the way down the coast. A terrific sight it was.

Flight Sergeant Rex Oldland
Lancaster bomber flight engineer, 405 Squadron, RCAF

We weren't allowed to fly over Southampton or Plymouth where we usually came back, we had to go right down into Cornwall and then fly all the way back to Bedford, by which time I think everybody had realised what was going on because we'd seen the invasion fleet out in the Channel. All the aircraft were down on the deck, all low flying, waking everybody up, right across country back to Bedford and back to our base, and even then the officer who was debriefing us said, 'Any activity in the Channel?' 'No.' 'You sure?' 'No. Never saw a thing.' 'Didn't you see anything at all?' 'No, nothing.' We used to pull his leg mercilessly, we really did.

The fifteen-inch guns of HMS *Warspite* firing on German positions, 6 June 1944.

Wing Commander Frank Metcalfe
Oboe controller, Pathfinder Force, RAF

The coastal batteries strung right across the French beaches could have blown the hell out of the invading fleet and it was our task to take them out and we did. Nine out of the ten didn't fire at all. Some of the gun crews must have fled under the sheer weight of the attack. Some were badly destroyed. Some probably couldn't get their supplies across – there was so much bombing all round the place. That was great to have achieved that.

Petty Officer Reginald Samuel Francis Coaker
HMS Urania (Royal Navy destroyer), off Gold Beach

As it began to get light, so of course they saw us, and they opened fire on us from the cliffs to the east of Arromanches. Having been in one or two other places on the North African coast, I thought, 'Oh, this is one where they are going to retaliate.' The shells started to come over and the spouts went up in the water. But as this was happening I can remember being in my position at the back of the bridge and I could hear, as clearly as anything, across the water from the four cruisers, the bugles for action stations and closing-up and they swung into position.

Engine Room Artificer Ronald Jesse
HMS Belfast (Royal Navy cruiser), off Sword Beach

I thought we were going to tear up and down at high speed blasting everything in sight but quite the opposite. We just stopped. And then it started. Bang! Bang-bang-bang!

Leading Telegraphist Reginald Heron
Landing Craft Gun (LCG) flotilla command boat, off Juno Beach

It started from the large monitors and battleships far out, firing way inland. And then the cruisers, destroyers, firing, say, ten to twenty miles inland. And then you had us, with the 4.7s. We were firing beyond the beach areas and further inland, say between five and ten miles inland. And then in front of us, going close in, were the LCMs, which carried light Bofors-type guns, attacking the actual beach emplacements, and of course there were the rocket ships, firing, I think it was, a hundred-odd rockets at a time. The whole thing was so enormously noisy and chaotic. Almost like an inferno.

Petty Officer Lawrence Alfred Moorcroft
HMS Urania (Royal Navy destroyer), off Gold Beach
Cruisers firing over the destroyers. Battleships firing over the cruisers and destroyers and the rocket ships. It seemed to us chaos. Never seen so many things firing. I was the one that went, 'Bonk-bonk, ding-ding,' and the gun fired. We had a stopwatch, an hour and minute stopwatch, they were all synchronised via radio, and the bloody *Grenville* fired two seconds before. I fired dead on 6.25. He fired two seconds before.

Telegraphist Kenneth Howe
Georges Leygues (Free French cruiser), off Omaha Beach
I was seconded to a Free French cruiser, the *Georges Leygues*, a very fast cruiser. I was in the radio office on the upper deck below the bridge directing the French gunfire on to targets and liaising with American ships on their gunfire. We were flying a very, very large tricolour, a French flag, which they said was for morale purposes. I could never understand for whose morale because the French crew wasn't particularly enchanted by it. It turned out it was for the people ashore who could see their tricolour flying on one of the ships.

Telegraphist George Lester
HMS Kingsmill (Royal Navy frigate and HQ ship), off Gold Beach
The *Flores*, a Dutch gunboat, she was part of the bombardment. Being of much shallower draft she came up and anchored herself not more than a hundred yards away from us and was belting away with her guns. You could feel every reverberation right throughout our ship as she fired.

Ordinary Seaman Robert Brown
Canadian seaman, HMS Belfast (Royal Navy cruiser), off Sword Beach
When the guns fired, on the decks below it would shake out half the light bulbs. They'd just snap out of their sockets and break on the deck. They were always replacing light bulbs when the guns were firing.

Engine Room Artificer Ronald Jesse
HMS Belfast (Royal Navy cruiser), off Sword Beach
A crash and a bang and a shudder. A crash and a bang and a shudder and a crash and a bang and a shudder. Not quite as fast as this, but monotonous.

There's a crash and a bang and a shudder. It's exactly the same sensation as a near miss: if someone is shooting at you there's a crash and a bang and a shudder and the ship shakes. And you get used to this till eventually it fades into the commonplace, if I can use the word.

Much more significant to our way of thinking were the horrendous outpourings of rockets from the rocket ships. We had landing craft fitted with a hundred rockets and when these went off with a 'Woosh! Woosh! Woosh! Woosh! Woosh! Woosh! Woosh!' they would all stream inland and there would be a vast series of explosions on shore. You couldn't help thinking that there would be nothing left surviving underneath.

Sub Lieutenant Anthony Swainson
LCT(R) commander, off Juno Beach

I was in command of a rocket ship. When we got within view of the beach one could see the whole thing clearly, there were pillboxes, and we did realise that there was a danger of us hitting mines as we went in. My best friend was on my port side in his ship and, alas, he hit one of these mines, which could have happened to any of us, and of course he went up in a huge cloud of smoke and a loud explosion. I just felt numb, I suppose, thinking, 'Well, there he goes. Oh dear, nothing we can do about it. Get on with the job, Swainson. Stop beefing.' And so, with more determination, we ploughed on and there was a German pillbox firing a flame-thrower at me and I fired off my rockets and destroyed it.

Lieutenant Richard Hill
LCS(M) commander, off Gold Beach

There was a need for a small shallow craft, armoured, that could attack shore emplacements on beaches. I'm not talking about the big heavy guns but machine-gun emplacements, machine-gun nests, firing from fortified houses and that sort of thing. They first of all adapted an LCA, which was really for transporting a platoon of men into the beach, and they gradually evolved to a Mark III LCS(M).

It was forty-one foot with a pointed bow, whereas an LCA has a ramp at the front. It had a well at the fore end, which housed a four-inch mortar, a smoke mortar and two machine guns. Immediately behind the well in which the two Lewis-gunners and the two mortar men were sited it had a coxswains' cockpit, which was entirely armoured, the whole vessel actually was armoured on its sides, and the coxswain had these slits around the cockpit so that he could see.

Immediately behind the coxswain's cockpit there was a twin .5 rotating Vickers machine gun, which was a pretty powerful weapon. In there you had a corporal, who was the gunner, and he had an ammunition loader in there and they were encased in armour. And behind them you had another Lewis gun mounted on a tripod and a smoke-making apparatus. The craft had a range of ninety miles and a maximum speed of nine knots if you were going flat out and a crew was one officer and nine men. Most of them were manning guns, and you had a stoker, a signalman and an officer, and we were the only three who were not manning weapons as such.

We went in. We could see our objectives, both of them were firing, our machine-gunner picked them up. The machine gun was the main target for the Vickers .5 but it was extremely difficult when (a) you are far out, because it was pretty low tide, and (b) the sea was quite rough. But our chap had practised quite a bit and I think he made pretty good use of what he had. We had tracer coming at us too but we did attack and we continued to attack.

Then we started to get absolutely showered with 88-millimetre shells. We were the only craft in this particular area and we were peppered and peppered and peppered with these 88s. You couldn't tell where they were coming from and I just don't know how we weren't hit. There was obviously great concern on the craft, because, I mean, we were being soaked by the spray of these things and one landed just in front of the bows. I shouted to the coxswain, and this is famous amongst my lads now, 'Make straight for where that shell landed, they never strike twice in the same place!'

At this stage the coxswain told me that the stoker had said that we were shipping water and that he couldn't cope with it with the bilge pumps. And not only that, we were having to avoid these underwater obstacles, we were having to change course quickly, we were having to reverse – the stoker must've had a terrible time down there.

Anyway, the message came through that we were shipping water and at the same time the machine guns stopped firing and I think that may have been a godsend in its way. I thought, 'The only thing to do is to pull out to sea,' which is what we did. We must have gone about two miles out to sea and we really were getting into trouble because the gunnels were almost awash at one stage. It became a choice now of chucking all the ammunition overboard and getting everybody down to the bilge pumps and we already had as many people as possible doing what bilge pumps they could operate.

But then this destroyer was out there and from the bridge an officer with a loudhailer said to me, 'You seem to be in trouble. Can we help?' Imagine, a destroyer talking to us, it was like looking up at a skyscraper to see this huge thing, and in the middle of a huge bombardment. I shouted, 'Yes!' He said, 'Come alongside but make it quick.' So we got alongside, they threw ropes down to us and we made fast. Another officer hung over the railings and said, 'What's the matter?' I said, 'I don't know. We're shipping water, I don't know how.' He said, 'Right, how can we get a hose into your craft?' I said, 'Well, the trouble's in the engine room, it can go straight in there, that's where we want it.' Within a matter of seconds they sent this big hose down, it must have been eight or ten inches wide, we put it into the engine room and we were buoyant in a matter of seconds.

While all this was going on, somebody had come down from the bridge and was just telling me briefly what was happening. He said, 'What area are you from?' I said, 'Arromanches, Le Hamel; and we've got to get back now because there's a spot of bother there still.' Meanwhile they had lowered a five-gallon tin of piping hot soup and the lads had got their mugs out and were all accepting it, very, very willingly, because we hadn't eaten – no one had wanted breakfast before really. Then they went off and just as they were going away the loudhailer came over the bridge, 'Good luck and God bless!' I always remember that. And off we went.

Petty Officer Reginald Samuel Francis Coaker
Ordnance Officer, HMS Urania (Royal Navy destroyer), off Gold Beach

No sooner had we opened fire on our target on the beach, the pillbox, and knocked that out, than almost simultaneously came in a wave of rocket-firing Typhoons and bombers and the whole beach seemed to erupt and was covered in sand and smoke. And in next to no time, where we had been right out at the forefront of the attack, we then were seeing soldiers going by us in these landing craft. The whole thing was so totally well organised. Wheeling overhead the whole time were groups of our Spitfires and Hurricanes: perfect air cover.

Major John Howard
2nd Battalion, Oxfordshire and Buckinghamshire Light Infantry

The barrage hit the whole of the coast from around seven o'clock onwards or before that. You could hear the coast being bombarded and then soon after seven the barrage lifted and it moved towards us, inland. And the whole ground shook. Those naval bombardments, on top of the RAF, were absolutely terrific. And we thought of those poor devils coming in by sea in those landing launches and we were damned glad we were where we were, relatively safe. We certainly wouldn't have wanted to be anywhere near the coast.

Private Philip Crofts
7th Battalion, Parachute Regiment

Even at this distance inland my eardrums were going in and out, I thought they would burst. On top of that there were huge shells passing over us and it felt like they were tearing the skies apart. And we then knew the seaborne forces were coming in.

Captain David Tibbs
Regimental Medical Officer, 13th Battalion, Parachute Regiment

Dawn broke, it was rather misty, and we could see the coast from where we were. Then about half past six or onwards one of my men called out and pointed and I looked towards the sea and there you could see, emerging out of the mist, a large number of craft. This was about two to three miles away so they were only small dots but it was a tremendous boost to our morale to see all this coming in. From then on there was a continuous rumbling from the coastal areas of the attack going on there, which was a great spur to us.

SWORD BEACH

Sword was the easternmost of the invasion beaches and stretched for eight miles from the Orne estuary at Ouistreham, in the east, towards the seaside village of St-Aubin-sur-Mer. Storming the beach, establishing a beachhead and pressing inland were the tasks of Major General Tom Rennie's British 3rd Infantry Division.

Guided in by a midget submarine and preceded by obstacle-clearance teams, the first elements of the Division to launch and make for shore were amphibious DD tanks. The first wave of assault infantry, men from the South Lancashire and East Yorkshire Regiments, hit the beach at 0725 hours: offshore reefs limited the attack to a tight mile-wide front west of the village of La Brèche. Many enemy strongpoints and positions had survived the air and naval bombardment, and the assault was made under fire from enemy field and coastal batteries, mortars, machine guns and snipers.

Movement off the beaches remained difficult throughout the morning. The early loss of many mine-clearing tanks meant exits from the beach were cleared only slowly. Meanwhile, the incoming tide caused further problems as follow-up infantry, commandos and vehicles continued to land, still under fire, and began to accumulate on a narrowing strip of dry sand at the top of the beach. Gradually the enemy positions above the beach were dealt with. Tanks and the arrival of commandos of Brigadier the Lord Lovat's 1st Special Service Brigade helped the process. By midday the traffic jam was beginning to disperse and the follow-up forces were following the assault battalions inland.

Lieutenant Commander George Honour
X23 midget submarine commander
We were on Sword Beach, about a mile and a quarter offshore, at Ouistreham. Our little operation was called Gambit. It was all part of the bigger operation and when we were given the code name we looked it up in the dictionary and to our horror it said, 'The pawn you throw away before a big move in chess,' which didn't encourage us too much.

We arrived on Sunday 4 June and confirmed our position through the periscope and sat on the bottom till nightfall. On Sunday night we surfaced, dropped our anchor, so we would stay in our position, hoisted our radio mast and we got a signal that the invasion had been postponed. So we had to retreat to the bottom again and wait until Monday night. One of the things we saw was a lorry-load of Germans arrive. They started playing beach ball and swimming and at the back of my mind I thought, 'I hope there are no Olympic swimmers and that they don't swim out a mile from shore and find us.' But here were the Germans having a Sunday afternoon recreation and little did they know what was sitting and waiting for them.

Should the worst have happened we had all kinds of plans so that we could get ashore and, if possible, contact the French Resistance and they would give us false passports and whisk us back through some unknown way. I personally don't think we would've got far off the beach if we had got ashore. I can imagine some great Hun with a rifle sticking his bayonet into you and saying, 'What are you doing?' or something like that.

The main tension was the postponement, because we were on oxygen fed to us automatically from air bottles and when we had the postponement it didn't say how long it was for. We had this awful problem: would we have enough oxygen if the invasion didn't come on Tuesday? Once we knew it was coming the tension went; we had a job to do and I think we just went ahead and did our job. We had enough food for about a week, I suppose, ten days; the air was the main thing. Interesting point: we had these extra big air bottles and the lightest ones they could find were *Luftwaffe* bottles, so we were using German air bottles.

On the Monday night we again surfaced and received a message that the invasion was on so once again we went and sat on the bottom. At about 4.30am on Tuesday 6 June we surfaced again and put up all our navigational aids: an eighteen-foot telescopic mast with a light shining to seaward, a radio beacon and an echo sounder tapping out a message below the surface. This was for the navigational MLs to pick up as they brought the invasion force in.

Lieutenant Graham Rouse
Motor launch commander

We were the ML on the port side of the convoy and there was another one on the other side. We were four or five hundred yards ahead of the convoy. We knew that on our beach a midget submarine would have gone in beforehand and remained submerged and when they got sight of us would surface and have various signals and devices to send back to me and my equipment so we could locate it. That was X23.

We were plodding on with all the equipment on and I reckoned we were on the right track. There were three pairs of binoculars on the bridge and the signaller with the telescope, all looking for the X23. I had not yet picked up any of his signals by sonar through our Asdic or the radio signal coming or the lights. But eventually the signalman saw a tiny green light and thank goodness we were in the right place, which was a bit gratifying because we dare not be any further east because we'd be too close to the River Orne and all the gun emplacements over there. I was greatly relieved to see him.

Lieutenant Commander George Honour
X23 midget submarine commander

We knew that the DD tanks would be launched all around us from tank landing craft and they would form up and swim ashore under their own power. They were in flotation bags, great big canvas bags, and carried two propellers. And sure enough they were launched all around us and as soon as the DD tanks had been launched we'd completed our task. We cut the anchor rope, we were too exhausted to pull up the anchor, and then we had to rendezvous with our escorting trawler.

Corporal Patrick Hennessy
Sherman tank commander, 13th/18th Hussars

The sea was very rough and the landing craft was heaving around. The door went down and the ramp leading into the sea went down and I was second tank off. Our troop sergeant went off first, he went down the ramp, nosed into the sea, straightened up, got out of the way and then off we went down the ramp into the sea and finally we straightened up too. I gave the order to drop the propellers and the propellers came down and engaged and we could feel them bite in the water and we started on our way following the sergeant's tank in front. You could see the shoreline briefly now and then from that low angle. As a trough appeared in the waves, so the tank slid into the trough; and with the engines racing, it managed to climb up to the crest of the next wave, where you could see what was going on, then down into the next trough. The wind was behind us and very strong and this was a bit of a help, I suppose, because it helped us toward the beach.

Corporal John Barnes
Sherman tank commander, 13th/18th Hussars

There's spray in your face. You're watching everything that's happening, you're seeing explosions, there's smoke screens being put up, and you're looking for that one light of the single submarine so you know you're on the right track. As the swell comes, you turn into it and ride it and then come

The view from a Landing Craft Infantry (LCI) approaching Sword Beach. Tanks and other vehicles of 27th Armoured Brigade and 79th Armoured Division can be seen crowding on the beach ahead.

back again. Desperately in your mind is, 'I must get to the beach, I must get to the beach.' You know that if you don't get there, you're going to sink in the water. You're in escape kit, you've got that basically prepared, the goggles, the nose clips and the mouthpiece around your chin, and you know that if you go down they're going to go in quick. Then you think, 'What's that black thing there?' and you're looking very hard because it's rough weather and you're wondering whether it's an obstacle that has a mine on.

Corporal Patrick Hennessy
Sherman tank commander, 13th/18th Hussars
Disaster struck one DD tank as he went off from another LCT. As he was going through the large doorway the ship rolled and as it rolled the tank lurched to one side and the canvas screen brushed the iron side of the entrance and slashed it. There was nothing they could do. They couldn't go back because there were other tanks to come off. They had to go forward. Nobody was sitting in the turret and as it hit the water the water gushed in through the screen and that tank sank. Luckily the crew got out. They had their rubber dinghy, which they jumped into, and they were saved.

The rest of us were still ploughing on through the water. We had some three miles to go and it was very tough going. The only one who was inside on my particular tank was the driver and he had to sit there keeping the engines running because if the engines stopped we were in deep trouble, so he was down there in the bowels of the tank. I had the rest of the crew on deck and we were making sure those struts stayed put. Water came in over the top of the screen from time to time from these large waves. We had a manual-operated bilge pump and the co-driver was kept very busy with this bilge pump and we were bailing with steel helmets and everything to keep the water down inside the tank.

Corporal John Barnes
Sherman tank commander, 13th/18th Hussars
Soon as the tracks hit the beach, the driver pulls the lever and the tracks take over and once you're out of the water the skirts drop and you're firing at everything you can see and you're moving forward all the time until you're off the beach. You're just doing the things that you've been taught. Getting there from the LCT, that part – two and a half miles at four knots – is the thing most

on your mind and you're praying a shell doesn't land on you. You've no defence at all until you get on the beach. Out of forty tanks, thirty-two made it. Those that didn't, hit something or they were either caught on something or the ramp came down too quick with it bouncing up and down. We had Mae Wests and those little rubber dinghy things: that saved a lot of men.

Midshipman Rene Le Roy
Landing Craft Obstacle Clearance Unit
The Germans had put in tremendous defences on the beaches in rows and rows and with very Germanic five-yard spacing. There was an initial row of tree trunks with mines on. The next was criss-cross girders and next was another row. So you had three rows of obstacles on basically all the beaches in Normandy. And Teller mines were fitted on some of them or some of them had French 75-millimetre shells with the nose cap changed to percussion caps for pressure, so you'd press on the shell and it would go off. Any landing craft coming in without seeing these obstacles could hit these fields.

Private William Edward Lloyd
2nd Battalion, East Yorkshire Regiment
'Heads down, in you go,' and everybody went dead quiet. The only thing that bothered me was what I was going to be like when we hit the beach. Was I going to hesitate or was I going to get out fast? Well, the boat behind us got a direct hit, one at the side of us got a direct hit and they dropped shells then either side of us.

Private Albert Holdsworth
2nd Battalion, East Yorkshire Regiment
Very frightening, very frightening; also you were feeling excitement as well. A knot in your stomach, you know.

Sergeant Desmond O'Neill
Cameraman, Army Film and Photographic Unit
We suddenly saw ahead of us smoke, grey smoke and mist mixed, and as we approached we saw obstacles in the water because the beach there is shelving, very shallow, for a long way out. But still there was no great sign of being attacked by anybody. Then we started noticing one or two plops in the water,

which must have been mortars, but nothing else. Then we heard gunfire, machine-gun fire, and then it seemed that once we got into the smoke we were in it. I immediately noticed over on the left a landing craft tank, which had come in alongside us and gone ahead a little, and it suddenly caught fire. The whole thing seemed so unreal. It's not like a battle scene as one would imagine it or has seen on a film since. It was a very unreal atmosphere.

Private Tom Barlow
1st Battalion, South Lancashire Regiment
You could see, and it was only years after I realised what it was, what looked like when you throw bricks into water and you get a little spurt of water shooting up. Well, you could see this happening in the water and at the time this is what I thought it was. It wasn't, it was bullets, but you just don't realise.

Marine Harry Wicks
LCT crew
There was an LCP with about twenty or something men on board – they're only wood, not armoured – and a shell dropped right off the side of it. We pulled alongside and tied up, Lofty and myself and Harry were getting the wounded out and then, of course, another shell dropped. Old Joe Wright, the old stoker, he was up the back and he had his arm almost severed, Lofty Crawford had a piece in the stomach and Harry got a piece in the neck. I got a piece in the arm, the back and the leg, but mine was the least. Mine was only superficial, you know.

They give you big wooden pegs and you knock them in the holes – if shrapnel tears holes in your boat you knock these pegs in – so we've got about fifty pegs in the holes and there's water coming in but we got back. They lowered a stretcher and we got Lofty in it, because Lofty was bad, he'd got it right through the stomach. As I say, there was nothing wrong with me, I've had worse blacksmithing. But having got in there they stitched me up and packed me full of penicillin and I found out I was allergic to penicillin, so I was worse.

Sub Lieutenant John Brooke
LCT crew
I went aft to find that one gun crew had been severely damaged. There was one stoker on the deck, severely wounded in his stomach, and the gunner in

the slings of the gun was lying back, I thought, unconscious. We got him out of the sling and realised he was more severely wounded than we'd thought: the top of his head had been blown off. Our commanding officer, he'd been severely wounded through the palm of his hand and up his wrist by a splinter. So as soon as we could, we turned and headed out of the melee and found a hospital ship lying off the main body of craft coming in. I know that three compares little with other ships' numbers but these were people we'd known, we'd lived very closely as a ship's company, two officers and ten men, we'd been together for a year. I'd seen wounded and dead men before but we were people, if I can say it, who'd become fond of each other and that hit me more than anything else.

Marine Edward 'Tommy' Treacher
45 (Royal Marine) Commando

We was four hundred yards from shore and there was such a crash on our boat and a shell had landed amongst all the chaps waiting to get off. They were lying there, they were wounded, they were dead; as a matter of fact we had twenty-three casualties on our boat, eleven dead and twelve wounded.

As we were getting closer the matelots were ready to push the ramps down and there was blood everywhere – there's no doubt about it, it was thick – and when the navy blokes was going to push the ramps down another shell hit us and it killed all four. As a matter of fact they were decapitated.

Then we had one of our officers and three other sergeants ready to push the ramps down. Now these people were not used to pushing the ramps down and once they were down they were all twisted and turned. God, it was in a state. We had to walk through this blood on the deck and it was really running, it was terrible, and as I was going to get off the boat I spoke to one of my friends and I said, 'How are you, Jasper?' And he says, 'How am I, Tom? How am I? I reckon I've broken both my legs.'

Sergeant Arthur Thompson
2nd Battalion, East Yorkshire Regiment

As soon as the craft hits the beach, the front drops and the centre group have to dash out straight away, otherwise the others can't get out. And this young Joe we had with us, he stood there and he was petrified, so nobody could move. Everybody is just shouting, 'Get out the bloody road!' and eventually I

MH 2664

Film still of British troops under fire on Sword Beach.

just pushed him out so that we could get out. By that time the beach was getting covered with dead and wounded, you were jumping over them as you went in, and that's when you start to say your prayers. I said my prayers when we got out of that boat and were going up them beaches, because there's that many laid about wounded and dead.

Marine James Anthony Kelly
41 (Royal Marine) Commando

There was a blinding flash and a terrible bloody smell of cordite and things like that and Charlie Hall was down on the deck and there was other fellows scattered about. I remember kneeling by Charlie Hall and blood was pumping out of his neck and right out of his combined ops badge that was on his shoulder – it was pumping out of all places. And I'd only just knelt down and was saying to him, 'Come on, Charlie, come on,' and this voice said, 'You're not supposed to stop. Get going.'

Private Lionel Roebuck
2nd Battalion, East Yorkshire Regiment

Each side of us there were wrecked boats, sometimes side on, sometimes upside down. There were bodies floating face down in the sea. There were men halfway up the beach who were in really peculiar positions, legs all over the place, really grotesque positions, and there were shells landing all around in the sea and on the beach. The sand seemed to drag on your feet. It just seemed you couldn't get going, what with the weight of your equipment and things like that.

Leading Seaman Henry Sivelle
LCI coxswain

The port ramp was down and they were being held back by machine gun fire which was trained on that ramp. Ahead we could see the machine gun post in the window of a house two hundred yards away. We reported to the skipper that this machine gun was holding our troops back and he said, 'Can you give them a ten-second burst?' I said, 'Yes,' and we gave them a ten-second burst and brought the house down.

Lieutenant Eric Ashcroft
1st Battalion, South Lancashire Regiment

About two-thirds to the high water mark I was knocked sideways when, so it would appear now, an 88-millimetre splinter struck my right arm. I was moving across the beach at the time fairly fast and I didn't think anything about it. I just kept moving.

Private William Edward Lloyd
2nd Battalion, East Yorkshire Regiment

Bullets just came at you like raindrops. You could hear them whistling and passing you and hitting the ground near you but you just kept going on. It was a gradual sloping beach, hadn't much to give us any cover. A few sand dunes and things like that but apart from that we hadn't much cover at all.

Sergeant Arthur Thompson
2nd Battalion, East Yorkshire Regiment

We lost our company commander and quite a number of officers on the beach. The company commander called an O group to arrange what we were going to do and they got killed. They'd formed a circle or something and I think a shell or a mortar dropped in amongst them all. After that we'd only some young lieutenants and we'd got to take hold of their hands and take them on with us because they had no idea, you see. It was one of the times where you've got to have someone who can just do things without getting excited or flustered.

Captain Arthur Rouse
1st Battalion, South Lancashire Regiment

Colonel Burbury headed for the sand dunes, there was a gap slightly to his left, and his gaunt figure strode across the sand towards this gap in the sand dunes. I followed him immediately and one or two people started to fall as mortar fire and machine-gun fire came across and fixed artillery firing along the line of the beach. I said, 'Keep going, they'll be looked after.' We didn't want people trying to help their friends.

Eventually we all assembled in the lee of these sand dunes, the commanding officer and me looking over. And he just turned to me with his map in his hand and said, 'Where are we, Arthur?' and then he was shot, immediately. His jaw went into spasms and he dropped down. I got down and turned round and the second-in-command had just arrived and I said, 'You're in command now.' The colonel was such an obvious target: he had a flag in his hand in case there was going to be confusion and he could be rallied round, he waved his map as well. I think he was hit by a sniper. Then the signals officer, Eric Ashcroft, came up with his arm in a sling and I said, 'You'd better get that seen to.'

Lieutenant Eric Ashcroft
1st Battalion, South Lancashire Regiment

I remember, when we were in the sand dunes, I was looking down and saw a procession of ants and thought, 'Goodness me, they're not affected by the war.' These silly thoughts you get.

Corporal Patrick Hennessy
Sherman tank commander, 13th/18th Hussars

Having got ashore, the next thing on the programme was to have been that the Royal Engineers would've arrived and started to clear the mines which were on the beach and put down markers so that we could come from the beach and drive inland avoiding the mines. They had a certain amount of trouble in their voyage across the Channel and so they were late and there we were, at low tide, sitting on the beach, firing away. The infantry were now coming past us ashore in their little landing craft and under cover of our fire they were going up the beach.

But we had landed on a fast incoming tide. We'd landed at low tide, so the longer we stood still and waited for the mines to be cleared on the beach, the deeper the water became. It wasn't long before the driver started complaining bitterly that, because we'd dropped our screen and the water was getting deeper, it was now coming in over the top of his hatch and he was sitting in a pool of water. He said, 'For God's sake, let's move on up the beach!' This was a failure on my part: I should've used my initiative and said, 'Go for it!' but I didn't. And as we sat there, wondering what to do, the problem was solved for us because a particularly large wave hit the stern of the tank and swamped the engine compartment and the engine spluttered to a halt and was drowned. Well, now we had a thirty-two ton tank and no power so we couldn't move even if we'd wanted to.

Men sheltering behind the build-up of vehicles on Sword Beach on the morning of
6 June.

So we sat there and fired and continued firing until such time as the tank became swamped. The water level inside the tank was rising and when the water got to the gun breach inside the turret we couldn't carry on. So we inflated the rubber dingy, took out the Browning machine gun and some ammunition and we got in the rubber dinghy and we had to abandon the tank and start paddling for the shore. By now, of course, the tide had come in so fast and so far that it was several hundred yards to the shoreline and it seemed a long way and the water was quite deep and it was being speckled with bullets. We were under fire all the time from the shore now and we used the map boards as paddles and there were five of us sitting in this little dinghy, trying to get ashore. We hadn't gone very far when we were suddenly hit by a burst of machine-gun fire. This punctured the rubber dingy which collapsed and threw us into the sea and we lost our machine gun and ammunition and one bullet hit the co-driver in the ankle so we now had a wounded man on our hands.

We were floundering around in the water and we started to splash our way into the beach and were trying to get the wounded man there at the same time. We lay there on the beach, swigging down hot soup and wondering what to do next, and I remember being suddenly approached by a captain in the Royal Engineers and he was very angry and he came up and said, 'Get up, corporal. That's no way to win the Second Front.' Then he pushed off on his business. Of course he was quite right and I felt a little bit ashamed about this. I finally found the Beachmaster, a Royal Naval lieutenant commander, who was a very busy man trying to organise things. I reported to him and said, 'Here we are, what can I do to help?' And he said 'You want to help me?' I said 'Yes, sir.' He said, 'Well, get off my bloody beach.'

Lieutenant Commander Edward Gueritz
Beachmaster

The task of the beach group centred on an infantry battalion and had added to it engineer, medical, transport, RAF and naval components, to enable it to carry out all the necessary duties of receiving men and vehicles from landing craft and ships, clearing them through the beach exits into transit areas and either then to storage depots or through to the operational front. The naval beach party element of this was to provide navigational marks to assist in the clearance of obstacles below the high-water mark, to mark any obstructions they could see and generally to provide the incoming landing craft with as much guidance as possible and expedite the unloading of them – their personnel, vehicles or stores – and clear them off the beach as quickly as possible. It was never straightforward. Things never go particularly well on exercises and it doesn't help when you're being shot at as well. We had considerable difficulty in clearing the vehicles off the beach, partly because of mining by the Germans and partly because we were victims of our own success in getting so much ashore and the exits were ill-suited to the volume of traffic. Mines were the chief hazard but of course vehicles do break down or 'drown' as the expression is. You can also create quicksands due to gunfire and that provides another hazard. We had to close our beach for a period because of the difficulty of dispersing the vehicles away from the beach area to their respective tasks.

Captain Julius Neave
Sherman tank commander, 13th/18th Hussars
That was the great problem: congestion. My brother had quite a lot of trouble clearing the exits. I met him on the beach, which was a remarkable coincidence. I was sitting in my tank and I suddenly saw his head appear over the top. He kept bobbing down as mortar shells came over, to get out of the way. I think it was 'Hello' and greetings: 'How are you getting on?' and 'What's happening?' A rather futile conversation. But it was rather rewarding as well because he was a very vital part; I think he had been about the first person to arrive on the beach. The great thing was to clear the exits from the vehicles that had got mined and push them out of the way and get on.

Marine James Anthony Kelly
41 (Royal Marine) Commando
I had a blue pennant with 'A Troop' on or a big 'A' in red and they stuck it in my pack at the back so that it stuck up over my head. I heard a voice shouting, 'All commandos this way! All commandos this way!' and he'd found an opening in the wire and was calling all the commandos and saying, 'Go on, get through there, quick, quick.' And when I got to him he said, 'Ah, here you are. Good. Wave that.' And he pulled this thing out of my pack and gives it to me. 'Wave that?' I thought. 'I'm a big enough target without waving that thing.' I honestly think I only gave it a couple of waves and he snatched it off me and he started waving and they shot him.

Marine Warwick Nield-Siddal
41 (Royal Marine) Commando

We grouped for about ten minutes on the beach until the Beachmaster, who was a naval officer, came along. The most calm man I've ever met in my life. Came along swinging a cane and shells were landing and mortars were landing and people were falling and he was walking through it. 'Come off the beach. Others have got to land. Off the beach.'

Marine James Anthony Kelly
41 (Royal Marine) Commando

I honestly wondered about this fellow as I ran past. He's just standing there, shouting, 'Over here! Keep over here!' Like a traffic copper, not a feather on him, in his blue uniform with gold braid. How long he lasted I don't know.

Able Seaman Kenneth Oakley
Beachmaster's bodyguard

Many of the landing troops would say, 'We must have a conference here, where are my unit?' Or, 'I've been awfully sick, can't we have a brew-up of tea?' 'No, you can't have tea here on the beach. Get cracking. Go inland. Knock a few Germans off and then have a cup of tea.' It was difficult. The chaos at the water's edge had to be sorted because craft was coming in all the time and, without someone there to continually move them and push them to go, groups would form and block the exits.

Sergeant George Rayson
1st Battalion, Suffolk Regiment

We lowered the ramp and out went a naval officer and out went our officer. They just stepped off into what they thought was going to be three or four feet of water and they disappeared and up they popped and they swam ashore. Of course no one else moved because half the boat couldn't swim. I said, 'Back off and go in again,' which he did, and we went in again. We didn't look any nearer but it looked all right. Nobody moved. Then I thought, 'If I go out of turn, like I shouldn't, they'll follow me.' So off I go, two more blokes follow me, and I never thought I was going to touch the bottom.

Eventually I shot up and the ramp was touching me back and the other two blokes come up and the bloody fool moved the boat forward. Course, they went round the corner, hanging on, and I went under the boat and I could feel myself going bump, bump, bump, bump, all the way along. Then I shot up and the boat was three foot in front of me. I started to stroke a bit but I kept going under because of all the gear I was carrying. I thought to myself, 'I'm never going to get out of this,' and undone me belt and got shot of the lot, including the Sten gun; all I got left was the steel helmet and two bandoliers of fifty rounds which I was carrying as spare and couldn't get off. Kept going under still. Anyhow, I got into something like a swim. Despite me boots, I could move slowly forward. Me steel helmet kept going over me face so I chucked that away as well. I started to get a bit exhausted so I turned over on me back and kicked out that way and eventually I touched the sand, I jumped up and ran a few yards and they'd all gone. Everybody on the boat had gone. Frozen stiff I was and soaked through to the skin and I'd felt a bit off anyhow.

I got up, I walked a few yards and there were six or seven South Lancs, dead. So I looked round and picked up a Sten gun, a couple of grenades which I shoved in me top pockets and some magazines which I shoved in me inside jacket pocket. I never bothered about equipment; I just couldn't get myself to take equipment off a dead man somehow. Steel helmet would come in handy so I put that on and off I go up the beach.

There was one of our fellows there, a stretcher-bearer, Harry Philby, and he said, 'Can I do you up?' I said 'What for?' He said, 'Well, look at you.' I looked down and I was covered in blood and he said, 'It's your nose'. I'd broken me nose, somewhere under the boat or other, and the blood pouring down made it look about ten times worse. I said, 'I'm all right. Which way did they go?' So he pointed which way they went and he helped me up on to the promenade and I got through the barbed wire. After a few minutes I caught D Company up. I asked them where A Company was and an officer pointed and I went across and found me own company. Of course, one bloke said, 'We know what you was doing. Swimming back. Didn't like the look of France.'

Private Leslie Perry
1st Battalion, Suffolk Regiment
On top of this pillbox was one of our chaps. I think he must've been a South Lanc. He'd run up on top of this pillbox with a Bren gun and was firing at the Germans in the fields and someone got him right between the eyes, there was a little hole in his forehead and a trickle of blood. And he was laying down

with his arms outstretched and his feet towards the top and his head towards the beach and I looked and I thought, 'My God, a little hole like that and he's dead.' I felt strange. I can't say I was frightened. When I saw him up there I must admit it hit me, but to me it was just like being on an exercise. I felt lonely, more than anything; though I had mates all around me, I felt lonely. I felt everyone was firing at me.

Lieutenant Commander Edward Gueritz
Beachmaster

There were of course people who found the landing very stressful. I remember there was a group of military policemen lurking behind an armoured vehicle and I encouraged them to go off about their business. I also met two men – and I've never seen this before or after – who were blue with fear. Again they had to be encouraged to take a grip of themselves. It was no worse for them than it was for anybody else.

Marine Derrick Cakebread
45 (Royal Marine) Commando

It was shocking really. What can I say? It was rough. All the mortars going and the shells and the people who landed before us, the East Yorks, to clear the beach – a lot of those were dead and floating. First time I saw a dead person, and it shakes you. There is no doubt about it, you're scared: the noise and seeing men falling in front of you and the people already gone.

Able Seaman Kenneth Oakley
Beachmaster's bodyguard

Mortar fire seemed to be passing over us and it seemed that we were so close that he could not depress to cover our area, which was fortunate for us. After a while, along came a DD tank and the hatch opened and a voice shouted, 'Where's the fire?' I pointed to the right and shouted, 'Two hundred yards, forty-five degrees!' Bang went the turret door; crash went the projectile; one shot finished the mortar fire. It must have ploughed right along their trench.

Film still of men of 4 Commando moving off Sword Beach. Cautious of enemy fire and carrying heavy kit, they are keeping well down.

Corporal George Sidney Kenneth Agnew
Sherman Crab flail tank commander, 22nd Dragoons
I ran slap-bang into an 88-millimetre gun emplacement which didn't take long to neutralise my tank. I was hit twice: one up the side and into the engine and one on the turret. The next thing we knew, we were standing in flames. The whole tank burst into flames. The only thing I could do was swing the turret round to make sure the driver and the co-driver could get out and I shouted, 'Bail out!' and we bailed out. I went along the sand dunes and there was another tank from another squadron and the commander had been sniped through the head. I came behind the tank and I shouted, 'Shove him out!' They shoved the body out and I got into that tank and went on.

Midshipman Rene Le Roy
Landing Craft Obstacle Clearance Unit
4 Commando came in, in five LCIs, with Bergen rucksacks which were all full of equipment, and they realised more than anybody as they were approaching the beach that the beach hadn't been taken and they thought, 'We attack.' So they came in and they passed through a wave of men on the beach, ditching their rucksacks and immediately firing their way forward. They came up in lines, straight up, passing us, passing through, attacking the pillboxes, attacking any buildings and within a period of ten minutes they'd disappeared and the beach organisation started to get up and move. It was quite incredible. Their role wasn't to capture the beach but that role had been greatly assisted by the commando advance.

Private Reginald Barnes
4 Commando
We made an immediate move to clear the beach and not to dig in or stay there. The first obstacles we came across was a sign saying 'Minen' and a whole lot of barbed wire, etc. There was suddenly a halt and Lovat shouted out, 'Come on, boys, what's keeping you? What's the matter? Move!' And a friend of mine, who had been specially trained for this type of thing, he ran forward. He knew he shouldn't cut those wires in case they were mined and would blow up so what he did, he threw a jacket on, threw himself on and let the boys jump over. And once two or three got through we knew it was clear, we broke away and we all filed through.

Piper Bill Millin
HQ 1st Special Service Brigade

Lovat looked round and seen me standing and said, 'Aw, give us a tune.' The whole idea was ridiculous, 'cause people were shell-firing and all kinds of things were going on at the time. It was mad enough the three of us standing there; we shouldn't have been standing, really, we should've been lying down. The whole thing was ridiculous and I thought I might as well be ridiculous as well. I said, 'What tune would you like, sir?' and he said, 'Well, play *The Road to the Isles*.' I said, 'Would you like me to march up and down?' and he said, 'Yes, yes, march up and down. That'll be lovely.' So the whole thing was ridiculous, in that the bodies lying in the water were going back and forward with the tide and I started off piping and going a few paces along. And the next thing there's a hand on my shoulder and a voice said, 'Listen, boy,' and I looked round. It was this sergeant I recognised and he says, 'What are you fucking playing at, you mad bastard? You're attracting all the German attention. Every German in France knows we're here now, you silly bastard.' Anyway, I walked away and of course there are other people up on the wall going, 'Hooray!' Cheering, you know.

Corporal Jim Spearman
4 Commando

Domineering the whole place were these tremendous big pillboxes. No matter where you went, you couldn't get out of range of them; they covered the beach very well. The fortifications were excellent. If you think of a pillbox, you can go up to it, go to a slit and drop a grenade in, but these bloody defences they had on the beach there had about a dozen slits in them. They were tremendous things.

Our job wasn't to stop and put them out of action, our job was to get off the beach, although of course some of our people did try to put some of these things out of action on the way. I remember one Lieutenant Carr. Terribly thin man but a very good officer. He deliberately went up to one pillbox and threw a couple of grenades in and I thought that was a very brave deed.

Nobody can know what it's like to be on a beach where you can do nothing, you're under severe fire and you've got to get off. It's only a person who's been through it a number of times can know you've either got to stay and die or get off and live. People doing it for the first time, no matter how many times you tell them, they don't realise it and nobody got off the beach. Of course, if you elongate yourself on a beach underneath cliffs or underneath a high road, you're much easier to hit. Standing up, you present much less of a target than somebody laying down.

I was shocked by the number of bodies, dead bodies, living bodies, and all the blood in the water giving the appearance they were drowning in their own blood for the want of moving. The whole place was littered like it. But having seen all the bodies on the beach doubled our determination. No matter what happened, we had to get off the beach. Once you get off the beach, you're out of the fire as it were. But it's a very hard lesson to learn and people won't bloody learn it.

The troops that landed in front of us, they had never been on an assault landing before. And I often wonder whether they were put there as sort of gun-fodder to distract attention for us to go in, because we were always the people who went in first, did a sharp, quick raid and got out again. It seemed to change here. They put those people in and they never even left the beach.

Private Peter Fussell
HQ 1st Special Service Brigade
The Royal Navy beach clearance people had been in front of us, they had cleared a narrow strip of mines through which tanks were going, and this was a great support to us as at least we had something to hide behind. If any snipers were around we could pop them off from either side – if we could see them.

Corporal Jim Spearman
4 Commando
Our first job was to knock out a gun battery at a place called Ouistreham, which was right on the east side of the landing. After that we were to take up positions in the Hauger area a few miles inland and defend that against all comers. If our boat had sunk I really don't know who would have taken over that job because there were no reserves for us. It was a very thin green line that we set up there.

Piper Bill Millin
HQ 1st Special Service Brigade
The strongpoint in Ouistreham was the casino. Well, this was captured eventually, mainly by 4 Commando, which included a French troop. Of course the local French people were delighted that there were French commandos with the British and they gave us help by pointing out the strongpoints which enabled the commandos to eliminate them.

Private Andrew Brown
6 Commando
Running up the beach I heard a 'moaning minnie' scream and one or two shells falling about so I dived into this shell hole and there was a bloke out of the East Yorks with a Bren gun there. I asked him what he was doing and he said he'd lost his mates and was digging in. I said, 'Well, if you dig in there you're going to die. Come along with me because if you stop on the beach you're going to die. You've got to get off the beach.' So he came along with me and he stayed with me to the end of D-Day, when he just told me he'd better get back and look for his mates. They took a plastering, they did.

Sergeant Arthur Thompson
2nd Battalion, East Yorkshire Regiment
We'd lost that many that the strength we had wasn't much strength at all, and when we got off the beaches we were getting shelled and mortared and God knows what. To move forward we had to go through some swamps and that was where we lost a lot. I remember one chap in particular. He was laid there in all this muck and he shouts, 'Thommo!' and I thought he'd fell over and couldn't get up because of the weight of his equipment, so I went and picked him up and he had no legs on. I just had to prop him up against some willows and asked him if there was owt he wanted and he said he could do with his cigarettes, so I lit him a cigarette and had to leave him. He'd just die, you see.

Private William Edward Lloyd
2nd Battalion, East Yorkshire Regiment
You didn't stop when someone got hit. You didn't stop to see what happened to them. You knew you'd got to get on.

Private Stanley Wilfred Scott
3 Commando

We went up the beach, straight over to the other side where the Germans had flooded it, and we lugged these bloody bikes through it. There was no cover and they was lobbing mortar bombs at us but they was just going 'Glump!' straight in the mud, cushioning the effect. Every now and then you would hear this 'Ka-ka-ka-ka' – you know, machine-gun fire – but if it didn't hit you, you didn't worry about it. There were blokes going down left and right. I stopped to have a few words with Johnny Johnson when he got hit. They took half his bloody ear off. He just went, 'Ah,' like that, and there was all blood. He said, 'Well, see you Scotty,' and went back down the beach and got on a boat. We carried on.

Sergeant Desmond O'Neill
Cameraman, Army Film and Photographic Unit

I started taking pictures of the troops coming ashore. Then I suddenly spotted two very tiny infantrymen marching along with a very tall German soldier who was absolutely terrified. He had a bandage round his face and there were these two – rather cheerful, I think they were cockneys – on either side of him. I said, 'Just a minute,' and they posed as though they might be posing in Piccadilly Circus for their picture, with this German in between them. It's a picture you're always told to look out for, captured prisoners. Very good for morale and all the rest of it.

I caught up with an infantry platoon who were making an attempt to get off the beach and all of a sudden there was a rattle of automatic fire, coming from where I know not, and I felt a searing pain in my left elbow. I didn't go down, I don't think I dropped the camera, I sort of crouched down and I looked to my left and the chap who'd been standing by my side, an infantryman, was lying on the ground and you could see right away that he was dead.

So I thought, 'This is a fine kettle of fish.' I got my field dressing out and wrapped it round and looked for a first-aid station. I saw the Red Cross flying over a bunker which had been captured by the initial assault troops who had used flame-throwers on it and I went up to the entrance. An RAMC corporal there said, 'What's the matter?' I said, 'I've been shot through the elbow.' He said, 'Let's have a look. Come inside.' I went inside and it was almost like a Hogarth painting. There were soldiers lying all over the place and some of them very badly wounded, you could see, with legs off and things like that. And there was a young RAMC officer busy operating and I remember thinking, 'That chap is going to learn more about surgery in the next half day than he will in the rest of his life.'

JUNO BEACH

Major-General Rod Keller's 3rd Canadian Infantry Division was tasked with assaulting and securing Juno Beach – directly to the west of Sword – and advancing from there towards the Caen-Bayeux road. The landings took place either side of the seaside town of Courseulles-sur-Mer and the mouth of the River Seulles.

Rough seas and the need to avoid offshore rocks meant that Keller's assault troops approached the shore behind schedule and were forced to negotiate, under fire, hazardous belts of half-submerged obstacles before their craft hit the beach. Problems were also caused by the failure of the preliminary bombardment to suppress a series of enemy strongpoints and positions and by the delayed arrival on the beaches of many Canadian DD tanks.

Losses among New Brunswick's North Shore Regiment, Toronto's Queen's Own Rifles, the Regina Rifles and the Winnipeg Rifles were particularly high. By the end of the day, Keller's men had suffered more than a thousand casualties, including 364 killed. Among the seaborne forces, only the Americans who landed at Omaha Beach suffered a higher casualty rate.

Once the armour was ashore and the beach exits were cleared and enemy resistance was quelled or bypassed, progress inland was rapid. Canadian troops penetrated further on D-Day than any other Allied force. By nightfall, though it had to turn back, a troop of Canadian Sherman tanks had crossed the Caen-Bayeux road: the only unit among the seaborne Allied forces to reach its furthest D-Day objective.

British assistance to the Canadians on Juno took many vital forms. Many landing-craft crews were British. AVREs and flail tanks from Hobart's 79th Armoured Division and Royal Marine and Royal Engineers obstacle-clearance teams worked to clear beach exits and paths. Further support came from the accompanying beach groups, composite units tasked with securing and organising movement into and off the beach, including medics and infantrymen who landed close behind the first wave of Canadian assault troops.

48 (Royal Marine) Commando, under the command of Lieutenant Colonel James Moulton, also landed on Juno Beach. Its objective was to push east through the village of St-Aubin and assault a formidable German strongpoint in the next village of Langrune, before continuing east again and linking up with 41 (Royal Marine) Commando who, it was hoped, would be pushing west from Sword. But obstacles and heavy fire from the shore turned 48 Commando's landing into a disaster and casualties continued to mount on the beach. By the time the survivors had fought their way through to Langrune, their strength was insufficient to carry the strongpoint that day. The link-up between Juno and Sword, meanwhile, was made only on 7 June.

Sergeant Keith Briggs
Landing Craft Obstacle Clearance Unit
The beaches had about three different rows of obstacles. The main one was the large one called Element C. They were like iron gates and they were situated just at low tide level so that when the tide came in they were covered by sea and each one had on it a mine or a shell with a fuse so that if you touched them they'd go off. They were between ten to fifteen yards apart and they were staggered so the rows were covered. And then, behind that, were rows and rows, continuous rows, of hedgehogs and then stakes driven into the sand. If your landing craft hit them, these stakes would make a hole.

We knew everything about those beaches long before we went there. We'd trained on bays of Element C. We'd trained at Appledore to cut bays of Element C down from an eight-foot-high object to a ten-inch object with explosive so that landing craft could run over it. And we knew all about those because people had been to different places in France and we'd got all their photographs of the beach defences. We were told exactly where we were going to go, our beaches were pinpointed for us, we were given photographs of the whole beach area and in my case it was Juno Beach, Nan Red. We were given photographs of the exact landing points and the houses on the beach and the exact beach area where we were supposed to clear a gap of six hundred yards. And we were going into Normandy at H minus sixty, which meant we were going in before the major invasion took place.

By the time we put to sea, there was a gale blowing, a storm blowing. Everything was terrible with the sea. We got to our point about seven miles off the French coast very early in the morning, probably about five or six o'clock in the morning, and we were dropped with our landing craft and its naval crew and had to get into our beach. Our craft was loaded with three or four tons of explosive; it was controlled by naval seaman, had Asdic gear for detecting underwater obstacles and so forth; and we went into the beach at Normandy. And as we were going into the beach, the sea was so rough, it was gale force, that our landing craft actually landed on one of the obstacles and had several holes knocked in it and the landing craft then sank on to the seabed. It was only in about three, four feet of water.

We got under the sea wall, a concrete sea wall, and looking through the apertures we could see German sentries walking about on duty. We could see German soldiers getting on transport to go somewhere or other; we assumed they were going out for the day or something like that. And we just sat there and waited for the invasion to take place, because, in actual fact, we couldn't put our explosive on the obstacles because the sea was too rough and we couldn't get at our explosive because it was in a sunken craft.

Private Frederick Perkins
5th Battalion, Royal Berkshire Regiment (Beach Group)
As we approached the beach there was all hell being let loose on Sword so by the time we got to Juno the Germans were aware that something big was happening. But that didn't take much calculation because there were thousands and thousands and thousands of ships out there in front of them. You can't imagine how many ships were there. You couldn't have got any more in. The corvettes, the destroyers, the Landing Ship Rockets were all starting their bombardment, and the bombardment was absolutely colossal. As we ran in, the whole seashore looked like a blue haze, there were smoke shells bursting to cover the landing, and it looked pretty hectic coming in under this barrage. Thousands of shells were whizzing over the top as one was coming in and the din was absolutely enormous, indescribable. All types of craft were firing. Even the landing craft that were coming in with tanks were firing their guns actually in the landing craft to help with the bombardment or at targets that they could see they could hit.

Lieutenant Ian Hammerton
Sherman Crab flail tank commander, 22nd Dragoons

There was this ripping sound, like calico being ripped apart, and a flight of rockets went up. You could hear it even above the radio and I saw a Spitfire flying along the beach and that suddenly disappeared in a puff of flaming smoke. It must have flown into the flight of rockets. You could see them landing on the shore, not on the beach but the land behind the beach, and the fire burning and the smoke, a tremendous amount of smoke.

Lieutenant Gerald Edward Ashcroft
LCT commander

I had the great pleasure of putting ashore the first tanks of the 3rd Canadian Division to knock out the pillboxes guarding the beach. We were constantly under fire from approximately half a mile off the beach. Shellfire, gunfire and, as we got closer to the beach, shrapnel and of course mortar fire. Being the port-wing ship of the flotilla we had no cover ourselves and we came under mortar fire and lost two men killed and three others injured.

Our greatest problem, though, hadn't been the gunfire so much as the fact that, owing to the invasion being postponed for twenty-four hours and being held up by bad weather, instead of beaching at the low water mark where all the beach obstacles would have been above water level, we had to beach through the beach obstacles: mines and stakes and shells fastened on to iron stakes. The infantry landing craft were coming in either side of us, blowing up in all directions on the mines. We backed away slightly and just let her drift, knocking off as many mines as we could with our big bow door, until we got two mines on stakes jammed within the door sections and had to pull away.

Boy Seaman Signaller Victor Longhurst
LCT crew

I was returning to the bridge when our gunners opened fire so we must have been quite close to the beach and I mentioned to the FO that there were no No 2s on the guns. Would he like me to act as No 2 on the guns? So he said, 'Yes. Carry on, Bunts.'

I went down and I remember going to the port gun and loading the port gun for the gunner, because they're strapped in, the Oerlikon gunners. I then went to the starboard gun and got a pan of ammunition out ready to load him up

Film stills of Canadian infantrymen of the North Shore Regiment disembarking from a Landing Craft Assault (LCA) on Nan Red sector, Juno Beach, at about 0805 hours on 6 June. They are under fire from German troops in the houses facing them.

when all of a sudden it seemed like all guns were trained on us. There were bullets flying all over or so it seemed. Unluckily the bullets hit the wheelhouse and ricocheted back and I got wounded and the coxswain inside the wheelhouse got killed because one of the gun ports was left open and a bullet hit him right in the forehead. I didn't know I'd got wounded. There was a lot of blood and I said to the gunner, 'Somebody's been hit,' and he said, 'It's you, you've been hit.' Then I looked and I'd got blood streaming down me arm.

Eventually I started to feel a bit groggy and went below. The next thing I can remember, the telegraphist came down and started to bandage my arm where I'd been wounded. Then the FO came and had a look at me. His remark was, 'Scars of battle, eh, Bunts?'

Corporal Thomas Edward Suffling
Royal Marine and LCA stoker

We were used to convey Canadian troops, the Winnipeg Rifles, on to Juno Beach. It was a very difficult landing and we became marooned on the beach. It was a funny sort of a tide, something like Cleethorpes'. It came in very slowly and if you missed it coming out again you were marooned. Gently shelving, the beach was; it wasn't a steep one where you could land and go off again, you sort of landed flat on the beach, and if you didn't get off quick that was it and that's what happened. We got the Canadian troops off and we got marooned.

In an endeavour to return to the LSI, that's our parent ship, my mates and I managed to float another LCA which was beached too and pointing nose-out and started to take it back. Bonzo Atkinson said, 'Everybody up forward to lift the back up and give the propellers a chance to turn.'

We had on board a Canadian with a hole in his foot. I was going to bandage the wound, I was having difficulty in opening the field dressing and I was bent down trying to undo this bandage and this officer bent down and said, 'Can you manage?' And as he bent down, we blew up. I don't know if it was a mine or a mortar but anyway everybody above the gunwales was killed by the blast. Everybody up front, this Canadian. There was two on the engine, there was two on the pumps, there was me bandaging this Canadian's foot and there was the officer: we were the only survivors. Then we just tried to get back to the beach as best we could.

People were running up the beach. A few dead bodies. Craft all over the place. Proper mayhem it was. We went into the shelter of the sand dunes and then we started getting sorted out, recovering. Then we started to see what we could do for the wounded on the beach. It was a while after, you know, when I'd sort of settled down a bit, that I realised that I'd started shaking like a leaf and I was a bit ashamed of it, to be honest. I thought, 'I'm a right 'un to be shaking.' And then I realised it was a reaction.

Private Frederick Perkins
5th Battalion, Royal Berkshire Regiment (Beach Group)

Suddenly we grounded and we were off. Down went the ramp and it was a mad dash for the sand dunes. Waves of Canadians had already gone in before us. On our particular beach they were Queen's Own Rifles and, when we got there, there were lots of dead Canadians laying about. As they'd hit the beach, beach obstacles were blowing up around them, landing craft were blowing up, hitting the mine obstructions on the beach, and the Queen's Own Rifles got caught with a crossfire by machine guns as they were advancing up a groyne. They lost the majority of one of their companies and they were laying there. It was terrible to see. We dug these hurried bolt holes in the sand and we got in there initially and set up gun positions, anti-tank positions, mortar positions. We were being mortared at the same time and sniped at especially.

Private Douglas Botting
5th Battalion, Royal Berkshire Regiment (Beach Group)

It was just a nightmare, a complete nightmare. I was eighteen years old. I expect there were others there who were eighteen years old but it was the first experience like that I'd ever had. I'd wanted to get there and have a go but when I landed and I saw people going down right and left of me I thought, 'What the devil am I doing here?' There's no joy in war. I mean, I come from a family of soldiers and I suppose you listen to their stories and when you're younger you watch the cowboys and all this business. And it's just not the same thing. Not the same thing at all.

Lieutenant Gerald Edward Ashcroft
LCT commander

On our particular point of the beach was a pillbox on the corner of the Courseulles harbour wall and the sea wall. When we were close enough to examine it through binoculars we could see that the gun barrel of the big gun was pointing westward along the beach and the embrasure on the north side was completely open. And when we were nearly to the level of the mines we saw the gun barrel come back in. Knowing full well that they'd have to swivel the gun barrel inside the emplacement, it was obvious that they were now training the gun to come out the embrasure directly opposite us.

I got the major in charge of the tanks to get his forward tank close up to the watertight door, got our bow ramp lowered, the watertight doors opened, and I arranged for the tank to train on to the pillbox and try to get the pillbox before the pillbox got us. Fortunately we hit the beach at full speed, the tank jumped out and came to rest, trained his gun as their gun barrel was coming out and the first shot went straight into the pillbox and it gave us no more trouble after that.

Before coming back off the beach, I couldn't resist the temptation to go ashore quickly and see what had happened to the pillbox. It was really an astonishing sight and it showed how effective a solid shot inside a pillbox really can be. There was literally nothing left but skin, blood and bits of flesh, all mixed up like a load of mincemeat. The solid shot had simply ricocheted round and round and round. Far more effective than a high explosive shell.

Sapper William Dunn
AVRE driver, 26th Assault Squadron, Royal Engineers

The landing craft stopped and dropped the ramps for us to come down and everybody straight away shouted good luck to each other. The first tank off was a Canadian flail tank and I had to follow him off. We came through this narrow gap they'd done for us, these people that had been there lying overnight, and then we had to drive up the beach.

The atmosphere in the tank then was a little bit tense. I was the only man who could see where I was going because the tank commander had battened down more or less because the shells and the bullets were coming across the top of us. My co-driver, Bill Hawkins, was sitting behind me and kept asking me what was going on, could he see, you know. My main concern as we came up the beach was seeing all the lads that had been shot down and were lying on the beach. I was a bit concerned in case I hit any of them. I only had a narrow visor to look through and I didn't know whether they were dead or whether they were alive or what, these people that were lying there. But in any case you had to pick your way through so you didn't catch any of them.

Lieutenant Ian Hammerton
Sherman Crab flail tank commander, 22nd Dragoons

Two flails flailed up to the sea wall and backed away as per the plan. A bridging tank came forward but the commander was killed by a shell which landed on the turret; it also cut the cable and the bridge dropped. So we then had to make use of the existing stone ramp off the beach which was sealed with Element C and barbed wire. That meant I had to drive up to the end of this ramp, which by now was underwater, and I had to fire at the Element C.

Now, in order to fire the gun, I had to blow the waterproofing off so I could rotate the turret a little. I was clear of the water level by this time but the business of firing at Element C is a lengthy one – it meant the commander sighting the gun through the barrel at every joint of the welding. You peer down the bore of the gun: we called it posting letters. So we fired HE and broke up the Element C. I then had to drag it out of the way because the other Churchill AVRE, he went up, he pushed the Element C to one side and drove to one side and blew up on a mine. But the Element C was still blocking the top so I had to attach a towrope to it and tow it down the ramp back out to sea. By this time the tide was much higher and just as I'd said, 'Right, that'll do,' the driver said, 'I've got water coming in and it's coming up to my neck. What shall I do?' I said, 'Bail out.'

We dismounted our machine gun from the top and got the tripod and boxes of ammo and grenades and dropped off into about five feet of water, which was very cold, right up to our necks. But the most difficult thing of all was climbing out of the water on to the ramp. The pull of the tide and the fact that our clothing was full of water and we were loaded down with grenades and things made it very difficult to get out, and there were various bodies floating about which didn't help either. But we did get out and we set up the machine gun on the top.

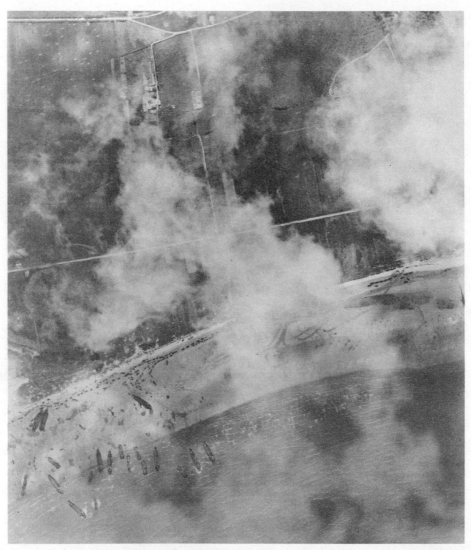

An aerial view, through clouds, of Mike sector of Juno Beach on 6 June. Landing craft and vehicles can be clearly seen.

Major Allan Younger
Commanding officer, 26th Assault Squadron, Royal Engineers

The waterproofing was fine and we got quite close to dry land when suddenly I found myself sitting on the bottom of the tank and I didn't know what had happened at all. I saw my wireless operator looking down at me and I said to him, 'What the hell have you done?' I just couldn't realise why I was sitting on the floor of the tank and I knew I ought to be looking out of it. He said, 'Sir, we've been hit.'

I realised the moment he started to speak that my hearing was very bad. What had happened was that a shell of some sort had hit the open turret hatch of the tank and it had burst there and knocked half the turret hatch down on to my head. Luckily I was wearing a steel helmet and there was a ridge down that and it had knocked me out and burst an eardrum. Otherwise it had not done me any harm. However, it had taken off the aerials from the tank, so I couldn't use the tank as a command vehicle any longer.

So we got on to the beach and I sort of pulled myself together and I realised I had to get out of the tank in order to command anybody and I got out and I ran across the open beach. There were quite a number of casualties already on the beach and there were little groups of Canadian infantry sheltering in the sand dunes. And I went up to this great conglomeration of tanks, I suppose about eight or nine of them there, at the entrance to what I knew straight away should be 2 Troop's projected gap.

26 Squadron's objective was to create two gaps and I had two troops to do this, each with some flails under its command. The first thing I did was to look out the commander of 1 Troop, Hewlett, to ask him what on earth he was doing there. I found him and he said, oh, well, his landing craft had landed there and so he thought it was best to go on in, which was not a very good answer. I told him to collect his men and get over to the correct gap that he was meant to be making which was another, I suppose, couple of hundred yards to the west. However, by then, his front tank, which was numbered One Charlie – our tanks were One Able, Baker, Charlie, Dog and so on in 1 Troop, Two Able, Baker, Charlie, Dog and so on in 2 Troop – was already through the sand dunes and was teetering on the edge of what looked like a huge crater. It was indeed a huge culvert, sixty-six feet across, full of water. And this tank was teetering on the edge of it and just as I came up I saw it sort of nudge into the crater, into the water.

Sapper William Dunn
AVRE driver, 26th Assault Squadron, Royal Engineers

The Germans had flooded the area and you couldn't see the culvert, you see. Tracks snapped, water started coming in the turret and, of course, with me being right at the front, I was last one out. Everybody had to get out a bit sharpish because the bullets were flying all over the place, I was starting to swallow water actually because it was all coming into the turret and, as my co-driver got out, he put his knees on both sides of me head, me temples, and as he came out he dragged me with him. Of course I had quite a bit of water in me stomach by then and Bill Hawkins, who was standing just outside the turret when we got out, he just hit me once in the stomach. He hadn't any time for any niceties or anything like that. He just brought the water up and that was it. Of course the bullets were still hitting the turret and so we decided that our best bet was the seaward side of the culvert. We had to jump off the tank and by that time Captain Hewlett had come up to see what was happening and he put his tank between us and the Germans and brought us back into the sand dunes.

He went away and left us then and we just lay down behind the sand dunes. Jim Ashton started to sing 'Kiss Me Again'. Like a father figure – he was a good lad – he always did this, tried to settle us all down. And he'd just started to sing when the mortar bombs came and dropped between us. It killed three outright, definitely. I was wounded. Bill Hawkins was badly wounded. The co-driver, he rolled over to me, he had a hole in his back that I could put me fist in, and he said, 'I'll call for help.' And he crawled away and I just saw him roll over after he got about a hundred yards from us and I was told afterwards that's where he died.

I rolled down into a minefield. In fact when I looked up there was a big board, 'Achtung Minen', straight above my head and I thought, 'Cor blimey.' I managed to get on to me feet and I ran about fifty yards, which the doctor said was impossible when I got home because I had five compound fractures in one of me legs. I said, 'Well, when you're frightened and there's bullets flying around, it makes you do queer things.' But me legs just gave way from me and I collapsed, I didn't know how badly I was wounded then, and two lads came and dragged me back. I told them Bill Hawkins was still up there and they asked me about the others and I said, 'I'm pretty sure the others are dead.' So they went up to Bill Hawkins and they took me back and laid me beside another sand dune and gave me a cigarette and a drink, and left me there.

The first one that came on the scene after that was a Canadian medical officer and he gave me an injection of morphine and put a card around me neck to say he'd given me morphine, then he took off. Then two Canadians came. I must have been lying with me eyes shut and they started going through me pockets and they took me watch out of these pockets and me whistle and I had a commando knife stitched to me trouser leg and they took that. Then I opened me eyes and one of them turned round and said, 'We'd better leave this bugger, he's alive,' and they took off. Then two lads from me own unit came and they carried me further back towards the beach and they brought Bill Hawkins down alongside me and they laid the two stretchers right between two Priest guns. Both of them opened up together and it just lifted the stretchers up and bounced them down.

There was an armoured bulldozer about fifty feet from us, we were lying on the stretchers there and we could see him. The armour for a bulldozer comes up round the side, round the driver, and a shell had hit the armour plating just where the driver was sitting and jammed him in. He wasn't wounded; it had just jammed him in. But he couldn't get out and the bulldozer was on fire and nobody could get near it. And that was my worst experience because you heard this man screaming and there was nobody could do a damned thing for him.

Major Allan Younger
Commanding Officer, 26th Assault Squadron, Royal Engineers
So we had this awful crater in front with this tank three-quarters of the way in it and it couldn't have been a greater shambles, really. The one way off the beach was blocked by this really horrible obstacle, no way of the Canadians getting any of their tanks inland.

The Canadians, incidentally, had lost quite a number of tanks. They were launched rather far out and it was such a windy day quite a number of the tanks had got drowned. But then they had persuaded some of the landing craft to beach and let them off on to dry land and they had mastered the beach by then. They fired straight into the embrasures of the huge pillboxes that were there and stopped the fire. They did very well. 1st Hussars of Canada was the regiment they came from and they were really a great help.

But then there was this awful mess of ours and the Germans were still free to fire at us behind the sand dunes. There were fairly high sand dunes at that landing place. So we had to make a plan and we decided the only thing to do was to nudge this tank right into the crater, drop one of our assault bridges on to the turret of the tank and then try and put a couple of fascines beyond that in order to make some form of crossing.

Jimmy Hendry's troop went ahead and did this and having got two fascines across it looked as though it was possible to get a tank over. I told one of the AVREs to get over there which it succeeded in doing and all the time we were improving the crossing because there was quite a lot of rubble there. I think there may have been a house there which had been destroyed or something. Also, quite early on, a farmer with a cart and a horse was seen, someone went down and asked him, told him, that we wanted his horse and cart, which he was delighted to let us have, and we used that. The cart was filled up with rubble from houses that had been knocked down in the bombardment and we continued throughout the morning improving this gap.

There was now a terrific build-up of stuff on the beach. We'd sorted out the chaos enough to try to get one of the 1st Hussars of Canada tanks across. He came across very, very slowly but he made it, so I went back and got hold of the infantry battalion commander and said, 'You can start going forward now because one of your tanks is over.' And a long procession of Canadian infantry started to go over and then we got another tank over.

Then a third Canadian tank had a go at it and you could see the driver wasn't very sure of himself and he got a track off the bridge and fell off on his side. But I'd thought this sort of thing might happen and this was why I'd got an AVRE over first because the AVRE had a very powerful winch on it and we got a rope to this Canadian tank, which was a Sherman tank, lighter than the AVRE, and towed him over on to the far side.

In the meantime we were repairing the mess and all the time it was being made better by rubble and stuff. By then some of the beach group had landed. In particular there was a field company who were engineers and would take over our gaps when we left so we made use of them. We were working hard to improve this gap the whole time and it got better and better until it was comparatively easy to drive a tank over.*

---

* Bill Dunn's submerged AVRE, One Charlie, was excavated in 1976 and stands today on display outside the village of Graye-sur-Mer, behind Juno beach.

Private Patrick Brown
33rd Field Surgical Unit, Royal Army Medical Corps

The Germans were firing mortars when we got on the beach and there was a beachmaster shouting through a loudhailer, 'Keep moving! Get off the beach! Don't clog the beach! Keep within the white tapes!' Things like that. We dashed on and started treating casualties. We carried on our backs Bergen rucksacks, which were full of sterilised dressings in waterproof packs, and all we could do really was to take off the old field dressing and put on one of these other dressings we carried. Some of the cases were rather bad and our major gave them shots of morphine. I had to mark on their forehead, 'M', time, date and amount. It was so chaotic. It really was chaotic. You only focused on what was in front of you, really.

We finally got into an orchard and waited for some of our gear to come along. The first one to come along was our three-tonner, which was called an assault wagon, and on there we had most of our gear. We started to unload and finally our members started finding us and we set up an emergency surgery. We had black-tarred canvas on the floor and we set up our actual theatre plus petrol-driven dynamos for lighting. The RAC chappies did the sterilising with these petrol stoves.

The casualty would come in wounded, covered in mud and dust and blood, and you'd have to cut off his tunic or wherever he was wounded. He was already on a stretcher and he was put on to the operating table. Then, according to his wound, he was given a general anaesthetic, we had anaesthetists with us, and they'd give them pentathol in the vein and then put the mask on, which was attached to a pipe down to a little machine, which was called a Boyles. It had air and drops of ether mixed up. Then you had to hold the man's chin up so that he didn't swallow his tongue.

They were mostly gunshot wounds. One or two were very bad from the mortars that came over; some of their limbs were really horrendous. We really did first aid to help these fellows and then they were picked up. The landing craft that came in took the wounded back to Blighty. And what was funny was that the French were still wandering around with all this mess going on, just wandering, looking at us, seeing what was happening.

Sick Berth Attendant Bill Fry
LST crew

Medical LSTs had to wait for the casualties to be brought aboard and as soon as the tide turned again we had to have the casualties aboard. We took an average of four hundred stretcher cases and maybe two hundred and fifty walking cases. Those went into the side cabins and the stretchers were laid out in the tank space. In between the time when the last tank went off the LST we'd turned the tank space into a hospital. At the rear bulkhead we had a folded operating theatre, it folded back like scaffolding poles, and behind it were all the things for an operating theatre: the operating table, the sterilising units, all the instruments, and as we were putting it up the sterilisers were being boiled. The rest of us, any of the ship's staff, would go round and pull out brackets on the wall. They were in three tiers and were pulled out and pinned and each set of two brackets took a stretcher so you had stretchers in three tiers. By the time we'd got all that ready the whole place smelled like a hospital because we also went round with sprays and things like that. And that happened just after the last of the troops had left. The funny thing – well, it wasn't funny when you think about it – was that by the time we did this the first wounded were on board again. Some of them had left the ship and as they'd reached the beach they'd been killed and wounded and the wounded were brought back immediately on to the ship before we were even ready.

Sapper Thomas Finigan
85th Field Company, Royal Engineers

We were carrying on in the minefields, picking up mines, searching for them, disarming them. We had Pioneer Corps people with us and after we'd disarmed these mines they would take them back along the beach and we would blow them up in situ, possibly about twenty at a time, away from the people who were landing on the beach. We used to get rid of the mines that way, blowing them up several times during the day. They were S-mines and Teller mines and also French anti-tank mines. On other beaches there were British mines: when we'd pulled out of Dunkirk, they'd used all the stores that were left behind to great advantage.

The chaps who carried the metal detectors ashore found it was quite useless using those, for the simple reason that there was so much shrapnel around that as soon as you switched your detector on you just picked up noise. So we had to do it the old-fashioned way, by prodding with the end of a bayonet. Once you'd got the pattern of a minefield, it made it quite easy. The Germans were very methodical at that sort of thing and they used to lay these in very good patterns and when you found that pattern it made your job a lot easier. You knew that there were probably three or four paces between each mine so your prodding then was a lot easier. You just went forward in lines carrying these white tapes that you laid behind you and you cleared an area maybe three or four foot wide and had another sapper beside you doing the same. So in the end if you had a dozen sappers you could clear fifty or sixty feet at any one time.

At the very beginning I was quite nervous. But we had a number of NCOs that had been posted into the unit who had seen service in North Africa and Italy and they were sent home to reinforce all the various units, so we had a number of NCOs who were battle-acclimatised, if that's the word. They were very experienced indeed. We had a sergeant, our reconnaissance sergeant, who had an MM and we looked upon him almost like God. He knew everything and he was very, very clever and he taught us a lot. We felt very confident in the minefields when he was around.

Sergeant Keith Briggs
Landing Craft Obstacle Clearance Unit
We cleared probably the whole of the beach area eventually by mechanical means with the Royal Engineers and the Canadian Engineers. We waited for the engineers to come in with their DD tanks and so forth and then we prepared, with them, to clear the obstacles manually. We swam out with wires, ropes and hawsers, attached them to the armoured bulldozers which the engineers were driving and we cleared a gap, as many gaps as we could, with mechanical means. Whilst we were working in the water it was mostly sniper fire with the occasional mortar landing in the sea around us but it didn't do us too much harm. Snipers were our biggest problem. German snipers in the houses above us were sniping all the time. It didn't frighten us so that we couldn't carry out our work. We weren't frightened to death. We carried on and did our job. We knew we had a job to do.

Carrying bicycles, a follow-up wave of soldiers from the 9th Canadian Infantry Brigade wade ashore at Bernières, on Juno Beach, shortly before midday on 6 June.

Private Frederick Perkins
5th Battalion, Royal Berkshire Regiment (Beach Group)
Sniping went on all day. Sniping from a church by what was supposed to be a woman – sniping at DUKW drivers as they came up the beach. She was picking off DUKW drivers at different periods during the day until they decided to knock the church tower off with a Bofors gun and that put paid to that. They said it was a woman afterwards, the girlfriend of a German soldier. He'd left her there with his uniform and his rifle.

Sergeant Kenneth Lakeman
Royal Corps of Signals
There was still sniping and things going on but the Canadians ahead of us, they'd done a fantastic job. Some of those regiments, the Chaudières, the Royal Winnipeg Rifles, those lads made the biggest inroad on D-Day. I think Canadians got about fourteen miles inland on the first day, which was the best beachhead of all, though they had to come back a bit afterwards. Incredible, those Canadians; I'm proud to have been a part of them.

Private Frederick Perkins
5th Battalion, Royal Berkshire Regiment (Beach Group)
We formed a body recovery party and we went picking up bodies laying about the beach area, because we knew very well that the tanks were coming in all the time and they could not leave these bodies about because they were going to get run over. It wasn't a very pretty sight to see these men who'd gone a few yards and dropped down; and the incoming troops wouldn't like to have seen that. So we decided to get these people off the beach areas and lay them up in the sand dunes and covered them over. Eventually we took all their particulars off them and documented them and put tags on them and then they were buried in shallow graves.

Driver Roy Hamlyn
282 Company, Royal Army Service Corps
Our work was primarily to see to the unloading of the ships and getting the ammunition in. Sometimes there would be a lull before the ships coming into position could accommodate you, so, instead of you just standing about doing nothing, you were told to do whatever had to be done. One of the first orders

I had was to pick bodies up from the beach. It drove home the horrors of what you were involved in.

One of the sad cases we came across immediately after the landing, when bodies had to be moved, were bodies in German uniforms with their throats cut. But they weren't truly the Wehrmacht at all, they were impounded labour from different countries from Eastern Europe that had been pressed into service for work on the Atlantic Wall. They weren't really true German soldiers. It's not a very nice story but it's reality. We had to assume that this was a little bit of Dieppe revenge. That's all you can say. It's not for anybody to condemn or to implicate. The burial parties told us their papers said they were Romanians or Yugoslavs or whatever.

Corporal Thomas Edward Suffling
Royal Marine and LCA stoker
We saw some of the lads bringing a few German prisoners out. Very old-looking people as well. Well, they'd said in the paper that they was using all the old ones up and that. They were very old. Well, I say very old: fifty, maybe? They looked it but of course it might have been their dirty appearance that made them look old.

Private Frederick Perkins
5th Battalion, Royal Berkshire Regiment (Beach Group)
There were quite a few prisoners. We didn't give them a lot to eat on the first day. We gave them some work to do, like digging holes for burials. Then we used them to get some of the wounded off the beach as well and then we used them to get some of the obstacles out of the way. Some were very young. Very few were arrogant. The SS type were arrogant. The others were just ordinary infantry units of the Wehrmacht sent there to do what we had been doing in Suffolk, really, as a beach defence unit.

Private Ray Burge
2nd Battalion, Devonshire Regiment
I was on a tank landing craft and I should have got off at Gold Beach but we got mixed up with the Canadians, my landing craft did, and when we first landed there was a Canadian officer there. We said, 'Where do we go?' All he said was, 'Keep going down there and remember Dieppe and don't take no

prisoners.' That was from a Canadian officer. 'Don't take no prisoners, just remember Dieppe.'

48 (Royal Marine) Commando
and the Langrune Strongpoint

Bombardier Ralph Dye
Royal Artillery, attached to 48 (Royal Marine) Commando
We were supposed to land on Nan Red sector, which was the extreme easterly end of Juno Beach, the Canadian beach, and there'd be a gap between there and Sword Beach where 41 Commando was going to land. We would move eastwards, capture a strongpoint at Langrune, which was the next village along, and link up with Sword Beach – link the two beachheads.

The troops going in were to be the North Shore Regiment: the New Brunswick regiment. They were going to take the town of St-Aubin; then our chaps would come in and leapfrog through them and then carry on to the east. The problem was, the North Shores went in and they had a terrible time because the bombardment hadn't taken out the coast defences. The Germans were sitting there waiting for them.

I recall the run-in. That was when I started to feel, 'This is it.' Up on the bridge there was a major of the North Shores absolutely pea green – seasick – and there was a sergeant of the North Shores down below and the major shouted to him, 'Get those men shaved!' And the sergeant said, 'The men are fed up with shaving, sir.' 'Get those men shaved!' And so, on the run-in to the beach, the Canadians were having a shave. I was impressed with this as we thought the Canadians had a very democratic attitude to discipline.

Sergeant Joe Stringer
48 (Royal Marine) Commando
The North Shore Regiment had a great deal of difficulty when they landed and their casualties were very high and we could see, as we approached, that there was still a lot of fire coming along from the left-hand side, whipping down the whole length of the beach. A lot of the North Shore Regiment had advanced across the beach to a wall and just piled up on this wall; it was under

fire from this left-hand side of the beach, our left-hand side as we approached, and they'd had a lot of casualties.

Marine Sam Earl
48 (Royal Marine) Commando
Most of us came up on the deck, just for the scenery, I suppose. We'd have been better off if we'd kept down below. When we got nearer the beach, the Germans started firing at us and the chap stood next to me, Joe Larkin, he was the first one killed. He fell down on my feet.

Marine Dennis Smith
48 (Royal Marine) Commando
As we got close in, all hell broke loose. We were under fire not only from ahead but also from the left because we were on the extreme end of Juno beach and for five miles to our left there were no landings taking place, so we were getting fire from the flank as well as from the front. And because the tides were running high the underwater obstacles were still underwater and one or two of the boats were holed and stuck on these obstacles, way out.

Sergeant Joe Stringer
48 (Royal Marine) Commando
Two of our craft were sunk on the approach to the beach and we lost a lot of men trying to swim ashore. Most of my section, as the demolition section, were carrying a lot of explosives in addition to our normal service equipment so we were heavily laden. I was the leading man on the left-hand ramp as we were going in; Lieutenant Curtis and Sergeant Bill Blythe, leading No 1 Section, were on the right-hand ramp, immediately exposed to the machine-gun nest at the far end of the beach. And our progress down the ramp was very, very slow, not like we would normally expect, running on to the beach off a flat-bottomed ramp. These ramps were floating about in the heavy seas, in as much that the matelots, the seamen on board the craft, were in the water holding them steady to allow us to get down. We were exposed and as I came down the ramp two fellows immediately behind me were hit by machine-gun fire. We lost a lot of men this way. As we'd approached the beach, our CO had had the good sense to get our mortars stationed in the bows of the craft so that

B 5225

Wrecked landing craft on the beach near St-Aubin, Juno Beach, where 48 (Royal Marine) Commando suffered heavy losses.

they did lay down a smoke-screen, which did enable us to get on to the beach once we were clear of the water.

Marine Dennis Smith
48 (Royal Marine) Commando

I got ashore through chest-high water, almost up to my throat, because our boat got stuck on an underwater obstacle and didn't beach properly. My job was to operate a signals lamp, an Aldis lamp. I'd met up briefly with the man who would be in charge of me, the Forward Officer Bombardment, and also the Forward Officer Observation and his two signalmen, both Canadians. We were a small group together and as a group we landed together and after getting ashore we were supposed to proceed close to the beach and call in any gunfire needed from the supporting ships. But everything went wrong from the point we landed. I hit the beach, made my way to the face of the wall in front and looked back for the two Canadian signallers I'd started off with, only to see either a shell or a mortar burst right close to them and they were both cut down.

Marine Sam Earl
48 (Royal Marine) Commando

I scrambled up and ran to the beach wall and I passed two or three dead and wounded. When I got to the sea wall, one man came running and stood near me. Another chap was running towards me, he got shot and went down, and the chap who was running behind him, Lance Corporal A____, he was awarded the MM in the Sicily landings, he stopped near the dead man. The dead man had a sniper's rifle and he cleaned the sand off and got down on one knee and he was firing at the strongpoint just down the beach.

We gave him a shout to tell him about a sniper up there. He fired one or two shots and then he got one bang in the forehead. Afterwards we looked at him. There was a hole there but the back of his head was gone, his brains and everything were gone. The chap stood beside me, he offered me a cigarette, he had a waterproof tin; I took one and I looked about and then he weren't there any more. He was dead. He'd got one in the side of the head.

I tried to move along. There were several Canadians lying there dead and wounded and I tripped over one. I thought he was dead. He was only wounded and when I kicked over him he groaned, and his mate, who was sitting there holding a rifle, threatened to shoot me. He was really going to shoot me. He pulled the bolt back and I had to run quick. He called me several names, I remember.

I kept running and running and then I saw a tracked vehicle coming from a ship and there were two of our chaps there. One of them, he'd got wounded and he lay there and this tracked vehicle came up, he couldn't move, and it ran over him and took his arm off. And the other chap, he bent down and tried to pull him and as he bent down a sniper got him, same place, in the head. When we went back two days after, to pick them up and bury them, we had a job to separate them two: the chap who was about to pick him up, his arms were round him and they were stiff.

Then there was a Canadian tank just off the beach. It had hit a mine and one chap, a Canadian, was stood there crying. That was all his mates in there, he said. They was all dead in there.

Sergeant Joe Stringer
48 (Royal Marine) Commando

There was a lot of chaos on the beach, lots of wounded lying on the beach, and the Fort Garry Horse tanks were coming in at this time with their hatches down and a lot of wounded were being badly mauled by the tracks. It was very, very chaotic and this is where Colonel Moulton really shone. He called us together, what was left of his commando. Of the five hundred who had left the previous evening from Warsash I think he assembled about 223 of us and we hadn't even started the job that we had been allocated, so it was a pretty rotten situation to be in. But we finally did leave the beach under the direction of Colonel Moulton, under his reassurance, and pulled together. We left our wounded on the beach being tended by our padre, the Reverend Armstrong, who himself was very badly wounded, and we moved off to our allotted task, which was a strongpoint at Langrune, another seaside village.

Marine Dennis Smith
48 (Royal Marine) Commando

I can recall the CO, Colonel Moulton, calling, '48, this way!' and we all made our way through the gap in the sea wall into the edge of the town of St-Aubin. We set up a signal station in a courtyard with high walls around and another signaller, a corporal, and myself, because we couldn't see who might be

On the roadside near St-Aubin, Canadian infantrymen and men of 48 (Royal Marine) Commando take cover from mortar fire.

approaching, went into two houses that were inside this courtyard. Being more experienced than me, having been in action before, he led me in. And I always recall that there was an old man and two ladies in this cottage. We told them we wanted to go upstairs and we took a bedroom window each, to control the road in case the Germans came. It was the ladies' bedroom and the man brought cider up for us to drink. And to me it's always been a joke that myself and my comrade were in a lady's bedroom drinking cider only within an hour or two of landing on D-Day.

Sergeant Joe Stringer
48 (Royal Marine) Commando

The moment we hit the road that ran parallel to the beach, we came under fire. Lieutenant Geoff Curtis, second-in-command of B Troop, was fatally wounded immediately we hit the road. But eventually after clearing a few houses we found ourselves in the rear of Langrune. We had more street-clearing to do, more houses to negotiate along this street, which we eventually did, and we got within striking range of the strongpoint.

Captain Perry then called an O group, which all senior NCOs attended, giving us his plans for attacking the strongpoint. We were in one of the last houses at the end of the street we had cleared and he stepped outside to take a last look and he was hit with a sniper's bullet, and we lost Captain Perry. At the same time they mortared us and another two of the sergeants were hit. That left Sergeant Bill Blythe and myself as the only two sergeants, and now our commander of B Troop was Second Lieutenant Rubinstein, a junior lieutenant who'd only joined us just prior to D-Day. So we were very badly hit.

Langrune strongpoint had been constructed of a dozen houses, a terraced run of houses, linked together with trenches and barbed wire round them and minefields in the gardens. A six-foot concrete wall barred the entrance and Colonel Moulton told me to get the explosives and have a go at blowing it. So my section and I retreated to a railway line we'd come over and scrounged some timber. We made a sort of a builder's hod and put the explosives, gun cotton slabs, in that, and we made our way down to the wall, under some considerable fire but fortunately not very accurate, got to the wall, placed our charge and fired it. But it wasn't very successful. I didn't have much hope as we couldn't bring enough pressure on it to make any impact on the wall.

But we were now immediately under the wall, my section and I, and the

Sergeant Joe Stringer, 48 (Royal Marine) Commando. This photograph was taken in 1945, by which time he had been promoted to sergeant major and awarded the Military Medal.

Jerries behind the wall were slinging over stick grenades. They were not very effective – these grenades were like a cocoa-tin, really – but they were slinging them over, and a bunch of them tied together to make them more effective dropped behind me. One of my men shouted out, 'Look out Joe!' and I turned my back to it, the natural thing to do, and both him and I were splattered with shrapnel. The amount of blood on my tunic indicated to me that I'd got a serious wound, I thought.

Colonel Moulton saw the difficulty we were in. He was concerned about us and called us to withdraw, which we did. When I got back I called for a medic to have a look at me and he looked very hard to find any external wounds. The only major thing he could find was that the lobe of my ear had been badly serrated and that was where all the blood was coming from, so it wasn't a Blighty wound. A few bits had gone into my rear end and my thighs which I carried for a number of years.

It was now getting late in the afternoon and things were getting very desperate. Apparently the Colonel had received instructions from the Brigadier that we were to hold what we'd got at all costs and make preparations for what was expected to be a counter-attack from a Panzer division that was approaching our way. So we were told to dig in, make some sort of fortification to assist us. This we did; but the counter-attack didn't take place.

I saw Moulton at various times throughout the day. He was with us virtually all the time, wounded though he was. Both his hands were wounded. There were lots of our officers who were wounded but they stayed with the troops. In point of fact, I think every troop commander was killed or wounded and most of the subalterns. Our officers took a hell of a pasting. Altogether it was a very, very sad day for 48 Commando, its introduction into the war. But as I think Colonel Moulton said, that was the day we finished our training, the day we came of age.

GOLD BEACH

Gold was the middle beach of the five assaulted on D-Day. Major-General Douglas Graham's British 50th Infantry Division was given the task of landing there along a five-mile front and establishing a beachhead and pushing forward.

For planning and command purposes, Gold was sub-divided into sectors code-named Jig and King. Jig sector lay immediately east of the seaside town of Le Hamel and the job of storming it was given to the British 231st Infantry Brigade. The attack did not go smoothly. Preceded by obstacle clearance teams, the brigade's assault battalions – men of the Royal Hampshire and Dorsetshire Regiments – hit the beach, on schedule, at 0725 hours. But the morning's air and naval bombardment had failed to silence several enemy strongpoints, and the incoming troops, lacking adequate armoured support, suffered badly, especially the Hampshires. Progress off the beach was slow. Many flails and other armour failed to get much further than the shore. Several hours passed before the infantry, with support from AVREs and self-propelled guns, got the better of the enemy defences.

The British 69th Infantry Brigade had the task of assaulting King sector. Here the preliminary bombardment had been more effective and the first assault wave of Green Howards and East Yorkshires landed with good engineer and armoured support. Though the attack was not made without casualties, by late morning the brigade was well established and moving inland. By then, too, Company Sergeant Major Stanley Hollis had performed the first of two feats for which he would be awarded the Victoria Cross; the second took place a little further inland, at a farm by the village of Crépon, shortly after midday.

JIG SECTOR

Leading Seaman Wally Blanchard
Landing Craft Obstacle Clearance Unit

I was ashore before four o'clock in the morning. I immediately started work. I think the tide was making fairly well. There was a diver working below me and I had what is now known as snorkel gear if I needed it but I worked virtually on the surface. There's a pier at Arromanches and I was working to the seaward side of that, our craft was tied up under it, and I went about my business. You had to be able to blow those charges but not before the bombardment started. Some of the bombardment, we think, was designed to land on the beach defences themselves and on the sand. Obviously some of them would fall in the water but that was a chance that had to be taken. The bombardment duly opened and we duly started blowing charges. The Germans would mistake them, we hoped, for the bombarding ammunition coming in. We didn't succeed in doing all of it.

Major David Warren
1st Battalion, Royal Hampshire Regiment
It was rather a grey morning and I suppose we got into the landing craft at about half past five because we had to get the landing craft lowered into the sea and circle about while we formed up in our flotillas. And it was just about first light, soon after first light, when suddenly this enormous armada of naval ships opened fire with a terrific noise. I think we passed the cruiser HMS *Ajax*, a six-inch-gun cruiser, and she let go just as we were near her. Very heartening if you were going the same way. We bumped around in the landing craft while we formed up for the run-in and I recollect that we'd had tea and rum put in for people to drink as we were going in. But a lot of people were feeling seasick and I think tea and rum was not the best thing.

Leading Telegraphist Alan Winstanley
Combined Operations Bombardment Unit
That was a sort of a time when everything really got quiet. It didn't really but in your mind it did. You were sort of so intent on knowing what you'd got to do, where you'd got to go, that it sort of obliterated most of the sounds from your mind. And I suppose there was a feeling of apprehension in not knowing what to expect. Would you hit a mine when you landed? Would you suddenly be mown down by hidden machine-gun nests that had kept conveniently quiet until the right opportunity came for them to do the most damage?

Private Richard Atkinson
9th Battalion, Durham Light Infantry
There were the usual pre-battle nerves. You were frightened, there's no doubt about it. There was a funny feeling inside your stomach and that. You didn't know what to expect and, by this stage, the war was getting along and you'd say, 'Well, I've been pushing my luck quite a lot.' All these thoughts running through your mind. You may not have said them to each other but they were there. You weren't the happy soul that you should have been. You keep saying to yourself, 'My number must be on one now.' And being wounded twice

before that, you see, you say to yourself, 'Next time, will I be so lucky?' You're shaking and you're saying prayers. I saw men that were as scared as I was and I was very scared. But you still went on. You just weren't going to let your mates see you were scared.

Lieutenant Edward Wright
1st Battalion, Royal Hampshire Regiment
The run-in was about seven miles, which is what we'd been trained for, but the weather conditions were very rough really for an operation of this sort. In the Landing Craft Assault, which was roughly one platoon per craft, there was a lot of seasickness and of course every succeeding wave poured a lot of spray into the boat.

Major Richard Gosling
Forward Observation Officer, 147th Field Regiment (Essex Yeomanry), Royal Artillery
We knew that we were going to get a bit wet and we weren't quite sure how many of us were going to get killed. We quite expected a lot of us would be killed but we were entirely confident. We were very well trained; we were so well trained, we knew exactly what to do. We had good equipment; we had maps and everything. We were all with our friends, which was the good thing. We knew that whatever happened, we were going to have friends with us.

Lieutenant Ian Wilson
73rd Field Company, Royal Engineers
All I can remember is this tremendous feeling of confidence, seeing the run-in to the point we were going to. A tremendous surge, you know. 'This is going to be all right. We're here.' Morale was high. The British Army had waited for four years to get back to France. I was still at school at Dunkirk time but the general spirit was there. We were going back to France and no way was anyone going to kick us out.

Sub Lieutenant Roderick Braybrooke
LCT crew
We went in and sort of fanned out into a line and of course there were the obvious problems – boats not quite sure where they were as opposed to where

they should be – and it was a question of really finding a space and getting in. There were LSTs, LSIs and assault craft going in at the same time and there was a lot of mortar fire coming from the shore. They'd got the range too as they were dropping mortar shells in a line. If you were lucky one exploded to the left of you and the next one to the right of you. If you were unlucky it landed right on top of you. And I remember one boat loaded with about twenty or thirty army fellows, an infantry landing thing, an open boat with a door that lets down, and they were just getting ready to go ashore and a mortar shell just landed on top of them. Little boats like that just sort of disappeared.

Lieutenant Ian Wilson
73rd Field Company, Royal Engineers
The sea was rough. I remember seeing one LCT beside us discharging its DD tanks, swimming tanks, into the sea and we saw six tanks, one after the other, disappear from view.

Gunner Ramsey Bader
Sexton (self-propelled gun) driver, 147th Field Regiment (Essex Yeomanry), Royal Artillery
The first tank coming off my LCT didn't make it. We were too far out, obstacles stopped the tank and those people were obviously drowned: the tank just sank. I was the next off, hoping we wouldn't hit any mines and obstacles in the water, but we kept going and we made the shore with our guns firing.

Trooper Kenneth Ewing
Sherman tank driver, Sherwood Rangers
One of the troubles was that there were gullies. On most beaches when the tide goes out you'll see lines of water, gullies. Well, some of these were quite deep and unfortunately that was what caused the problem. Some of them, they touched down, they lowered their screens and they went forward and went down into a gully and of course that was it.

Leading Seaman Wally Blanchard
Landing Craft Obstacle Clearance Unit

The Germans had done all sorts of things. They'd left a lot of the pre-war beach kiosks and things like that on the promenades, left them all in position. Only of course they looked like kiosks but they were really pillboxes either painted to look like they were before or heavily reinforced. And they did indeed open fire as soon as the landing craft appeared and I engaged what looked like a beach kiosk where I'd seen what I took to be an Oerlikon or heavy machine-gun muzzle emerging from the slot. I had it covered and I fired straight into it. I managed to subdue whatever was going on there, by which time the infantry landing craft were in.

Private Leslie Gibson
6th Battalion, Border Regiment (Beach Group)

There was everything flying about, there were these cross-girders with mines on the top and the first chap I saw was a rubber-suited frogman, minus a leg, lying on the beach. Of course there was lots of other debris. We were very lucky because we did have a shell ricochet under the boat.

Sergeant James Bellows
1st Battalion, Royal Hampshire Regiment

Suddenly we grounded. I think it was a sub-lieutenant, he dropped the ramp, and we were a hell of a way off the shore and the waves are coming by the side and I thought to myself, 'They're pretty bloody high for shallow water.' It was nice, smooth, what you get in fairly deep water. So I said, 'We're not in shallow water, you know. We're in deep water here.' But this sub-lieutenant, he said, 'We've grounded.' Course, all sorts is going on all around but we were in our own little world here and I'm having an argument with him about the depth of the water. So he calls for a stick. One of the matelots comes down, he puts it in the water and he says, 'Four foot six.' I said, 'You must be bloody joking. You're in deep water, we're on an obstacle.' He wouldn't have it. 'No we're not,' he said. 'I'm in charge of this ship. I'm the captain.' Little sod. I said to all my chaps, 'Now, look, this is going to be a bloody wet landing.'

Major Richard Gosling
Forward Observation Officer, 147th Field Regiment (Essex Yeomanry),
Royal Artillery

I was a very simple boy, you know. I hadn't been out of England in my life
before then and there I was wading ashore in France to fight the Germans.
Extraordinary. We weren't trained for that at Eton or Cambridge. But anyway
we were full of enthusiasm and we started to wade ashore and the water got
gradually shallower and there was a lot of forward shelling, our Essex
Yeomanry guns fired over our heads, a lifting barrage.

As we got nearer and nearer we could see one or two flashes from German
guns on the other side and then we heard something and because I'd been
born in the country I thought it was a swarm of bees. It wasn't. It was German
machine guns firing on fixed lines overhead. We got through the deep water
over our balls and then we could see the German machine guns furrowing the
sand – there was wet sand in front.

We were supporting the Hampshires, the assault infantry, so I was with the
colonel, Nelson-Smith, and he said, 'Lie down.' Well, he'd been a soldier all
his life, I'd never been a soldier before, but I didn't know what the idea was, it
was bloody wet to lie down, so we weren't very keen on that and we started to
run across the wet sand. We could see the sand dunes just in front of us, fifty
yards in front of us, and one or two people were shot and suddenly there was a
great 'Bang!' just behind me. And exactly like playing football at Eton, when
a boy had kicked your legs away from you, suddenly I found my legs kicked
away from me and I was lying on the wet sand. Poor old Nelson-Smith, the
colonel, was next to me. His arm was shot through the elbow. I could just
hobble. One leg was all right. I limped through and we got up into the sand
dunes and were able to throw ourselves flat on the ground.

We were just under the sand dunes and we could hear these Germans firing
their machine guns through the rushes just over our heads. I wasn't really
frightened because so much was happening you couldn't be frightened. My leg
was numb. It was full of small pieces of splinter but it wasn't really hurting. I
had a first field dressing, Sergeant Brace took it and wound it round and cut
my battledress. I said, 'For Heaven's sake, I've got to pay the quartermaster if
that gets damaged.'

So we lay there for a little bit. Then a chap next to me, a Hampshire
corporal, he put his head up to look over the sand dunes to see what was

happening and as soon as he did that he was shot straight through the chest. A little bit later I thought I should look over – I was the officer. I had a wonderful old revolver which had belonged to my uncle Seymour in the Boer War and it had some bullets in it and it worked, too, so I crawled up the sand dunes with my gammy leg and peered over the edge and there was a bloody German, just the other side. I didn't like the look of him, he didn't like the look of me, and I fired my revolver hopefully in his direction and then I slid back again. When I looked up again he'd gone.

Private James Donaldson
2nd Battalion, Devonshire Regiment
One thing I remember – very outstanding – was 47 (Royal Marine) Commando, who were part of our brigade for this individual landing, coming past us, soaked to the skin. A lot of their landing craft had turned over but I've never seen men so resolute as these commandos.

Brigadier Sir Alexander Stanier
Commanding Officer, 231st Infantry Brigade
47 (Royal Marine) Commando had a terribly rough landing. The seas got rougher as the tide came in and they lost seventy men before they actually reached the beach. Then, when they got on to the beach, they found none of their wirelesses would work. How their commanding officer collected them, I don't know. He must have had a megaphone and shouted; sent people hither and thither; perhaps even put a flag up, I don't know. I saw the commanding officer for five minutes while they were assembling just behind the sand dunes and him worrying about where his men had gone to and getting his wirelesses and things and trying to get a move on. They were very independent, if I may say so. They knew what to do and they were quite happy to get on with it.

Lieutenant Edward Wright
1st Battalion, Royal Hampshire Regiment
When we got to the dunes on the far side of the beach we discovered a minefield which we knew was there but we hoped it would have been breached by our armoured flail vehicles. But when we arrived it hadn't been breached at all so I had to decide whether we were going to try to make our way through the minefield or go up or down the beach. We'd always been

A knocked-out flail tank of the Westminster Dragoons on Gold Beach after D-Day. An abandoned DD tank can be seen in the background.

trained: 'Get off the beach.' And by that time there was a lot of machine-gun fire coming down. It was very unhealthy. I lost two of my platoon, killed.

But we were very lucky. When I'd just made my mind up that we had to go through that minefield, a prospect I didn't like one little bit, a flail tank appeared on our left and began to flail through the minefield and got through to the far side. This was actually in the area of the 1st Dorsets to our left but I wasn't going to fuss about that and we went through that breach and we got through. It was clear afterwards, when I had time to look at my map, that we'd landed about two or three hundred metres to the east of where it had been intended that we should. In the event that proved very fortunate because the further west you went the more unhealthy it was. The main trouble was coming from an enemy strongpoint at Le Hamel and those who landed closest to Le Hamel got the worst of it.

Major David Warren
1st Battalion, Royal Hampshire Regiment

I realised that we should have to 'gap' our way ourselves, cut our way through the wire, and we started to do that. Meanwhile the casualties were piling up because the fire was very strong and it was raking along the top of the beach where people were trying to get. This particular beach was enfiladed: that is, there was a German position at the end of it and they could rake the whole beach with fire. Also there was a gun, which appeared to be some sort of anti-tank gun, and that of course was in concrete and steel. This position, at Le Hamel, where we landed, was going to cause us a great deal of trouble. It had excellent fields of fire and the Germans in fact did not show much signs of giving up.

Captain Arthur Warburton
Sherman tank commander, 147th Field Regiment (Essex Yeomanry), Royal Artillery

I got my tank on to the beach road behind the sand dunes and when I looked back to the sea I found the sand dunes were full of Germans still running about. They'd camouflaged themselves and they must have been well under cover when all this bombardment was coming down and there was the pillbox at the end still firing, still shooting at things coming in. Then it changed its ideas and saw my tank coming along this beach road and I thought to myself,

'I'm bloody sure that thing's pointing at me.' I could see this thing, about 150 yards away, so I shouted at my driver to pull out the fire extinguisher, by instinct, and at that very moment the thing hit me and cut my engine into about fifty pieces. But we never caught fire. I saw many, many Shermans hit and I never remember seeing a Sherman hit without going straight up in flames. I then saw one of the regimental self-propelled guns coming ashore so I got hold of him, the No 1, and I pointed out to him where this pillbox was which was within good range for him. I said, 'Blow that damned thing up, it's just hit me.'

Sergeant Robert Palmer
Sexton (self-propelled gun) commander, 147th Field Regiment (Essex Yeomanry), Royal Artillery

He yelled at me, 'Sergeant! Quick! See what's happening? You've got the best gun nearest to that! Put that out of action!' I climbed over the side of my self-propelled gun, got down on to the road, on this unmade road, walked along the road till I got level with this line of trees. Then I looked across and with my field glasses I could see ever so easily what it was. There was this enormous monster of a place and it looked like a big, big mushroom. And as far as I could see, the only bit that was likely to be of any help to us, if we could get there, was their gun aperture point, where their gun barrel came out. The rest of it, if you hit it, you'd only be bruising the concrete, so we'd got to try and get one in that aperture.

I said to my crew, 'There's no good us going up there like all the others have done, we shall simply be number seven if we go up nice and steadily. We've got to do something different and take them by surprise.' So I said to the driver, 'When I say "Go", go. Put your foot down and go.' Now those things weighed something like thirty-five tons but they would do about thirty-five miles an hour. And I said, 'When I tell you to stop' – a tap on the head, that's the signal to stop – 'I want you to immediately turn 45 degrees to your offside.'

So what happened was, I hit him in the back, which was the signal to go, and off he went. We flew across as fast as we could and we got away with it, we caught them by surprise, they weren't able to pick us up. We did about eighty yards past the trees. I tapped the driver on the head; he stopped and immediately turned 45 degrees to his right. The gun layer, who was going to fire the gun, he could see quite clearly what the target was and I'd instructed him to travel with the gun already loaded and the safety catch off, which you shouldn't do normally, to save us seconds of time. And as soon as the driver stopped and steered it to 45 degrees to his offside, the gun layer, with his wheels, was able to manoeuvre it on to the thing accurately and fire. And as soon as we had almost stopped bouncing, as a tank does when you stop suddenly, he fired immediately and the first shot actually hit.

From where I was, I could see we'd hit the target but it hadn't gone in the narrow bit that we wanted. It was a fraction high and a fraction to the left. So I ordered him to deflect one to the right and drop twenty-five yards and fire again. So he fired again and, would you believe, the next one was kind enough to go right in the actual aperture. Now, if we'd practised it all the morning we couldn't have got better than that, it was marvellous. That went in and of course exploded inside and put the gun out of action. About four people struggled out of the back of this emplacement with their hands over their ears. Poor devils, I felt sorry for them. Obviously they were badly knocked about.

Major David Warren
1st Battalion, Royal Hampshire Regiment
We had managed to gap our way off the beach and we'd got over the mines and so on and then I met a tank, an AVRE, a Royal Engineers' assault tank, specially equipped. This particular one had a mortar-like gun on it, called a Petard, which fired a large bomb. So I spoke to the commander of the tank, I told him I wanted him to support this attack on Le Hamel, and the tank came forward and it fired the bomb into the buildings and when he did that we assaulted it and went inside and it was silenced. And that was a great relief to all concerned because there was a lot of landing craft having difficulties on our beach. They could now come ashore; the beach masters could get things organised rather better.

Lance Corporal Norman Travett
2nd Battalion, Devonshire Regiment
No way could we possibly advance until this troublesome pillbox had been destroyed. We laid there in our wet trousers and water oozing out of our boots for what seemed ages. Eventually it was silenced. That was where I saw my first dead Germans, up there in that pillbox. Gruesome. I thought those chaps had probably been called up for service like myself and had no wish to be

Troops inspect a knocked-out German 50-millimetre anti-tank gun emplacement on Gold Beach, 7 June 1944.

where they were. They didn't stand a chance, really. Not there. What could they do?

Private Leslie Gibson
6th Battalion, Border Regiment (Beach Group)

We were pinned down behind a jeep. There was a big concrete building, it had been a convalescent home for German soldiers, and they'd left a lot of snipers behind in the building. To the right of me was some high ground in the direction of Arromanches and I could see a tank blazing in the distance, bodies round it. And this soldier, I don't know what regiment he was in, came up. He had a leather jerkin on which was smouldering. I thought, 'He don't know what he's doing,' and when I got closer to him I found out that he had no face at all, it was just a balloon, it must've swelled up in the tank when it got hit and the heat had blown his face up. Anyway, I got hold of him and took him back to the first-aid post, told him to keep his head down. I don't know if he heard us but he did keep his head down a bit.

Lieutenant Edward Wright
1st Battalion, Royal Hampshire Regiment

We'd had quite a lot of casualties and a lot of the supporting fire we had expected hadn't materialised but I personally had never expected it to be a walkover. I had hoped that we would do it with fewer casualties and to that extent it was a disappointment, but we had achieved what we had set out to do and we had got all our objectives, so that was a plus.

Sergeant James Bellows
1st Battalion, Royal Hampshire Regiment

Just off the beach there were two or three little cottages and opposite these cottages there was a road that led from the beach and one of our men had been killed and his mates had just dug a hole and covered him. The reason they done this was because, if they hadn't, it was more than probable he'd have been run over by all sorts of things, tanks, you name it. It was a humanitarian gesture, you might say. And as I was walking by, out of one of those cottages came an old lady. Goodness knows how old she was. Skirts were touching the ground. And she hobbled across the road and in her hand she had a posy of flowers and she placed them on the grave, kneeled, said a prayer, got up, gave the sign of the cross and then walked back to her cottage. It was one of the most moving sights I think I saw in the war.

KING SECTOR

Lance Corporal Alan Carter
6th Battalion, Green Howards
It were very quiet on my landing craft except for one young lad. I always remember him. Fresh-faced, he'd only be about eighteen, and I heard him say to one of his mates, 'I hope I get a Blighty one.' That was about the only thing said.

Private Dennis Bowen
5th Battalion, East Yorkshire Regiment
Once you get down into the assault craft you can't see out of it because it's all metal and the front, which is like a ramp, is up in front of you. So you've got to get up to look over the side, if you were daft enough, to see what's happening. Everybody's got enough sense to stay in the bottom where it's quite bulletproof.

Corporal Alfred Church
2nd Battalion, Hertfordshire Regiment (Beach Group)
Everybody was sick. There was probably a foot of seawater and sick and everything else in the bottom. But of course as soon as the shells started coming over you forgot that sort of thing.

Private Dennis Bowen
5th Battalion, East Yorkshire Regiment
The noise is absolutely horrendous. It's not 'Bang! Bang! Bang! Bang!' It's a continual roar of sound, constantly, without stopping, and all the time you can hear people shouting out orders. '4896 follow me!' 'My maximum speed is 22, I'll keep up with you!' All that sort of stuff. Everything's very exciting. Your heart is pounding like mad. You can't really think of it as something where you're going to get hurt, you're going to get killed maybe, or lose a limb or whatever. It's all very, very exciting. But if somebody had actually picked

you up out of that boat and took you away to where it was quiet and said, 'Now, what's happening?' you'd have said, 'I've no idea. I'm on a ship that's going to land and there's going to be Germans there and we're going to fight them.' That's really all.

Lieutenant Michael Irwin
LCA(HR) commander

It was H minus one minute. The destroyers were bombarding and then precisely at the moment we arrived off the beach to do our job, about twenty or thirty yards from the beach, the bombardment lifted and we let go our spigot bombs and there was a tremendous explosion. I went to port and then along came this LCT that beached and out of it came the flail tank. And the most incredible thing was that there wasn't a shot fired. It was absolute peace, probably for a minute or two minutes. Then this tank waddled up the beach, the flails started off, there was an explosion as the waterproofing was blown up, then there was black smoke from the tank as it received a direct hit. There weren't any flames for a moment but they were obviously all killed inside.

Sergeant Neville Howell
73rd Anti-Tank Regiment, Royal Artillery

The skipper rammed full pelt at the shore, presumably hoping to get well up on the shore so we would get a dry landing. Unfortunately, we could see that we were heading straight for beach defences – I think they were called hedgehogs – and we ran straight at a couple of these things. They had shells on the top pointing in our direction and as we hit the shore there was a terrific blast. This wasn't unexpected at all, we could see what was going to happen, and I think some of us even gave a little ironic cheer. The blast blew us backwards and unfortunately it blew a hole somewhere, flooding the engine room and damaging the landing ramp, and we started to drift out to sea again. The skipper was calling out over his loudspeaker to other craft coming in, trying to get somebody to push us a bit further into the shore. Some smaller assault craft were coming in alongside of us and some of them were hitting beach defences and being blown to pieces.

Lance Corporal Alan Carter
6th Battalion, Green Howards

They said 'Prepare to land' and we picked up our weapons. One of the sergeants picked up his Sten gun and with the rocking of the boat he put a bullet through his wrist. He was our first casualty. The second one was my sergeant. He was very heavily loaded, he stumbled and he went under the landing craft and that was the finish of him, you see. I was last in the section and I said to the lads, 'Where's the sergeant?' 'Oh, he went under.' Well, I'd liked him a lot. You could trust him, he'd do anything for you, I was more or less raw and he knew what to do. At any rate, I went through this three-foot of water. There was a 'Plop!' beside me. I think a mortar or a shell had went into the sand and of course with it being wet and that it hadn't gone off. Kirkpatrick came to me and he gave me the maps and binoculars and he said, 'You're platoon sergeant now.' He was wounded. I noticed he had a bandage.

Corporal Percival Tyson
5th Battalion, East Yorkshire Regiment

We were under shellfire and machine-gun fire, we had quite a few shell bursts near the landing craft, and I remember the sailor shouting, 'Get off the bloody thing! Get off the bloody thing!' He wanted to get out of it, bring in some more.

Corporal Alfred Church
2nd Battalion, Hertfordshire Regiment (Beach Group)

We lost one fellow going in that drowned. Several we had to pull out because they fell over. You see you were carrying all this ammunition, you had four or five pouches full of ammunition; you were actually carrying sixty pounds of equipment with you. So that's half a hundredweight of equipment on your back, you're running with that through the water, plus you're carrying your rifle as well. Several went down and we'd pull them back on to their feet. Our orders were, 'Stop for nothing. If anybody falls down, too bad. You've got to go and clear that beach, because there's stuff coming behind you.'

Trooper Joseph Ellis
Churchill Crocodile tank driver, 141st Regiment, Royal Armoured Corps

One of the navy men had a big pole with markings on it. He dipped the water at each side of this ramp and said, 'Right, No 1 tank off.' He went off, straight forward, sunk. The crew got out, left the tank, swam back. No 2 went out, turned to the left, he went down. There was ten tanks on and No 3 went to the right and he went straight through on to the beach so they said, 'Right, follow him.' We left them, them two tanks. You couldn't do nowt about them.

Sergeant John Clegg
Centaur tank crew, 1st Royal Marine Armoured Support Regiment
The ramp goes down, the engines have already been warmed and off you go. All sorts of noises are coming through your headphones. You can hear possibly bullets splattering against the side of the landing craft and your tank: pitter-patter, pitter-patter. That you ignore. Your sole object now is to get through the water and on to the beach.

Whatever angle you've come off the tank landing craft is the angle that you'll steer through the water until you get out the waterline. Otherwise, if one tries to turn the tank in water, it's possible you'll take a track off. So whatever angle you come off, that's where you're going for the next two or three minutes, which seems an age.

Now you're on the beach, you press the switch to drop your reserve ammunition off, you blow some of the waterproofing off the rear – this is all done by explosive bolts – and now all that you've learned in the months previously is brought into being. You know where your targets are if you're in the right place, you're already looking for places that you can identify, and once you've identified somewhere you just carry on doing the job that you've trained for years for. And this is your revenge for Norway.

Trooper Ronald Mole
Sherman tank gunner/wireless operator, 4th/7th Royal Dragoon Guards
We got ashore. We were all strung out, the nineteen vehicles in the squadron. Anything that moved we were giving it a burst. And there was an AVRE, an Armoured Vehicle Royal Engineers. It was a Churchill with what they called a Petard – it had a shortish barrel that fired a forty-pound charge of dynamite, a blockbuster – and this thing came up and passed us and I was watching it go in front. It had gone something like fifty yards up the beach when suddenly there was a flash and sixty tons of metal just disappeared in front of our eyes and then down came a sprocket, a piece of track, flames licking the sand. A whole Churchill tank had literally disappeared in front of our eyes. I gather

there must have been a ton of dynamite on board and this had been hit by an 88.

We were given a brief to attend to a house that was reinforced with a pillbox and this was spraying the beach and the poor old infantry were really catching it. So I was firing into this thing with HE and not making any headway so we switched to armour piercing, the idea being that if I could make a hole and put an HE through the hole, that would be it.

Now, my tank commander, Sergeant V____, from Cardiff, he was stood up behind me and he had the turret flap half open and he was looking through his periscope and he said, 'Hang on a minute, Ron. I can't see anything for the dust.' He stuck his head above the turret and he was dead. He was shot right between the eyes. His right elbow hit me on the neck, his left elbow hit the gun, he sagged and his knees hit me in the kidneys and when I turned I could just see blood running. It wasn't splashing, just a gentle run, and there it was on the bottom of the tank, just coagulating in a small pool and getting thicker and thicker. My immediate reaction in my innocence was to say, 'I wonder where that came from?' leaning back, to climb out and have a look. Fortunately, my chum, the operator, an ex-Nottingham city policeman, he leaned across the gun and shouted, 'Don't be a BF!' He was the one who saved my life, because I was as green as grass.

Private Dennis Bowen
5th Battalion, East Yorkshire Regiment
We got up about fifty or sixty yards up the beach and there was a sea wall with a road built along the top of it, a tarmac road. Obviously it was a position of cover so we ran up there and got underneath the edge of this road which was like a sea wall about three feet high.

More reinforcements came up and of course it reaches the stage where there are more and more people getting on to the beach till you were literally forced over the wall. Everybody was reluctant, naturally, to get up on to the road: the road was on a fixed line of enemy fire and was being fired on. But one soldier, I don't know who it was, got up on to the top of the road and shouted, 'Come on, you're going to be here all day. Let's get over this bloody road, let's get over.' And then, just as if everybody had decided all at the same time, we got up on to the top of the road. And as soon as we got on to the top of the road the men who had obviously been in action before began firing. I

British infantrymen of the 7th Battalion, Green Howards, cross King sector of Gold Beach at about 0830 hours. Sherman tanks, an AVRE and other vehicles can be seen on the water's edge.

couldn't see any enemy; but as they ran across the road they held their rifles at their hip and just fired towards where obviously there were Germans. We got across to the other side, which was a wet area, and the sergeants were shouting, 'Don't hang about, keep going! Keep going forward! Keep going forward!' And that's the time that we began to see German soldiers.

The German soldiers didn't seem to be organised at all. I suppose the ones that were organised were the ones we didn't see. But the ones we did see, and the ones we shot, just seemed to be blindly running into any sort of position. They had trenches and pillboxes and things. Some of them were already putting their hands up. In the excitement, of course, they unfortunately were the ones who got shot. You never think of a prisoner. Somebody's shooting at you and you see people coming out and they suddenly put their hands up. All you see is a figure of a man in an enemy uniform and you don't particularly lay on the sights, take aim and shoot, you just blindly fire in his direction. And as soon as the magazine is empty, reload and continue firing, without counting the rounds or anything. Just keep banging away.

I can remember firing and seeing people fall and you know that if you haven't hit them it's somebody alongside you that's hit them. I suppose that you think that they're going to get up again, especially if the man's got a weapon in his hand. The German soldiers, some of them, were within fifty, sixty yards of us, running across to get into their positions. And if one got up and ran, everybody fired at him and of course he'd just go down in a lump. Some of our men were being hurt as well and I remember men were stopping to pick them up and I can remember being screamed at, 'Leave them! Leave them! Don't take any wounded back; leave them! Just get forward!' So the lads who were wounded were left, they were picked up by the people coming after us. But we were the assault troops and I realise now that if we had stopped to bandage up our wounded the action may well have been lost.

Corporal Alfred Church
2nd Battalion, Hertfordshire Regiment (Beach Group)

A lot of the troops who we killed and captured, they were all sorts of nationalities. They weren't necessarily Germans. Somebody tried talking to them in German and they couldn't talk German. They were Polish and Czech and God knows what. When they saw what was happening they used to drop their arms a bit sharpish and surrender. But of course we didn't know what they were. They wore the same German uniforms.

Sergeant Neville Howell
73rd Anti-Tank Regiment, Royal Artillery

I saw a number of prisoners gathered. They had been part of the German forces but most of them were obviously of some other nation. They looked like Mongolians to me and I believe that a number of people of that type had elected to go over to the Germans and do their pioneering work or man some of the beach defences.

Sergeant John Clegg
Centaur tank crew, 1st Royal Marine Armoured Support Regiment

We cleared the beach sufficiently by approximately ten o'clock in the morning, which was very good going. We had been told, unofficially, that our casualties would be eighty per cent. Fortunately we got away much lighter than that.

Lance Corporal Alan Carter
6th Battalion, Green Howards

We went on up the road and we came to the first house. There was a movement in the first house and we stopped and got ready to sling a grenade in and all of a sudden an old Frenchwoman came out. She was pointing out to sea and tears were rolling down her cheeks. I knew what she was asking, she was saying, 'Is this the real thing? Is this the liberation?' I nodded me head. Then her old man appeared with a bottle and it warmed us up, 'cause we were wet through.

Company Sergeant Major Stanley Hollis
6th Battalion, Green Howards

We had to take a coastal battery at Mont Fleury. I was in charge of a group of two-inch mortars laying down smoke but I noticed that two of our platoons, running up to attack the guns, had gone past a pillbox. This was only about a foot above the ground but I spotted a Spandau machine gun in the firing slit. I went along with my company commander, one of the bravest men I know. They fired at us, but, once we were on top of the box, grenades and Sten guns killed some of them and when I went down inside with my Sten gun I got half a dozen prisoners. It was a big place, two storeys deep, and we got all of the equipment intact. So that made things just a little safer for the rest of our company in their attack.

The fighting all through D-Day was fairly warm and one piece of trouble we ran into was on account of some dogs I noticed at the end of a country lane. There was nobody there but the dogs were wagging their tails. When I went along with the major we found a German field gun supported by machine guns in a farmyard. Elements of D Company attacked from some farm buildings but every time our lads got up to the next wall they were knocked out by machine guns. I tried to get the gun crew with a mortar but they started blazing away with the gun at a hundred yards, open sights, and big stones were flying all over. The gun concentrated on one of our Bren groups and things looked bad for them, they couldn't get back, so I tried again with a Bren and this time the German boys got so worried they left our lads alone and we all got back safely.

Now these don't sound like VC affairs and I don't know if they really are. I do know it was the sort of thing that was happening all over in the first five days in Normandy and jumping into a pillbox full of Germans wasn't so wonderful when you saw your own lads fighting like heroes every side of you. And when you saw lads you knew dropping dead, you wanted to do something to smash the guns that had done it. Just after we were out of the water on D-Day I saw one lad go down wounded; now he saved my life in Sicily and he comes from Middlesborough too. That sort of thing makes you forget to be scared. I've always been scared when we've gone into action – with the BEF at Dunkirk; Alamein to Sicily – but if your lads see the sergeant major's got his head down, well, it's a bad do, isn't it? So that's the way it goes, and things like snipers' bullets on your cheek and being blown out of trenches and looking into German gun muzzles, they don't count as much as you'd think when you've got men like that round you.

I'd like them to know that their telegram was the first I'd heard about the VC. I've sometimes heard that chaps who get medals inspire the other men. It wasn't like that in my case. My officers and men, they inspired me.

Company Sergeant Major Stanley Hollis, Green Howards. A veteran of Dunkirk, El Alamein and Sicily, he was the only man to be awarded a Victoria Cross on D-Day.

OMAHA BEACH

Nine miles west of Gold, Omaha Beach stretched four miles from Port-en-Bessin to the town of Vierville-sur-Mer. Flanked by cliffs and dominated by a grassy ridge running parallel to the shore, it was naturally suited to defence and the German fortifications there were strong and well placed. Assaulting it was the task of the United States Army's experienced 1st Infantry Division, together with the 29th Infantry Division and men from two Ranger battalions.

Rough seas swamped almost all of the DD tanks launched out at sea and capsized several landing craft before they got anywhere near the beach. Closing on the shore at 0630 hours, the first wave of infantry found the German defences largely untouched by the air and naval bombardment and quickly came under very heavy and accurate fire. Casualties mounted rapidly, movement up the beach seemed suicidal, though there was nowhere else to go, and the next wave, which began to reach the beach at 0700 hours, suffered much the same fate.

In the face of all of this, the infantry managed, nevertheless, to push forward in small groups and start to take on the enemy defences. Progress was slow and losses were very heavy but as the hours passed the Americans fought their way on to the ridge and up the cliffs. A few tanks that had arrived safely helped reduce the enemy positions, as did naval gunfire. Eventually key exits were taken and the infantry began moving inland. By nightfall the beachhead was a mile and a half deep and the Americans had lost at least two thousand men killed, wounded and missing. Recent research has suggested that the figure may have been many hundreds more than that.

Though largely unknown, a significant number of British personnel were engaged in supporting the Americans on Omaha and witnessed what happened there. The roles they performed were important; a large number of landing craft, including many in the initial assault waves, were British-crewed, while trained British teams did what they could, both on the shore and in the sea, to make paths through the mines and obstacles.

Sub Lieutenant Jimmy Green
LCA flotilla commander, aboard HMS Empire Javelin
(Royal Navy Landing Ship Infantry [LSI])

I wasn't very pleased to be woken up at half-past three on the morning of 6 June because my call was for four o'clock. But Able Seaman Kemp, who woke me, said, 'Please, sir. Would you go along to the flotilla office? There's been a change in time, they want you to go earlier'. So I went along to the flotilla office and I was told then that the time of launching had been brought forward from 4.30 to four o'clock. So I scrambled to get ready, got all my equipment, got my guns, snatched something to eat and went up on deck.

My job on D-Day was to land A Company of the 116th Regiment in front of the pass at Vierville-sur-Mer, which led off the beach. The beach at Omaha had cliffs all the way along it and couldn't take vehicles. The vehicles had to go through a pass, which was at Vierville-sur-Mer, and it was the job of the 116th Regiment to capture that pass so that all the vehicles, guns and heavy equipment could get off the beach.

It was the first time we'd actually taken in an inexperienced assault group. Previously we had been working with Rangers who had previous experience of landings and were a pretty tough group, a tough-looking lot, they looked as though they could take care of themselves. Now the 116th were a very pleasant lot, like country boys, they looked like Somerset lads, they looked like farm lads, very pleasant, very open, wanting to be friendly, though we didn't have much chance of speaking to them.

At four o'clock it was still dark, pitch black, and the ship was rolling. It had already come to anchor at its point about fourteen, fifteen miles off the Normandy coast but it was rolling in the very heavy seas and it didn't seem to me as though the sea had abated much since the previous day. Certainly there was quite a sea on, roaring along the side of the ship, and we were going from side to side.

When I arrived on deck the American troops were already there. They'd been called early and were waiting to be loaded. The LCAs were bound into the side of the ship so it was a fairly easy process for the troops to step from the deck, even though it was rolling a bit, on to the deck of the LCA. Then they'd go down into the well of the boat and sit down as they'd been instructed and as they'd practised on exercises. So they all got on board and sat down in their three rows, with a terrific amount of kit, ready for launching into the sea.

They were very quiet when they got on board. They weren't talking very much amongst themselves. It was probably going into the boat, which was a bit unnerving, and they weren't encouraged to make a lot of noise on board because we had to carry out our communications, so they were talking in whispers amongst themselves. But they weren't high-spirited. I think they were realising that this was it. They were thinking, you know, 'How am I going to react? What's ahead of us?' What talking there was, it was quiet and subdued.

Whether the commanders passed this down to their troops, I don't know, but all the commanders, all the leaders of the invasion force, were told that a third of us were expected to lose our lives in the first wave. And originally my wave was to go in an hour before any other wave approached the beach so we were given the tag of the 'suicide' wave among the flotilla. It was jokingly given, I think, but we were proud to accept that, although we all expected to come back.

Sub Lieutenant Hilaire Benbow
LCA commander, aboard HMS Prince Charles (Royal Navy LSI)

We had ten LCAs, Landing Craft Assault, hoisted on the davits of the *Prince Charles*. They were like iron matchboxes, square, and the idea was that two or three of them would go to Pointe du Hoc. On that point there was a gun battery which threatened the anchorage and it had to be silenced or stopped, so these Rangers, under a Colonel Rudder, were to go and assail the cliffs of this high point and capture the gun position. They had all sorts of ingenious equipment, grappling irons and ropes with rockets on, all sorts of things to get up the cliffs. I really don't know why they didn't drop paratroops, you know, but anyway it was to be assaulted from the sea. I shook hands with Colonel Rudder and wished him good luck as he went down the scrambling net of the *Prince Charles* into these LCAs. We set out about an hour or so later and headed towards the main shore.

Sub Lieutenant Jimmy Green
LCA flotilla commander

We formed up in our formation of two columns and set off in the direction of the beach according to the course that we'd worked out and the speed we'd worked out and we had an American patrol craft with us as our escort. About five miles off the beach he left us and just after that I came across a group of landing craft tanks.

I didn't know anything about these. I said to Taylor-Fellers, the captain of A Company, 'What the hell are these doing here? We're the first to go in and these LCTs shouldn't be here.' He said, 'Oh, yes, they should. They're supposed to go in ahead of us.' I said, 'Well, thank you for telling me. I had no indication.' And I said, 'They're not going to make it.' They were really ploughing into the waves, they were going as fast as they could, but they were only doing, what, five knots to our eight, and they were shipping water and they were not going to make the beach by six-thirty. So I said, 'We've got to go in and leave them behind. Is that all right?' He said, 'Yes, we've got to be there on time.'

As we approached the beach we heard a terrific noise. All the major bombardment had ceased but these were some rocket ships, landing craft rockets. They were supposed to land their rockets on the beach ahead of us, again something that had escaped the planners telling me, but the rockets just went up in the air and landed a good quarter of a mile off the shore line. A terrific firework display but absolutely useless and I shook my fist at them. They'd come all the way from England to the Normandy coast and shot their rockets up in the air and disappeared and I wasn't all that pleased because I was beginning to make out pillboxes on the beach and it looked a pretty formidable beach for the troops to take. At that moment, just before I gave the order to form up, an LCG, a landing craft with guns, opened up and hit one of the pillboxes from about a thousand yards out. It really let rip.

I turned round to give the order to come into line abreast, I was signalling with my flags, and LCA 911 disappeared beneath the waves. Stewart waved at me. I shouted back at him, 'I'll be back to pick you up!' I don't know whether he heard it. Everybody had life jackets on and they were bobbing about in the water but I had instructions, I had to get there on time, and I didn't have room. My instructions were quite clear. 'Don't pick up anybody from the water. Get to the beach on time.' But it went against the grain to leave people in those seas with life jackets and the Americans with all the equipment they had with them. It really did hurt to go on but I had to do it.

Leading Seaman John Tarbit
LCA coxswain

Two of our LCAs were swamped and sank and the Americans, when I got up to them, were all floating upside down in the water. Because they had so much equipment around their necks, the only place for their life belts was around their waist. Of course what they should have done was push them up under their arms and drop their other equipment, but they hung on to their equipment and they were top heavy and you could see seventy backsides floating in the water.

The first wave of DD tanks were, like us, dropped in the sea several miles out and of course they were worse off than us. They were lower in the water and they only had canvas dodgers around to stop the spray coming in and it was so rough they were just swamped. The Americans thought they were going to have these DD tanks to shelter behind at the same time as they landed but of course it didn't come about. They had no protection. The only protection they had was a tin hat.

Sub Lieutenant Jimmy Green
LCA flotilla commander

We were told that the beach would have craters on it so that the troops would be able to shelter. It was going to be a wide sandy beach with obstacles but the American air force the night before was supposed to bomb the beach and cause craters and the bombardment was also supposed to do something of that sort. But when I gave the order go into line abreast there were no marks at all. There was a virgin beach stretching for three hundred yards with not a sign of any place where the troops could shelter: they had to cover an open beach with the Germans waiting for them in the darkness of the cliffs. Although at half-past six it was lightish, it was still a grim, depressing sort of morning and the cliffs looked very foreboding and sinister and we knew that Germans were there because they were popping mortars at us.

I spoke to the captain of A Company of the 116th and said, 'There's the beach, where exactly do you want to land?' He said, 'I want to land to the right of the pass, just there, and I want the other group to land to the left of the pass so that when we go up the beach we can converge on the entrance to the pass.' So I gave the order to go full speed ahead, we saw the beach ahead of us, we made for the spot and we crunched to a halt, because the beach was very shallow, about twenty-five yards from the shoreline. I didn't expect to hit it just there, so there was a bit of a shudder, we all staggered a bit. We lowered the ramp and the Americans started to file out in single file.

Taylor-Fellers, the captain, went first, followed by the middle rank, followed by the port, left-hand, rank, followed by the right-hand rank. This was as practised. But they had to go out in single file because it was a narrow door and they plunged into surf and they were going up and down and they had to keep their weapons dry so they had to hold them over their heads. One minute the surf was round their ankles, the next minute it was under their armpits, and we had to keep the boat steady as they were getting out to assist them in their disembarkation.

Surprisingly, because we were particularly vulnerable, the Germans held their fire at this point. We couldn't fire back because we were so involved in keeping the boat straight and the troops were in the water without being able to get at their firearms. There were a few mortars popping around us but nothing else opened up. It was almost an unearthly silence while the troops got out. And I was surprised that when they got out of the craft and made their way in single file on to the beach they didn't go charging up the beach, they in fact formed a firing line along a ridge and faced the Germans. The obstacles were about fifty yards up the beach and then a further two hundred yards from the obstacles were the Germans in the cliffs. Nothing, no craters, no shelter, did they have. Originally I was going to cover them with my machine guns as they went up the beach but they didn't go, they lay down in a firing line to get themselves sorted out. They were in a line facing the Germans, lying prone, with their rifles pointing toward the cliffs, in one line running parallel to the shore.

We pulled off and my coxswain said, 'Sir, there's some of our blokes on the beach.' I said, 'There can't be,' but there were. They were from the Rangers' craft that had been hit by four mortars as it went in – sank the craft, killed a number of the Rangers and wounded some of the crew – and they were on the beach waving frantically at me to go and pick them up. Obviously they didn't want to be there and I don't blame them. I was toying with the idea of leaving them because my first thought was for those poor people floating about in the water, Petty Officer Stewart and his crew and all the American troops relying on their life jackets to keep them afloat in this terrible sea. But I couldn't leave the naval ratings on the shore so I went in and picked them up.

Then I went back to where the 911 had gone down and where all the Americans were floating about in the water. I found then that the naval people had been picked up by an American patrol craft going by but he'd left all the Americans still floating about. So we picked them up, one by one, which was difficult because they were quite big blokes and they had all this kit which was soaking wet and the LCA has about two or three feet of freeboard to haul them up. In most cases we had to cut their kit off them with seamen's knives to haul them aboard. I thought we'd rescued everybody but they told me that their radio operator had gone to the bottom because he had his radio equipment, which was very heavy, on him. But everybody else on that boat was picked up. We took them back with the others to the *Empire Javelin*.

When I left A Company on this ridge, some three hundred yards away from the Germans, the tide was lapping at their feet. They couldn't stay there long, the tide was coming in – it comes in at a rate of knots on that beach, it really does flood in. They had to move and, as they went up the beach, the Germans with their machine guns opened fire and wiped them out. Practically all of A Company, the first wave, were wiped out. There were very few survivors by the time the second wave came in. All the people I landed from my boat were killed including the captain, Taylor-Fellers. Practically all of A Company had perished within minutes of walking up the beach. They had no cover, no craters to get into, and as they walked up the beach they were just sitting targets, well, standing targets, and down they went, mowed down by machine guns. They didn't have a chance.

It's lived with me ever since. I can still see those fresh-faced boys getting out of the boat. It comes back to me from time to time, you know, that I was a link in their death. I know I had to do my job, they had to do their job, but I was in some way responsible for putting them there and it does haunt me from time to time. It does haunt me. I still see their faces.

Sub Lieutenant Hilaire Benbow
LCA commander

The idea was that when the assault on Pointe du Hoc had been a success we would get a success signal and follow in and sort of enlarge the force there. But seven o'clock came and we had no signal from them and we waited for a quarter of an hour and still no signal so our instruction was to head in to Vierville. There was a very prominent spire of the church of Vierville and that was our bearing. It was pretty rough and I had the Americans baling out with their steel helmets to get the water out of the LCA because it was coming over the door, and they were very seasick. They had all their weapons and all their wireless stuff in cellophane or whatever it was in those days, plastic, to keep it dry.

Because we had delayed by this quarter of an hour and the weather was so rough, we reached the obstacles. We were supposed to have landed when the sea was seaward of the obstacles, all these poles and crosses and so on, but with the delay the tide had gone in amongst them so to land the troops we had to get in amongst the obstacles. And the craft on my port side hit one of these poles with a mine on the top and in the twinkling of an eye I looked to my left side and there were all these bodies, like statues in a shop window, in various poses, jet black, in what was left of the bowels of this landing craft. It must have been one of the craft from my ship. I never quite worked out who it was because I didn't really know the names of the fellows; I'd only been on that ship about six days and I just didn't know their names. We carried on, straight on.

Leading Seaman John Tarbit
LCA *coxswain*

Although we had been training for eighteen months it never prepared you for actually being under fire. It was only on D-Day morning that it really hit us, I suppose, how horrendous it was going to be. It was on such a gigantic scale and everyone was firing at once and there was smoke and flame everywhere. What took my mind off a lot of it were the weather conditions, the rough sea. To keep the LCA going and stop it from being swamped took your undivided attention, to steer the thing and keep it afloat. You weren't able to stand back and see what was going on around you for the majority of the time. It was only when we got in amongst the beach obstacles that it really hit home that we could be in a lot of trouble, because there was so much firepower going on.

When I started to find my way through the beach obstacles, about a hundred yards from the beach, the Germans started to shell us with mortars. I was so naive to think that they were actually firing at us that I turned round to this young American lieutenant who was standing beside me and I said, 'Look at that. Your destroyers are shelling short, aren't they?' But of course it was German mortars and one of them hit my craft in the engine room, smashed the cylinder head on one of the engines, and it stopped the engine.

We were drifting broadside on to the beach and at the same time the Americans were trying to get off the craft and the machine guns were killing them before they could get to the shore. There were bodies floating in the water amongst the beach obstacles. There was a lot of machine gun and mortar fire and the port side of my LCA was like a pepper pot. We managed to get the other engine going and we managed to claw our way off the beach on one engine. We brought off one American with us because he'd been hit while he was in the landing craft but he died on the way back to the ship.

I hadn't really thought a lot about the Americans until then. But they were prepared to step out of the protection of the landing craft into the water amongst these beach obstacles and at the same time they were being killed off by the machine guns and mortars, you know, and none of them refused to go. It amazed me. I had the greatest respect for their courage. They did what they had to do, even though the odds were against them.

Sub Lieutenant Hilaire Benbow
LCA *commander*

We grounded some distance off the water line. It was a sand bar. We heard the crunch and we revved up our engines and there was smoke at the back and it didn't move and then of course they had to say, 'Well, we can't stick here and be mortared. We've got to get out.' We downed door and the troops all went forward and the craft sort of tilted, the bows went under the water, and it filled with water even more so than with the waves coming over. These craft were petrol-driven and the water got in the engine room and we couldn't get the engine started.

We got out. It was obvious to me that we were not going to get back to the ship, so: over the side. There was nothing we could do. We had no arms; we had no food; we had all intended to go back to our ships. We stayed in the water up to our necks and one felt safe. You could see all the explosions all around you but being under the water, though it was no protection at all, you felt it gave you protection. After being in the water for about an hour or so we decided that we should get on to the beach and we hollowed out troughs in the shingle to drain ourselves off because we were sopping wet. Of course everything was noise and smoke around us.

Eventually we got across the beach. There was a bank and then sort of a

EA 25992

Allied landing craft off Dog and Easy sectors, Omaha Beach, photographed from a B-26 Marauder of the United States Ninth Air Force.

country road and then the walls of bungalow gardens, so we got behind the shelter of this bank and crouched there. There was still fire coming over. The distinctive feature of Omaha Beach was these bluffs, this high land. The others, Sword and all the other beaches, had promenades with residentials on but this had these cliffs on which the Germans were situated and were firing down on the beach.

It was getting on, then. I suppose ten o'clock. We'd left the ship about five and we were getting hungry and these Americans who were also crouching behind this bank very kindly gave us bits out of their rations, biscuits and lumps of cheese and stuff, and that kept us going because we had nothing. The beach seemed to have been closed and I had the feeling that the invasion had failed and that I was going to be a prisoner of war and I was thinking of my parents at home having breakfast. I think we then crossed the road and got behind the shelter of the walls of these bungalow gardens and by then the American troops were getting through the bungalows and presumably scaling these bluffs.

The day dragged on and I saw some very badly wounded men. I saw a chap with his chin off staggering along. We gave out all our handkerchiefs because of course the first-aid personnel had been killed as well. I did have in my possession a little tin box of morphia injections but I didn't give those up. I felt I might need them for my own men.

I'd lost my sea boots in the water and I was in bare feet. I couldn't spend the day in shingle, so, when there was a lull, I crawled back to the water's edge where there was literally a wall about two-foot high of dead bodies all along the surf line. The sea had washed all their clothing off and they were naked, their shirts and so on had all disappeared, washed off by the surf. And the strange thing too was they all had cropped heads and as the sea came inwards the hair lay flat and as the sea receded it all stood up on end so you had all these coconuts if you like, the hair on these heads, going backwards and forwards. I took a pair of boots off one. His toes looked just like mine. I took his boots and went back and put them on.

Stoker Albert Rogers
LBV crew

We thought we had to beach straight away but we got stopped and I suppose we laid off about a quarter of a mile. The coxswain had his own binoculars and we had the naval issue binoculars and we could see what was going on. People running along and going down and not getting up. It was just like being in a ten-pin bowling alley and they were knocking all the pins down together. Something I'll never forget as long as I live.

We were then told to get out the way: an American boat came up and threatened to shoot the coxswain if we didn't move. And being as I was on the Lewis guns I said if he pulled the trigger I'd cut him and the rest of his crew in half. I would have done if he'd pulled the trigger and shot the coxswain. Then a bloke on another of the ships there, wasn't a big ship, it was about the size of an LST, he got a loudhailer and shouted down, 'What's the trouble?' I shouted up, 'He's trying to shoot our coxswain and I'm going cut him in half if he pulls the trigger.' Well, he told him to lower his pistol and hand it to the coxswain – the coxswain had always wanted an American .45 – and off they went. Then this naval officer on this landing craft, he had all scrambled eggs round his hat, he asked us to move, politely, as we were causing chaos because we were so low in the water that they couldn't see us until they were nearly on top of us. We went down to Utah.

Leading Seaman Wally Blanchard
Landing Craft Obstacle Clearance Unit

We'd heard an enormous amount of firing coming from our right – to use the civilian term, starboard to us – along the beach and it was, of course, Omaha. We knew who was going in on Omaha and some of the conveyance of the troops ashore was being carried out by the Royal Navy. This is not generally known but British naval personnel were also on Omaha Beach. Some were there for the same reason as we were on Gold and they were still on that beach along with United States combat engineers, trying to disable explosives and mines, when the first wave of landing craft came in and came under very heavy fire from the German defences, which were very well sited.

We were ordered up to give support. Well, we naturally thought that we were going up there to do what we'd been doing. We might get involved in fighting but the first, primary objective was to disarm whatever mines or explosives we could lay our hands on, to broaden the landing craft front so that you could get more landing craft in. Unfortunately, when we got there, there was an enormous firefight taking place and we had no alternative but to join in.

Leading Seaman Walter Blanchard DSM, who worked to clear mines and obstacles on Gold and Omaha beaches on D-Day. This photograph was taken in 1945, when he was serving in HMS *Newfoundland*.

We got in the water. Practically the first thing I became aware of was a lot of objects in the water and the peculiar colour of the water and the froth. I think everybody that was ever on that beach knows what I mean by this. The noise, the confusion, the stonk were overpowering. You had a heavy bombardment taking place in the sea. You had the cries and the screams, an awful lot of young men, bodies, nudging you in the water. I became, by turns, very afraid, then, as you do, you settle down and I became colder and more angry. The Germans were standing up shooting at them. They were throwing grenades down at them. I thought, 'This isn't right.'

There was a landing craft which was abandoned. I crouched alongside it and I opened fire along with other people. I was aware that there were comrades of mine also in action and exchanging fire. I don't know how long this went on. I have no idea. I remember a lad clutching hold of my ankle. He was an American, badly bleeding. I had a knife on; I cut his equipment off him. The first landing craft that came in on the other side of me was fortunately a Red Cross one, one of ours, bearing ambulance marks. Not that the Germans cared about that, they fired at that as well; after all, they were defending their beachhead. I managed to get a few lads into there.

A surprising thing happened: I don't know how long I'd been at it but I was given ammunition from Americans coming in. Seeing the weapon I was using, they dropped me off spare clips, a whole box of Remington ammunition. I noticed the flashes of course and some of them were 2nd Rangers, which upset me even more because I had trained with some of them.

Now and again there'd be a little lull and I'd spot something that had been uncovered that looked suspiciously like a mine and I would deal with it if I could. I thought, 'I don't want some poor sod to tread on that.' There was enough going on as it was.

And something comes over you. Your actions are almost automatic. I was clipped more than once by bullets or ammunition. It didn't seem to matter. Nothing really hit me. It was pinging and clanging off you like rain. Tracer flying in all directions. Grenades. None of them came near me fortunately but an awful lot of people were being killed on that beach. The Royal Navy decided not to put them in the water where they were told to but were driving them right up the beach and turning them round, to try and give them some cover to get off.

This seemed to go on for an interminable time. Eventually the Rangers did it. Somehow they got off that beach. The other troops were still pinned down but the 2nd Rangers went up that damned cliff. They took an awful lot of casualties trying to do it.

I found a bit of space and was able to get on with some mine clearance and one or two more of our mine people appeared but I think we took quite a few casualties along that beach. Then I was withdrawn from there and repaired to one of our depot craft to get cleaned up, get some food, get a bit of sleep and go back in again to my own beach, Gold Beach, which by this time was secure. There was still fighting going on for Omaha but they had more or less got a good foothold. But that was a terrible, terrible experience. Bear in mind that I had no idea I was going to be an infantryman when I joined the navy and that's basically what I became for that time. I only thank my lucky stars that I knew how and when to use weapons.

During the course of that particular day, that peculiar day, somebody tapped me on the shoulder and when I turned round it was a German. My Remington carbine was up his nose in an instant but he was only trying to surrender. He too was paralysed with fright; he'd been wounded; it turned out he was a German military policeman, a much older man than us, obviously conscripted into the army. I covered him so he wouldn't get hit again, I put him into one of the Red Cross landing craft, a Royal Navy one, and our lads took care of him. And before he left he got something out of his tunic pocket and pressed it into my hand. It looked like an Iron Cross; it turned out to be a German police long-service medal, which I still have to this day.

That's how action is. There's so much confusion; surprising things happen. You look along the beach and suddenly you see a whole warship, a minesweeper, she's struck a mine, she seems to go up in the air and disintegrate completely. People scream, they shout. They call out for mothers and Lord knows what. They all seem younger than you. I was eighteen.

Sub Lieutenant Hilaire Benbow
LCA commander
We spent the afternoon making our way slowly along this beach to where activity was happening, things were coming in and going out and so on. One quite large ship had been somehow beached and grounded, bows-on, to the beach and we came round the bows and that was a shock, because there were all these bodies, stretcher cases, laid out in the shelter of this great ship.

I was the only British officer around and a lot of British naval ratings who'd been shipwrecked in the same way as we had, either blown up on a mine or hit a sandbar or something, they all came to me. I had sixteen of them at least, maybe more, some from my own ship, others from other ships, and I got them all down to the water's edge and I went aboard this American LCT and said, 'I've got a party of British naval ratings here. Could you take us back to England?' 'Yes, all right.' So I said, 'Come on, lads,' and we walked up the ramp and on board this LCT.

As we left we listened to the radio and there was Howard Marshall, the sort of Richard Dimbleby of his day, with a very deep voice, very slow. He was commenting on the success of it all and how it was all going so smoothly and to plan and I could have smashed that radio because it was so untrue as far as Omaha was concerned.

Overnight they transferred us to a large troopship and that came back within sight of the Isle of Wight and then all the way round the coast to Tilbury and we were debriefed in Tilbury. I knew there was great restriction on telephones but I was in an office and there was a telephone and I dialled up my mother and father and I got through and I said, 'Hello, I'm safe, I'm here.'

Commander Felix Lloyd-Davies
HMS Glasgow (Royal Navy cruiser)
Omaha was of course quite the worst and bloodiest landing of the whole lot. At one-thirty that afternoon the American 1st Division and other troops were still on the beach and hadn't got off, having suffered incredible casualties. They had over two thousand men killed and wounded on the beach. We closed in as far as we could until the ship was practically aground and with the destroyers started bombarding the emplacements with broadsides of six-inch, and the other ships were doing the same. Eventually the Americans got off the beach but they were only about a mile-and-a-half inland when dark came.

Brigadier David Belchem
21st Army Group planning staff
It was a tremendous achievement of the American infantry that they hung on and, incidentally, justified the policy of utilising highly experienced divisions in a sandwich formation with new, unbaptised divisions. The 1st US Infantry

Division, which I think was one of the best in the Allied armies, was involved in this and only a division of that calibre could have done it. Assisted by the Rangers, by the way.

Sub Lieutenant Jimmy Green
LCA *flotilla commander*

I remember getting back on board the *Javelin* and offloading the troops we'd brought back, the people we took out of the water and the LCA crew we'd picked up off the beach. We made sure they were off-loaded and people went to the sickbay to get their wounds dealt with.

And then I don't remember a thing after that. I must have flaked out. I must have gone and had something to eat but I don't remember it. Don't remember talking to anybody at all. In fact the next thing I remember was when the *Empire Javelin* entered Plymouth Harbour to the sounds of the sirens of all the ships. We'd lost a third of our craft in Normandy and they could see the vacant spots on the davits where the six LCAs had been and they knew where we'd been, and they really gave us a welcome I shall never forget.

UTAH BEACH

Utah was the westernmost beach of the invasion. Thirteen miles west of Omaha, it was a low-lying strip of coastline, nine miles wide and backed by dunes and marshland, at the south-east corner of the Cherbourg/Cotentin peninsula.

A successful thrust here, hoped the D-Day planners, would lead in subsequent days to the isolation of the peninsula and the capture of the important port of Cherbourg. The United States Army's 4th Infantry Division was tasked with making the assault, forging the beachhead and reaching the US 101st Airborne Division, which, with the 82nd Airborne, would have dropped inland during the night to secure the western flank. The first landing craft hit the beach at 0630 hours. The British contribution to events on Utah was primarily in the form of naval assistance, which included many landing craft crews. These were employed not only in taking men and armour to the shore but also in landing stores.

Of all the beaches assaulted on D-Day, Utah was the least costly to take.

It was not problem-free: early confusion was caused by strong currents and poor visibility, which led to many units landing in the wrong locations, and by the mining of several command landing craft. Fortunately, the Americans met light opposition only. Accurate naval gunfire had silenced many of the enemy positions while many soldiers found they beached in places considerably less fortified than their planned landing sites.

Once ashore, engineers and others worked hard to clear paths off the beach, but it took time. Reinforcements and the incoming tide caused congestion, as they did on other beaches, which compelled some units, to their cost, to try to find their way forward through minefields before they were swept. By one o'clock in the afternoon, however, the 4th Infantry was through and advancing inland and firm contact was soon made with the 101st, which had secured the beach exits despite a badly scattered drop. Well before nightfall and for the loss – according to recent estimates – of around three hundred men killed, wounded and missing, the 4th Infantry Division was ashore in force and had achieved the majority of its D-Day objectives.

Sub Lieutenant Herbert Male
LCT crew

We were attached to the American Assault Engineers. We were loaded with tanks and we went into Utah about twenty minutes after H-hour: H-plus-twenty. We saw not one German aircraft over the beaches all the time I was over there. There were lots of mines on the beaches and obstructions that had to be got through but we had a team of underwater divers who'd disposed of most of those anyway. We weren't bothered at all. We had a free run into the beach. Everything went not bad at all. I'd do a D-Day once a week than go back to Tobruk once a year.

Lieutenant Richard Charles Bird
LCT crew

We went into the beach at 8.45 in the morning. It wasn't as bad as I thought it was going to be. We were expected to be lost but although we got a lot of shellfire it wasn't too bad and all our flotilla got off actually.

The fellows we took were very good. They were the 22nd Infantry and they were like American commandos. Very good, they were, very good. Real professionals. They were a bit like Errol Flynn; they went running up the beaches. We wanted to get off, of course, and I remember the old captain was going around shaking hands, saying, 'For God's sake, get off,' because once we got rid of all our vehicles and so forth we were allowed to come off. We had to form up and go right down all the beaches to the Sword area.

Stoker Albert Rogers
LBV crew

We went straight in. We beached there. Then we had a row. All of a sudden military police came up, what they called 'snowdrops' in the American Navy. 'You can't beach there!' Then a two-and-a-half ringer [Royal Navy lieutenant commander] came up and said, 'What's the trouble?' I told him. He said, 'What have you got on there?' He sent the snowdrop to have a look and he came running back and he said, 'They've got jerrycans of petrol!' This two-and-a-half ringer said, 'How many is there?' I said, 'Five hundred.' Now, where these trucks come from, I don't know. But they were there unloading those jerrycans of petrol like nobody's business.

Lieutenant Richard Charles Bird
LCT crew

The organisation was terrific. It was no good having all the vehicles one end of the beach and no petrol. We were all carrying different things so you had to go in on your spot because they had it all organised, where the petrol dumps were going to be and so forth.

Tom Treanor
War correspondent

We came sliding and slewing in on some light breakers and grounded. I stepped ashore on France, walking up a beach where men were moving casually about carrying equipment inshore. Up the coast, a few hundred yards, German shells were pounding in regularly, but in our area it was peacefully busy. 'How did you make out?' I asked one of the men. 'It was reasonably soft,' he said. 'The Germans had some machine-gun posts and some high-velocity guns on the palisades and made it a little hot at first. They waited until the landing craft dropped their ramps, then opened up on them while the men

American soldiers of the US 7th Corps wading ashore on Utah Beach.

were still inside. In a few cases we took heavy casualties. Then the navy went to work on the German guns and it wasn't long before they were quiet.'

The general lack of fortifications at this point was astonishing. The barbed wire consisted of four single strands such as we use at home to fence in cattle. A man could get through by pushing down on one wire and lifting up another, provided they weren't booby-trapped. The engineers and beach battalions, however, had blown gaps in the wire through which we could move vehicles. A few dead lay about and some wounded were here and there on stretchers awaiting transport to ships out at sea. All up and down the broad beach as far as I could see, men, jeeps, bulldozers and other equipment were moving about like ants. A few columns of black greasy smoke marked equipment which had been hit by shellfire and set on fire. The German shelling continued steadily at various points up and down the beach but so far had not reached the area in which I was walking. It would work over an area, then move on to another. It was accurate, landing for the most part close to the water's edge, and I saw one small landing craft catch fire after taking a hit. Men came scurrying out of it into water waist-deep. From time to time there were huge concussions as the engineers set off demolitions. The ground would shake and the troops would throw themselves violently on the ground.

I climbed a rock embankment and came to a piece of flat land where hundreds of men were digging slit trenches. When they got down about a foot-and-a-half they struck water. Some of them were lying in the water and I asked them if there was much shelling. 'There is when there is,' one man said. 'Right now there isn't; but when it comes, it sure comes.' I asked him what German fortifications he could point out. He showed me some tunnels at the top of the palisade – the palisade rises above the beach along this stretch of coast. There were five or six positions I could make out, nothing particularly formidable.

I walked over to an aerial, which seemed to mark a command post. A colonel and a major were sitting beside a slit trench half-filled with water and I said to the colonel, 'Sir, I'm a war correspondent.' He looked up from a map, fiercely, and the major said, 'I think you'd better stop back later. You might try going up that path there where you see those men, if you can make it. Watch out for mines. It's heavily mined.'

A long column of men was winding up the palisade on a narrow path. They weren't moving. At the skyline they seemed to be knotted up. To reach the palisade I joined a column who were wading across a slew. The water came nearly to their armpits and they had to hold their rifles and equipment over their heads. The water was rather warm but the bottom was a slimy mess. When a man got to the far side of the slew he would always stop, in a maddening way, holding the rest of us up. We shouted angrily but when we got there each one of us stopped too: the reeds on the far bank were loaded with mines. One man lay at the top of the bank, dead. The mines had been marked with bits of paper and soldiers at the top advised us just how to climb so as not to venture into dangerous ground. There were more dead men along the narrow path that led up to the palisade.

The column had stopped moving and I began to step past men, following a captain. Suddenly a voice said, 'Watch yourself, fella. That's a mine.' A soldier sprawled on the bank was speaking. He had one foot half blown off. He'd stepped on a mine a short time earlier. Now, while he waited for litter-bearers, he was warning other soldiers about other mines in that vicinity. I can stand the dead but the wounded horrify me and I only looked at him to thank him. He looked very tired but perfectly collected. 'What you need is the medics,' I said. 'I'll try and get them for you when I go back down.' 'Yeah,' he said. 'But how will they get up here?' He was right. The pathway was so clogged with men and so heavily mined that it was impassable. The engineers would have to get up there first.

The column didn't move forward. The captain I was following stopped and so did I. I asked him his name and he said he was Louis Hilly of Cincinnati. 'It looks like they shell around here a bit,' I said, pointing to some shallow craters. 'No,' said Hilly, 'those are all mines.' At the top of the palisade the knot of men had gotten to its feet and it looked like the line might move. One man darted over the skyline and almost immediately afterwards we heard the speedy burst of a German machine gun, then a few stray rifle shots. The bullets cracked overhead and everyone instinctively ducked lower. These were some troops who had never seen combat before and the bullets must have seemed close to them, although we were a hundred feet below the skyline.

The line remained stationary and I looked down the beach and the sea. Landing craft of all descriptions were sliding in through the low surf disgorging men who moved through the water with amazing alacrity. As soon as they got ashore and saw the men moving about calmly they seemed to steady down and began to walk quietly themselves.

I waited a spell longer and the line didn't move so I began to make my way down the path again. It was slow work. The soldiers were so alarmed that I would step on a mine right next to them that one man told me to walk on his back rather than step off the path. I promised I would try to get the engineers up to disarm the mines. While I was going down the slope the Germans began shelling our area. It was hard not to throw myself down on the ground willy-nilly but the thought of those mines kept me from it.

I took a last look at the greatest armada in history. It was too immense to describe. There were so many transports on the horizon that in the faint haze they looked like a shoreline. Destroyers were almost on the beach occasionally jolting out a salvo that was like a punch on the chin. Farther out, but still incredibly close to the beach, sat our huge battle-wagons and cruisers. Overhead, formations of fighters swept swiftly through the air with nothing to do. During this entire day I never saw a German plane or spoke to a man who had seen one.

I reached a small command post on the flat where a dispatch had just been handed to two captains. It said that our troops were a mile inland, but we could still hear small-arms fire: they were apparently being harassed by snipers but so far had met nothing heavy in the way of emplacements or an armoured force. Just as I reached the beach the German artillery came down in earnest. I dived into a slit trench but a man was in ahead of me so I ducked under a bulldozer where I felt very safe. The only trouble was that I didn't want to get out from under the bulldozer after the shelling had stopped. The stuff was coming in close enough to send pebbles flying in and I felt pretty badly shaken for a period.

Pushing Inland

We heard the sound of bagpipes, and the firing all stopped.
It had been noisy, what with us firing at Jerry and Jerry firing at us,
and then you could hear the bagpipes.

Securing a foothold on the Normandy coast was not the only British aim of 6 June. Troops landing on Sword and Gold, as on all Allied beaches, had been set additional objectives for that day. Consequently, as each beach was brought sufficiently under control, the assault and follow-up forces began fighting inland to achieve them.

Advancing south from Sword, British commandos of Lord Lovat's 1st Special Service Brigade made swiftly for the Orne River and Caen Canal bridges. Lovat's orders were to link up as quickly as possible with the men of the 6th Airborne Division holding on inland. If that could be accomplished, the commandos were to cross the bridges and take up positions alongside the paratroopers.

The principal thrust from Sword was aimed at the city of Caen. A series of enemy strongpoints and gun batteries – the British code-named many of them after motorcars – were to be neutralised en route. One, Hillman, proved particularly formidable. Prolonged resistance there slowed the whole southward advance. So did a counter-attack by elements of the German 21st Panzer Division. Although, by nightfall, a forward troop of the Staffordshire Yeomanry had made it as far as Lébisey, a mile from Caen, most of the city was not to fall to the Allies until 9 July.

Inland from Gold, the men of the 50th Infantry Division successfully made contact with Canadian troops from Juno and in the evening captured the coastal town of Arromanches, which had been identified by the planners as a good spot for a Mulberry harbour. The division's main objective, though, was the important road junction at Bayeux, eight miles from the coast. British troops reached the edge of the town that evening and it was occupied, peacefully, the next day.

REACHING THE AIRBORNE

Piper Bill Millin
HQ 1st Special Service Brigade
I was up front playing the bagpipes, Lord Lovat behind, the rest of the troop stretched out behind, and all along the side was these tall poplar trees and piping away there I could see a sniper in a tree on the right-hand side of the road. Then there was a flash and the sound of a shot and I looked round and Lovat was on his knee so I stopped playing. Next thing, about half a dozen commandos rushed past me firing at this character, he was struggling down the tree by this time, and then he disappeared into the cornfield. I could see his head bobbing up and down. Lovat was shooting, his rifle was blazing away, and then we stopped and Lovat sent some commandos into the field to drag the body out and we dumped him at the side of the road. Lovat said, 'Well, start playing your pipes again, piper.' He wanted the Paras to know that we were coming.

Private Stanley Wilfred Scott
3 Commando
We was the leading troop of the brigade, 3 Troop of 3 Commando. It's down in several books as 3 Troop of 6 Commando but everybody makes the same mistake. Five of us somehow got in front. One was Campbell; one was me; one was Jimmy Synnott, I think; Ozzy was another one. But there was five of us – a little detached party – like yellow jerseys going first. Not that we wanted to, we were just going.

At Le Port opposite the church we passed a Para sitting with his leg up on a chair. He had a shattered leg and he was guarding this little knot of prisoners and as we come along, like, he looks at us, didn't he? And what he said was unprintable. British Army language. Something like, 'Where the flaming hell have you been? About time.' There was none of the bagpipe-playing and cheering and all that crap.

Commandos move inland from Sword Beach.

Anyway, we turned left past Benouville and we're looking down the road at the bridge, we're about seventy-five yards from the bridge, and it's like a beehive. There was rounds hitting it from all sides, there was rounds ricocheting off and splatting and hitting. Nobody's round it. Everybody has got their heads down – it's no good standing. Most of it's coming from the maternity home in Benouville. The Germans was in there.

Somebody says, 'Get on your bikes and go like the clappers. You'll probably get away with it.' Well, you're soldiers, you're there to do a job. 'OK, let's go.' We all jump on our bikes and away we go, pedalling like bleeding mad. I shot across that bridge and on the right-hand side there was a German vehicle burning and I shot behind that, and that's solid, that's protection. Jimmy Synnott and the others went to the left-hand side where there was a dip, like a ditch. They shot into there and got down. Campbell was just the unlucky one. He got clobbered. He got hit straight through the neck, fell down in one big lump, him and the bike and all that. We wasn't there long as the rest of 3 Troop of 3 Commando come up.

Private William Gray
2nd Battalion, Oxfordshire and Buckinghamshire Light Infantry
It was while we was in Le Port that we heard the sound of bagpipes, and the firing all stopped. It had been noisy, what with us firing at Jerry and Jerry firing at us, and then you could hear the bagpipes.

Corporal W. R. Howard
2nd Battalion, Oxfordshire and Buckinghamshire Light Infantry
Lo and behold, probably five minutes later, chaps with green berets came streaming along the road who happened to be Lord Lovat's commandos. Walking along with Lord Lovat was his piper, Bill Millin, blowing the bagpipes, and we just sat there and watched in amazement as these green-bereted commandos came along. There seemed to be an endless stream of them. There must have been six or seven hundred of them moving through.

Piper Bill Millin
HQ 1st Special Service Brigade
I stopped immediately across the road from the café and there was a right battle going on and huge columns of black smoke. Even where I was standing

I could hear the shrapnel or the bullets, whatever, hitting off the metal side of the bridge. The wounded were being carried up from along the canal banks and into the cafe. It was a real hot spot. Lovat went forward to speak to John Howard and he said, 'John, today we are making history.' Then Lovat came back to me and said, 'Right, we'll cross over.' I put my pipes on my shoulder and he said, 'No, don't play. Wait until you get over.'

Private William Gray
2nd Battalion, Oxfordshire and Buckinghamshire Light Infantry

We were firing from near the churchyard at Le Port, firing across the bridge into the trees where we suspected the snipers were. We couldn't see them, we just did all we could to help the commandos get across the bridge, but they were under quite heavy fire and we saw loads of commandos killed. They were in single file dashing across in sections from one side of the bridge to the other side but they were getting heavy casualties. They set up a Vickers on the corner of the bridge and were spraying the trees alongside the canal, the side where the gliders had landed. In fact I've heard since that some snipers had got in amongst the three gliders and were using them as cover.

Major John Howard
2nd Battalion, Oxfordshire and Buckinghamshire Light Infantry

A lot of them wore their green berets instead of their steel helmets and there were rather more casualties for that reason than there might have been. But their job wasn't to fight around the bridges, it was to get across the bridge as soon as possible to help the Sixth Airborne fighting the other side of the river and they did that pretty well. They certainly didn't hang about the bridges because there was too much shooting going on.

Piper Bill Millin
HQ 1st Special Service Brigade

We got to the other side and Lovat said, 'Right, play now and keep playing all the way along this road, about two hundred yards, until you come to the Ranville Bridge and keep playing right across that. No matter what, just keep playing.'

Piping along the road, we come to the Ranville Bridge. It was a narrow bridge, metal sides with open railings, and I could see two Airborne on the other side in a slit trench dug in. And as I'm piping along I've got my eye on those two chaps and they were going, 'Get back!' and pointing to the sides of the river, meaning that this bridge was under fire. So I looked round at Lovat and he's walking along as if he's out for a walk around his estate and he was going, 'Carry on, carry on.'

I piped along that bridge playing the tune 'The Blue Bonnets over the Border' and got over and the two Airborne chaps in the slit trench were looking at me like I were crazy. And then Lovat came over, there's several casualties following him on the bridge, and from across the road appears this tall Airborne officer, red beret on, marching along with his arm outstretched. And he said, 'I'm very pleased to see you, old boy,' and Lovat said, 'And we're very pleased to see you, old boy. Sorry we're two and a half minutes late.' We were more than two and half minutes late. Well, that's the famous words of the link-up of the Airborne and the commandos.

Private William Edward Lloyd
2nd Battalion, East Yorkshire Regiment

We got a section dug in with the Sixth Airborne before the commandos got there. There was a company that set off and about nine men got through and Sergeant Thompson was there dug in on the River Orne with those nine men. They was only the few that got through out of a company of men. When you talk about Lovat we get annoyed 'cause everybody has the idea that the commandos went in first on Pegasus Bridge, which is wrong. Admittedly we wasn't there in strength but we was there. Tommo will tell you he watched Lovat and his commandos walk on to the bridge.

Sergeant Arthur Thompson
2nd Battalion, East Yorkshire Regiment

When we got there, there was lots of firing going off but you couldn't see where it was coming from. We just got ourselves dug in and remained there all night. And I tell you what, that place will never be forgotten because we were bitten to death. It's all swamps around that side. The only thing we could find that would give us any peace was anti-gas ointment so we used nearly all this anti-gas ointment, rubbing around our necks, our knees and our arms and whatever, and our knees swelled up like footballs. It's not bloody pleasant.

THE DRIVE ON CAEN

Captain Darby Robert Houlton-Hart
2nd Battalion, Lincolnshire Regiment
We went over with these airborne collapsible bicycles. It was intended, I think, that we were to cycle up the Orne canal and perhaps get as far as Caen, the first day. Of course, when we got ashore – a pretty average shambles – everything didn't go according to plan and we dumped all our bicycles and reverted to being ordinary old infantry soldiers.

Private Lionel Roebuck
2nd Battalion, East Yorkshire Regiment
We set off through an orchard, and the orchard, because of all the shelling, was amazing. All the trees had had their branches ripped off completely. It was just a load of trunks sticking up and all the branches were strewn around the ground.

We came across a Bren carrier that was smoking and there were the bodies of two dead chaps inside. It had obviously been hit by a shell and then set on fire. There was nothing we could do for them so we just went past. All the animals as well, the cows and the horses and everything else, they were all laid on their backs with their legs stuck in the air just like posts, all stiff and bloated. Then I saw my first dead commando. He was laid out at the side of the road. He was the first dead chap I'd seen really close to. He'd got flesh just like a wax dummy, the flesh, so cold and solid.

When we went into the village of Colleville, which is just a few hundred yards further on from where the dead commando was, a few more of my mates popped up from over the wall. Arthur was one of them and a lad called Winterbotham from Leeds and they looked over the wall and they warned us, 'Careful, there's a sniper up in a high building over in the village.' Just then I noticed there was a woman stood in a doorway just on the right-hand side of the road and she had a small child with her and she just stood there even though the shelling was going on. She was dressed in dark, drab clothes with a long black skirt and she didn't say a word to us as we went past. She had a real depressed look on her face, really unhappy, no greeting, just looked as we went past.

Troops and vehicles wait to move forward from a point just beyond Sword Beach.

Private William Snell
1st Battalion, King's Own Scottish Borderers

As we passed through one village a thing that has always stuck with me was that I looked up and there was a pair of legs stuck on the telegraph wires and I looked along the pavement and there were bodies of East Yorkshires, dead. Some of them were without heads, without legs.

Trooper Berkeley Meredith
Sherman tank driver, Staffordshire Yeomanry

The fields of Normandy are divided by hedges, which are called *bocage*, and are very good for sheltering infantry or if you want to shelter behind and just peer over the top. And we saw some movement in the *bocage*, we guessed it was a platoon of enemy infantry, so we shot at them with machine-gun fire. There seemed to be some movement still but no response so we edged out to look over the hedge. What we'd done was to hit some poor old French cow which was in agony. Another ludicrous thing was that in Normandy, in the heat of battle, we felt that we couldn't leave this wretched animal in its agony. We tried to depress the machine gun but we were too close to it, so I took the breech-block out and then we sighted this poor animal down the barrel of the gun and put it out of its misery.

Sergeant Major Russell King
2nd Battalion, Royal Warwickshire Regiment

In front of us was a big gap in a hedgerow and I remember this tank in front just flame-throwing this gap and, when we got up, there was this bloke, charred, like a bit of bloody coal, stuck up against a tree. Terrible.

Captain Darby Robert Houlton-Hart
2nd Battalion, Lincolnshire Regiment

We got into position behind a hedgerow. Another officer and myself were the only two who had been in the Dunkirk thing – none of the others had seen any action – and we were being shot at so I thought it was my duty to try and see who was shooting at us. I went to the end of the hedgerow and by a big tree I searched the ground with my binoculars. And I'd half turned to go back when I got a whole burst of Spandau fire which hit the rifle I was carrying which shot up in the air. I thought I'd been stung by a bee, but I hadn't: I'd

Passing a memorial to French dead of the First World War, British troops press inland from Sword Beach.

had a finger removed and the top of another one. And that was me. I was patched up by the stretcher-bearers and I was told to shove off. I went back to the field dressing station and I felt a bit bogus there. I remember taking tea round to some wretched fellow who had been in the Tank Corps and he was all burnt and was lying on a stretcher.

Private William Edward Lloyd
2nd Battalion, East Yorkshire Regiment
I took part in the attack on Daimler, which was a big gun position, a 155-millimetre gun. When we attacked Daimler I think they'd had enough. We came from the backside of it and we flung a few grenades in and I think the gunners had really had sufficient and we took about seventy prisoners there.

Private Lionel Roebuck
2nd Battalion, East Yorkshire Regiment
In the blockhouse there was a picture of Hitler in a frame about two-foot by two-foot-six on the wall by the desk. I smashed it to the ground with the butt of my rifle in anger. To think that that chap had caused all this trouble for us.

Corporal John Barnes
Sherman tank commander, 13th/18th Hussars
The infantry were held down so we were told to come back and help out towards the front of Morris. The squadron leader told Mr Smith to take five tanks and go and see if we can make an impression, see if we can't force Morris to surrender by pumping more rounds of ammunition into the steel doors. So we set off across this field in arrow formation and half way across I got hit twice, another tank got hit and Corporal Collins' tank got hit, and we turned round and got into a safe position. I think they were only two-pounder guns as they didn't go through my tank, they hit the side, but one driver had his eyes taken out and Corporal Collins had his leg taken off.

Corporal Arthur John Blizzard
1st Battalion, Suffolk Regiment
B Company took Morris. Morris was easy. Hillman was where we lost quite a few.

Private Leslie Perry
1st Battalion, Suffolk Regiment

The American air force was supposed to bomb Hillman on the morning of D-Day but they said that there was low cloud and they couldn't see it properly and not one of their bombs hit the target – they landed in fields all around it. And we were supposed to be supported by naval gunfire from one of the destroyers but the Royal Navy forward observer coming off the landing craft was hit and knocked out on the beach with his signaller. So no messages got back to the ship and we got no naval gunfire, so it had to be taken using just infantry and sappers. We had two tanks that was firing at the steel cupolas over the machine-gun positions but the seventeen-pounder anti-tank shells were just bouncing off.

Sergeant George Rayson
1st Battalion, Suffolk Regiment

We was the first platoon supposed to be in this Hillman attack. It must've been the size of a bloody football pitch, really, with several guns on the top, which we couldn't see. It looked as though they'd piled up dirt and then built this place in the middle, like. There was an underground barracks, electric light, a hospital; everything was done there. I think there was about twenty gun emplacements on the top, machine guns, and round it triple Dannet [wire] and a thirty-foot minefield.

We'd trained for this so we knew exactly what to expect. We had an engineer officer and two men and they cleared the mines from the first lot of wire, about six foot wide, and put some white tape out. The idea was to run through there, you see. And along came these D Company blokes and put a couple of Bangalore torpedoes out. I don't think they went off at first, as the officer had to go back. Anyhow, they blew a great big void and we ran in.

Well, the first two blokes got killed to start with. Right opposite was a machine gun in a turret, the turret was made of glass of all things, and all the guy in it done was put the gun down right where we were and killed the first two, a corporal and a private soldier. Of course we all got down quick and he couldn't get the gun down further, otherwise he'd have had the lot of us. We laid there quite a long time and suddenly everything went quiet. The bloke had disappeared inside. The company commander came running over and he said, 'Come on, Rayson.' There was six or eight in front of me and they turned inside that gun by the bank and I got fired at and I threw myself down on the ground. Landed behind the corporal that had already been shot. Cor, his head. Just a mass of blood, brains and bone.

Private Leslie Perry
1st Battalion, Suffolk Regiment

One of our chaps, Jim Hunter, he was in a sunken road very close. He got up close to the wire and then when they blew the second lot he was laying up the bank. And this German kept firing this machine gun and it kept spattering him with earth and he said to his mate, 'I've bloody well had enough of this,' only his language was a little bit stronger than that as British soldiers sometimes use. He said, 'I've had enough of this, I'm going to have a go,' and he picked up his Bren and advanced on this German position firing as he went. He said afterwards, 'There was bullets spattering all around me but I was so annoyed I just didn't care.' This German saw him coming but he ducked down and he dropped a couple of grenades in the emplacement, then he jumped down into the zigzag trench and as he turned one corner of the trench a German came round the other. They both fired together and Jim is only about five foot two and the German's bullet went right through his helmet and out the other side and creased across the top of his head. He got the German in the chest and killed him and he carried on and got one or two others and cleared the position. He was awarded the DCM for what he did.

Sergeant George Rayson
1st Battalion, Suffolk Regiment

I found myself in a deep trench. Course, the others had gone up the front, I was in there all alone and I couldn't see over the top, I wasn't tall enough. Talk about feeling lonely. And I went up and kept zigzagging and eventually I caught the few up ahead of me. I said, 'What you all stopped for?' There was a corporal amongst them and he said, 'Round the corner, Captain Ryley, Lieutenant Tooley, Corporal Stares, they're all dead.' Apparently they went round the corner and got a burst of machine-gun fire.

Of course we didn't know what to do, really. We was there trying to work things out and Jerry chucked some stick bombs and they just missed us. One or two of our blokes threw some stick grenades back and that quietened them down and everything went quiet. And we were just deciding what to do when the runner came round the corner and he said, 'You've all got to get out as fast as you can!' Cor, we didn't want no telling. I beat all Jesse Owens' records going out there. I did and all. What had happened was, they'd decided it was too much and got hold of some more tanks.

They got the tanks in a line and we went behind the first tank. That went up the slope and turned right and the other went straight up and the other turned left, there was a group of men behind each and we took the place without a lot of bother after that. The tanks blew up all the guns and Jerry done a bunk down below.

Corporal John Barnes
Sherman tank commander, 13th/18th Hussars

There were a lot of slit trenches around Hillman and you couldn't get the guns down so a lot of crew commanders just threw grenades in the trenches. You wasn't worried. It wasn't like it was before: 'Play up and play the game.' You didn't care who was in there – they got it this time.

Corporal Arthur John Blizzard
1st Battalion, Suffolk Regiment

Next day we had to bury the dead and if you're a young fellow and you haven't buried the dead before it's the biggest pain of all. What we done was, we got the Germans and buried them as well as we could and took their tags off and our own boys' tags and sent them back. We were all that day burying the Germans. It was a terrible battle, this Hillman.

Inside Hillman I saw a big metal cupboard in the corner and opened the door and it was crammed with bottles from the top to the bottom, and when I picked one up it was five-star brandy. I said, 'Look at this, Alec.' He said, 'Is it all right?' I pulled the top off and stuck my finger in and tasted it. After me and him had drunk the first bottle, I said, 'We feel better now, don't we?' And he said, 'Yeah.'

'Hang on,' I said. 'There's a door here.' And I pulled the iron bolt back and opened the door and there they all stood. Sixty-odd Germans, I counted. There was Alec and me and the commandant of the area with his hands above his head. He gives me his camera, he gives me his dagger and he says, 'Kaput.' Well, he could have 'Kaput' us as easy as pie if he'd wanted. But I lined them all up and marched them down the road to the platoon where

Inland from Sword Beach, an M10 'Tank Destroyer' provides support for troops of the 2nd Battalion, East Yorkshire Regiment.

Sergeant Booth took over and I never heard another word about it. Only lies in books about how they were taken.

Private William Edward Lloyd
2nd Battalion, East Yorkshire Regiment

Me and a lad called Heslop was taking some prisoners and there's this officer stopped us and said, 'Where you two going?' We says, 'We're taking these prisoners to Brigade HQ,' and he said, 'Well, B Company are very short of men, so one of you has got to go to B Company.' Before I could say anything, this Heslop turned round and said, 'I'll go to B Company.' That left me with these two prisoners.

Every time their hands dropped a little bit I just tipped them with a bayonet and how they managed to keep their hands up I don't know. But if they hadn't kept their hands up there was no two ways about it, there was only one answer and that was to shoot them. Because, let's face it, the Geneva Convention is all thrown to the wall when you get into action. I don't care what anybody says, it's all thrown to the wall.

Trooper Berkeley Meredith
Sherman tank driver, Staffordshire Yeomanry

We saw some prisoners of war. There was no way we could stop and deal with them and they just wandered on. They looked jolly relieved to be going in the direction they were going with their hands up. I don't think they were very high-quality troops.

Further in we were signalled to by a German who wanted to surrender. To this day I don't know why we did it but we stopped. We didn't know what to do with him. There were no ground troops with us to whom we could hand him over, we weren't prepared just to let him wander in case he did any damage to anybody further back, so we'd got two options. We either finished him off or we could take him with us. In the event we put him in our turret. That tends to amaze me now. But he did as he was told because I'd got my pistol out and we got rid of him very quickly when we came across some infantry.

Lieutenant Lionel Knight
Sherman tank commander, Staffordshire Yeomanry

My troop were down in a dip prior to going up a lane to Lébisey when a counter-attack came in from the Germans which would basically have cut us off. But the rest of our regiment, which was behind me, could see it coming and they were able to fire down on the incoming tanks fortunately and we were OK. Well, we went up the lane and the first sighting I had of a German on French soil was when a motorcycle-sidecar came round the corner at the top of the hill. I let off a few shots at him but he got in a dip and the last I saw of him he'd tumbled off into the wood leaving the bike and sidecar there.

Trooper Berkeley Meredith
Sherman tank driver, Staffordshire Yeomanry

There were a few infantry lying ahead of us on the road, dead. Further up, beyond which we couldn't see, there was a bridge over the road with an archway. I think it was the railway that led through that area into Caen but going ahead on our own we would have been completely exposed without support.

The wood we were in was Lébisey Wood and I think it was as far as any unit got on D-Day and for this our commander, Lionel Knight, was awarded the MC. But tanks don't stay out in woods or the open at night, they laager, and we withdrew then to an area where the whole squadron laagered together. But on that first day we'd reached Lébisey Wood and it took us another month of hard bloody fighting to get back to that same point.

Lieutenant Lionel Knight
Sherman tank commander, Staffordshire Yeomanry

I think it was about another four to six weeks before we got to Caen eventually, but, if we'd had another infantry regiment that day, we could have done it. Still, there we are. That's war, isn't it?

311

THE PUSH FOR BAYEUX

Major John Mogg
9th Battalion, Durham Light Infantry
We came toward the beaches about nine o'clock in the morning: we were the reserve battalion of the reserve brigade. It was a scene of a lot of activity by the beach brigade trying to make holes through the mines; there were flail tanks trying to flail up the mines. There were one or two carriers that had been brewed up; there was the odd tank that had been brewed up. There were medical stations set up by the previous battalions. There was not a great deal of shelling. We had no casualties at all. It was almost peaceful. You heard an awful lot of noise going on ahead of you. Destroyed pillboxes were another thing you saw along the side of the beach, destroyed either by our Typhoons or our naval fire or artillery fire or by tanks.

Private Richard Atkinson
9th Battalion, Durham Light Infantry
It was noisy and the smell of cordite stuck in your nostrils. Cordite and death. And there was a lot of smoke hanging around. The Beachmaster was there. I can remember him shouting, 'Get off my bloody beach!' And I says, 'I don't want to be on your beach!' That was to relieve the tension.

Lieutenant Herbert Jalland
8th Battalion, Durham Light Infantry
We were intent on just getting through, getting away from the beach, the emphasis being that we must get to Bayeux. Nobody wanted to stay on the beach because we knew that it wouldn't be very long before German artillery ranged on it or German bombers came. We were expecting a real humdinging do and I don't think I was alone in wanting to get away from that particular spot as quickly as possible.

Private Richard Atkinson
9th Battalion, Durham Light Infantry
Montgomery's orders were that you had to be inland. You were told, 'When you come off the beach, go up this little ramp, turn sharp-left, de-waterproof, drive on to the road and from there you start.' Up to the road you had orders

and from there you were on your own. You'd see an officer or maybe bump into one of your sergeants and you'd say, 'Have you seen any of our lot?' 'Follow the signs.' And you picked them up. There'd be a stake stuck in the ground with a 'TT' pinned on it or there'd be a doorway with a 'TT' and an arrow-point on it. Things like that. By this time the Division was charging inland, going hell for leather.

Major Patrick Barrass
2nd Battalion, Essex Regiment
You've got to remember that we all came off different landing craft. I was all right with my company and half of somebody else's company but that half company had to marry off with its other half coming off another LCI, so there was quite a bit of reorganising to be done before we could all get into our proper groups ready to advance. We then started to carry out what we had gone over there for, which was to make for Bayeux. I remember that A Company started off first on bicycles and carriers. They went ahead and the rest of us followed. St Suplice was the place we were aiming at which was about five miles away inland towards Bayeux. We weren't really sure where the enemy was so we were going in battle formation. We were in file behind one another and we went up this dusty road, moving in file on either side.

Lieutenant Philip Branson
5th Battalion, East Yorkshire Regiment
As we were going down the street, a gendarme of all things appeared on a bicycle, pedalling furiously towards us and waving his hands, obviously trying to indicate to us that the Germans were still in the village. I remember him clattering to the ground with another burst of fire but it was a worthy effort of his to give us some indication.

Private Harry Pinnegar
2nd Battalion, Gloucestershire Regiment
Our instructions were to get on our bikes as soon as possible and rendezvous in an orchard. That was where we had to rendezvous to get together, get the platoons together, and get moving. Well, we got to the orchard all right, minus a lot of men that was wounded and one thing and another, and there happened to be a German tank unit there. They were on an exercise and I

After landing on King sector of Gold Beach, a convoy of RAF vehicles pauses in Ver-sur-Mer before heading inland on the afternoon of D-Day.

don't think really they were fuelled up with ammunition because they were taken by surprise. Unfortunately, the biggest weapon we had was a PIAT gun. There was no heavy artillery, no vehicles, no tanks, all that we had was infantrymen, but we fortunately happened to put out one tank. One of our boys in the unit done it, blew the tracks off a tank there, which jammed up one of the exits for the tanks to get out. So the tanks were going round and round trying to get out of this wood and we were riding on these tanks waiting for them to open the hatches so that we could drop phosphorus or 36 hand-grenades in.

Private Jack Forster
6th Battalion, Durham Light Infantry
You would go forward for so long then stop, have your breath, have a look round, find out what's in front of you, then go a bit more, pushing up all the time, quietly, until you come against some resistance. When you come against resistance, that's when you called on the tanks or the guns or something to get rid of it. You weren't rushing right forward.

Private Dennis Bowen
5th Battalion, East Yorkshire Regiment
Occasionally you have to stop because the line gets out of line and you get too far forward or too far to the rear and people are then held until they all get back into line again and at that time you always get the same command, 'Dig in! Dig in!' Which means, 'Scratch a little hole to get into.' You don't actually have to be told after the first time – you realise that if you dig a hole and get into it you'll survive. Then along come the NCOs, 'Get forward! Get forward!' and you get out of your little hole and go forward. And the one thing you do is when you find a French shovel, which has a much bigger head than yours, that's the one that you get because you can dig a lot quicker. Life or death depends on whether you can get into a piece of bulletproof cover and you get into the bulletproof cover by digging it.

Brigadier Sir Alexander Stanier
Commanding Officer, 231st Infantry Brigade
I could see the Devons going up this brook called La Gronde Ruisseau, it was only a stream about as wide as a pocket-handkerchief, towards Ryes. It had a

certain number of willow trees along it and there was green corn, wheat, which of course gave quite a lot of cover again to the German snipers as they were withdrawing. It wasn't the number of bullets being fired, it was the odd bullet that killed an odd man and it all adds up, particularly officers, because these blinking snipers could see the leaders running about. The officers and the sergeants have to move about.

Sergeant William Baker
2nd Battalion, Devonshire Regiment
The Germans fought very well. After you get past the houses and that, you come into what they call 'close' country. It's all hedgerows. It's not open warfare like you trained quite a bit for; it wasn't like that at all. You had to stalk hedges. You daren't go out into the open fields because Jerry had these Spandau machine guns and he had them perched in little corners.

Lieutenant Philip Branson
5th Battalion, East Yorkshire Regiment
We approached this German position. We were all right moving along a sunken road on the side of this meadow but eventually we came to a gate, which we'd got to pass in front of, and it was obvious that in any kind of holding position the gate would be pinpointed by one of the German guns. Nevertheless, we'd got to get round, and we used the normal technique of a cloak of chaps running over the gate quickly and then another group. And as the second or third group went over we did encounter Spandau fire.

There was a big Yorkshire content of men from Hull and one of their qualities is that they have a kind of stoicism mixed with a strange kind of humour. And a lance corporal, as he went over the gate, he was caught by the gunfire and he came bouncing back clutching his backside, cursing that the buggers had shot him in the backside, or a little stronger than that. Immediately there was a temporary halt while we pulled his trousers down. He was pouring with blood. We were trying to put a field dressing on – where we were going to put it, I don't know, somewhere – and his friend had a good look at his wounds and then announced with some triumph, 'It's all right, they've missed them.' As if that put everything right.

Corporal Percival Tyson
5th Battalion, East Yorkshire Regiment

If it was too bad we got a tank up. In those tanks there was little bells you could press at the back and the bloke would talk to you and you would tell him, 'To your left, two o'clock.'

Private George Nicholson
7th Battalion, Green Howards

One Spandau had us pinned down but they got a tank up and it only fired one shot. When we got to it, there was one, oh, he were a mess. It had turned him inside out. The other one looked as if he hadn't been touched except for his brains out, but this bloke had been absolutely filleted by the look of him.

Sergeant Robert Palmer
Sexton (self-propelled gun) commander, 147th Field Regiment (Essex Yeomanry), Royal Artillery

We go along this track and there's this officer standing there waving his arms and he came over to where we were and I leaned over the side of the turret and spoke to him. He said, 'Down there, you see those two great big houses, posh-looking houses? They're both heavily fortified and they're both making a nuisance of themselves. They've already knocked out about six Bren gun carriers and killed a lot of our ground troops so please deal with them.'

When we got near them, fifty yards away, within easy range anyway, I could see that they weren't ordinary houses at all. They'd been piled up with masses of concrete all round the windows – the windows were deep-set because of the heavy amount of concrete they'd got added to the original. I could see movement in the upstairs right window of the first one so I said to the layer, 'Put it in the upstairs right window.' So he fired the first shot, that exploded and within seconds a whole pile of people, ten, maybe twelve, came running out of the side door of the ground floor, and as they did of course the infantry boys from the Hampshires collected them as prisoners.

Telegraphist Harry Siggins
HMS Ajax (Royal Navy cruiser), off Gold Beach

I always remember being told we were going to fire on Bayeux – we had grid map references – and that as soon as it was possible we should be receiving specific targets from spotting planes. My job was to mark the grid reference given by the spotting plane. I had to write this on a piece of paper, immediately hand it to the gunnery officer who would immediately transfer it to the gunnery table and the gunnery officer would then decide what type of shell he was going to fire. The ranges would be set, the fuses would be set, the gun ready signals would light up in red and the guns would fire. And so it came: the first order was given to fire. I remember now the guns firing. 'A Turret, ready! B Turret, ready, sir! X Turret, ready, sir! Y Turret, ready!' Up go the lights. Firing gongs: 'Gong! Gong! Gong! Gong!' Off the guns would go. 'Phrmmmmm!' Off the shells went.

The spotting plane and I were dealing in RT, plain language, talking to each other, and I distinctly recall that amongst the first of his targets were enemy pillboxes. He said, 'Enemy pillboxes, grid reference so-and-so and so-and-so.' I took the grid reference down and passed it on and the necessary action was taken. First of all a ranging salvo was fired. Then he came back with a correction: 'You're too high, you're too high, come back fifty, come back a hundred.' I passed that on and back we came. 'Now up twenty, now up twenty.' The correction was put on the guns and then we fired another salvo, another turret fired. 'That's it, that's it; give them the lot, give them the lot, give them the lot.' And the whole four turrets, eight six-inch guns, belched out. 'Marvellous. They're running, they're running, they're coming out. They're running out, they're all going backwards, keep firing, keep firing. Up ten, up twenty. Keep firing, that's it.' And so it went on.

Then a fresh target was picked. He said, 'There's tanks, there's tanks. Tanks in a field. They're in a hedge. Take this bearing.' He gave me a fresh bearing and the grid reference map was taken down and it was quickly checked and then we took out the tanks. 'You've straddled them,' he said. 'You've straddled them now. Now twenty this way and thirty that.' This was the procedure which was gone through. This was D-Day for me. Here we were, what, must've been seven miles off the shore, picking off individual targets, on D-Day itself. And the day wore on and eventually I got a relief. I always remember mugs of tea and corned beef sandwiches. Ah! Tasted like chicken.

Private Dennis Bowen
5th Battalion, East Yorkshire Regiment
By the middle of the afternoon some of the men were beginning to talk about food. I hadn't even had a drink of water by then. I never even stopped. I just seemed to be constantly running forward, firing and firing, digging in, getting up again, running forward, digging in again, running forward, and firing and firing.

Sergeant James Bellows
1st Battalion, Royal Hampshire Regiment
I witnessed something that you only expect to see in training. These two men were firing with their Bren gun across Arromanches, which was still in German hands, to a road leading out on the opposite side stopping anyone from getting in or out. And the gun jammed. They both slithered to the bottom of the hole they were in. With a Bren gun you've got a wallet with various parts and various tools for various stoppages and they opened the wallet, as on par for parade, took out their tools, stripped their gun, cleared their fault, put it back together again, closed the wallet, even put the little straps through their brass links, then went back up the hill and carried on firing.

Lieutenant Edward Wright
1st Battalion, Royal Hampshire Regiment
We went through Arromanches. I think most of the Germans who had been in there had gone. And we pressed on beyond Arromanches to our allotted areas and by the evening we had arrived in the approximate area of where we were supposed to form this defensive ring round the bridgehead. There had to be a certain amount of reorganisation because the battalion had suffered quite a lot of casualties: I think the final figure for killed and wounded was just under two hundred.

My platoon was allotted a position on the outskirts. There were some quite nice villas on the outskirts of Arromanches and we were instructed to dig in there, which we proceeded to do. I had a little difficulty there, which surprised me. I was busy digging when from one section position I heard voices raised in argument and I heard a female voice saying, 'I demand to speak to the officer in charge.' I was very surprised to hear this and I went over to see what was going on and I found there a lady who declared she was English. I'm sure she was. And she pointed an accusing finger at me and said, 'Your men are digging up my flowerbeds and making a whole mess of the place and it's quite unnecessary. I demand that they stop.'

I was a bit put out by this. Momentarily I thought back to these stories we'd heard about the German invasion of the Low Countries in 1940 when they were said to have employed paratroop saboteurs dressed as nuns. I wondered for a moment whether this was one of those but quite obviously she wasn't. But she was very smartly dressed and very insistent. I thought, 'Well, I must put a stop to this,' and I told her very curtly that I was not going to have any of this nonsense and I asked if her house had a cellar. She said it had, so I said to her, 'Well, if you don't want to be shot, go down there and stay there until I tell you if you can come out.' She was very incensed by this but off she went down to her cellar and that was the last I saw of her.

Major Peter Martin
2nd Battalion, Cheshire Regiment

Long before nightfall we got to a place quite close to our D-Day objectives, a place called Esquay-sur-Seulles, when the brigade was told to stop and just patrol forward to the main Caen-Bayeux road. As everything was dead quiet I went up to Rucqueville, which is just short of St Léger, and had a look and everything was dead quiet there. I then went forward on to the main Caen-Bayeux road and everything was quiet there and I said to my driver, an excellent young chap, 'Shall we just potter down to Bayeux and liberate it?' He said, 'What a good idea, sir.'

So we set off cruising down the road to Bayeux, which I thought by now must be in our hands. But we got slower as we got into the built-up area and then a Frenchman standing on a corner whistled through his teeth and said, 'Boche! Boche!' and pointed down the road. So we did a quick about turn and came back again, only to be attacked by an American fighter plane that machine-gunned us. We managed to get into the ditch just in time and the only damage to the jeep was a bullet through one of the tyres. So, in this slightly built-up area outside Bayeux, with the Boche somewhere quite close, we did the quickest wheel change that I think has ever been done outside of a Grand Prix meeting and got back to join up with headquarters.

Major Patrick Barrass
2nd Battalion, Essex Regiment

The CO sent out patrols towards Bayeux to find out what was going on. It was getting dark when they came back and they said the Germans were still there. They didn't know in what strength but they'd got fired on. And it was decided that there'd be not much point in trying to launch an attack that night, we'd do it in the morning, in daylight. Our objective had been Bayeux but not necessarily on D-Day itself; I think we'd been given latitude to D-plus-one. One of the things I can remember before it got dark was seeing the spires of Bayeux cathedral enchantingly sticking up over the trees.

Private Harry Pinnegar
2nd Battalion, Gloucestershire Regiment

We had a lot of scrapping as infantry soldiers do, advancing and one thing and another, and we lost a lot of men. We lost our platoon sergeant. We lost our platoon corporal. I was one of the senior soldiers and I took over the platoon and we went all the way through and we got as far as Bayeux. In the history books it says that Bayeux was taken on D-plus-one but my platoon, my section, was in Bayeux cathedral at seven minutes to midnight on D-Day. That is history because that is true. We were in there on the night of D-Day.

Holding On

It was very terrifying and unusual to have bullets whipping over
you and shells going off and there was such a lot of banging
that they may have had some mortars opening up on our position
too. There was a hell of a shindig around.

Stationed outside Caen, the powerful 21st Panzer Division was the only German armoured division in a position on D-Day to counter-attack the Allied landings. Billeted in villages east of the Orne, a few scattered sub-units found themselves able to engage the British 5th Parachute Brigade almost as soon as it had landed. By noon, stronger and more organised forward elements of the division were also in action, while German infantry on coastal defence duty continued to fight hard for a way through to John Howard's bridges. Meanwhile, east of Ranville, James Hill's 3rd Parachute Brigade, bolstered by the arrival of Lord Lovat's commandos, was engaged against German infantry attempting to sweep in from the east.

The British had expected these counter-attacks and managed to hold them. Even so, the fighting was fierce and casualties were high. The pressure scarcely eased when German commanders redirected much of the 21st Panzer Division to counter-attack the British and Canadian landings on the coast and sent tanks to drive a wedge between Juno and Sword.

In the end, British armour and anti-tank guns repulsed part of that thrust and the few panzers that reached the coast turned round and returned, unable to exploit their tenuous advantage. By then, the panzer crews had had the dispiriting sight of more than two hundred gliders sweeping in overhead to land behind them in the fields around Ranville. This was the evening arrival of the British 6th Airlanding Brigade: a welcome boost to the morale and resources of the Airborne hanging on inland.

The D-Day experiences of men of 41 (Royal Marine) Commando show how another German unit was prepared to take the offensive against the Sword beachhead. While the principal British push from Sword was being made towards Caen, the Commando's assigned tasks that day were to push west, neutralise a series of enemy positions along the coast and make contact with Allied forces advancing from Juno. In the town of Lion-sur-Mer, however, it found itself reeling from a strong counter-attack by a determined group of German artillery and grenadiers.

THE ORNE BRIDGEHEAD

Captain John Sim
12th Battalion, Parachute Regiment
I went forward to establish what was known as a forward screen position on a hedgerow three hundred yards in front of the company positions. We started to dig in to a hedgerow facing to the south, towards Caen, and we had about an hour and a half of digging hard with our entrenching tools and the odd pick and shovel.

It was a quiet morning. We noticed the RAF flying around above us, the odd aircraft with their white-striped wings giving us cover. We watched our front, being very still in our little holes, not moving. Then at about eleven o'clock that morning I noticed through my binoculars a group of about fifty soldiers debouching from a little copse about four hundred yards in front of our positions. They looked very much like our own lads. They had round helmets on and camouflage smocks and I thought they were perhaps a group of our own parachute soldiers who had been dropped afar and were coming in to join us.

This group moved across my front from left to right and then suddenly they deployed in extended line and advanced towards us through the fields, long grass, grass as high as the knee almost. We allowed them to come closer and closer. This was all part of our plan. They were enemy, I'd realised that: they were coming at us in a threatening manner and as they came closer one could see that they weren't British parachutists. There was a little cattle fence in front of us, going parallel to our hedgerow, and we planned that until they reached the cattle fence we weren't going to open up on them. So they came closer and closer and when they reached the cattle fence I fired my red Very pistol straight at the middle of them and we all opened fire and the enemy went to ground.

We engaged their fire for a little while and then ceased fire and I heard the sound of officers' orders, in German, working its way to my right, down towards the River Orne, and I thought they were probably going to attack my position from the right side. There was a pause. We couldn't see any enemy to shoot at so we didn't shoot. And suddenly, to our surprise, two self-propelled guns came towards our position as if from nowhere, from dead ground in front of us. These two SP guns came side by side and stopped in front of our position about seventy yards away, short of the cattle fence, and they started to systematically open fire on my positions and there was nothing we could do other than keep our heads down. I thought to myself, 'What a wonderful target for our six-pound anti-tank gun: point-blank range,' but nothing happened. And in the middle of this noise and the explosions a soldier came along the ditch from my anti-tank gun position, crawling up to me on his hands and knees. He saluted me on his hands and knees and he said, 'Sir, the gun's unserviceable, we can't get it to fire. It must have been damaged in the glider landing.' So I told him to go back to his position and open up with his personal weapon when he saw the enemy.

I felt a bit numb. It was very terrifying and unusual to have bullets whipping over you and shells going off and there was such a lot of banging that they may have had some mortars opening up on our position too. There was a hell of a shindig around. But then, as happens in war, suddenly silence reigns: no more shooting; no more noise. And to my surprise one of the hatches on one of the SP guns in front of me opened up and out stepped a German officer arrayed in his service dress, belt, peaked hat, leather boots. He quietly got out and stood beside it and started to light a cigarette. He only had a couple of puffs, I think. Somebody in my section shot him and he fell to the ground and disappeared from sight. I don't think we killed him because later, when we walked round that area, there were no German officers' bodies lying around.

Next, my sergeant, from the right-hand flank of my section, came up to me and said that he was the only one alive in his little area and he had run out of ammunition. What should we do? Well, there was no point in staying there any longer. I called out for any soldier around me who was alive to come and join me and I planned to get the hell out of it. There was my batman, he had a nasty gash in his cheek: he'd been shot in the face. There was a soldier on my right, dead, with his rifle up in his shoulder pointing towards the enemy. And after this call only this sergeant, my batman and two other soldiers came to me and I decided that the five of us would withdraw back to our positions. So this was what we did.

I reported the situation to my company commander. Quietness remained in our hedgerow, there didn't seem to be any movement, so we decided to reoccupy the position. Another section from C Company and I went back and we found that the enemy had withdrawn. There was no sign of any infantry. The two SP guns had moved out of their position and had gone round towards B Company and I gather, an hour or so later, both SP guns were shot and dispatched by the anti-tank guns of B Company.

So we were able to reoccupy the forward hedgerow position in peace. There were one or two wounded around. Our stretcher-bearers came up and we got our wounded back. There were quite a few dead; there was a dead German soldier in the hedgerow. I found myself at a loose end so what I decided to do was to remove the dead. I got a couple of soldiers from C Company and back in Le Bas de Ranville we found a handcart, then the three of us whipped this handcart up to the hedgerow position and we loaded up about four British soldiers including a sergeant, Sergeant Milburn, and the German. And with these four or five dead we went with this handcart back into Ranville and I laid the dead along the cemetery wall, by the church, and returned to the company.

Sergeant William Higgs
Glider Pilot Regiment
I was watching the bushes until my eyes were aching. All of a sudden everything was moving and we could see that the tanks were coming, a squadron of tanks. And it was the most marvellous thing. It came across our arc and nobody breathed, we were all camouflaged, and we let them get into the middle. And just as though a squadron commander or RSM had said 'Fire!' all the guns opened up and we knocked that squadron of tanks right out. Later on General Poett said it was the most marvellous thing because it made the Germans withhold their armour, wondering what was going on, and that delay may have been a great help to the invading forces landing on the

Captain John Sim MC, 12th Battalion, Parachute Regiment. This photograph was taken in 1945.

beaches. After that we were mortared and shelled. When they knew where we were we had a terrible time.

Lieutenant Richard Todd
7th Battalion, Parachute Regiment

By midday the battalion was in a pretty poor state. A Company, which straddled the road coming up from Caen, had taken very heavy casualties earlier in the day, attacked by forward elements of 21 Panzer Div, tanks. They were saved by a corporal who got fed up with being shot at, got out of his foxhole, ran down the road firing from the hip and actually attacked a tank. Tanks don't like being sprayed by small arms fire because they have cracks, which they closed up, and he got near enough to it to throw a Gammon bomb and, with a bit of luck, it blew a track off. That tank slewed across and blocked the road and that's what saved A Company.

Meanwhile we could hear the voice of the company commander encouraging chaps. What we didn't know was that he was lying in the window of a first-storey house in Benouville with one leg mangled. It was his second-in-command, Jim Webber, who got through to us eventually to tell us the position and ask if he could have some reinforcements because they were hanging on by their teeth, they didn't know how long they could keep going. He had been shot in the lung but we didn't know it at the time because his webbing equipment covered all the blood and signs of wounding there. He insisted that there was no way of reaching A Company except by the way he'd come and he insisted on going back with the relieving section. We sent an officer and a few chaps, ten or whatever it was, back down to A Company to help out, and it was Jim Webber who led them back.

B Company was in Le Port. They were pinned down by quite well-ensconced Germans and movement was very difficult. They were just behind our headquarters position and they were really, really pinned down, particularly by snipers in the church tower. But we had this Corporal Killeen, an Irishman. Well, Corporal Killeen had a PIAT, a shoulder-firing anti-tank missile – very inaccurate, not very strong, very cumbersome, but quite effective if you happen to hit the right place. He mouse-holed through cottages, got from one to another, till he got to within range of the church. Later he described all this to the great BBC war correspondent, Chester Wilmot: 'I got to within range of the church tower and I let fly with a bomb and I hit the church tower, knocked a bloody great hole in it. So I fired a few more times, and each time I hit the tower, and I made a real mess of that little church tower. I stood up and there was no firing. I walked across to the church – I reckoned it was safe for me then – but, oh, God, I was sorry to see what I'd done to a wee house of God. But I did take off my hat when I went inside.' Absolutely true. He was a devout Irish Catholic boy. And there were twelve dead Germans in the tower. He'd killed the lot of them.

Captain David Tibbs
Regimental Medical Officer, 13th Battalion, Parachute Regiment
Fierce fighting was going around while the Germans tried to recapture the bridges over the canal and the river and Le Bas de Ranville itself was almost in the front line. The Germans were only a few hundred yards away from Le Bas de Ranville and attacking it fiercely all the time, just as Ranville itself was under counter-attack from the Germans who were beginning to send in elements of the 21st Panzer Division.

The scene around the Field Ambulance, which was occupying a chateau in Le Bas de Ranville, was extraordinary. We were, the 5th Parachute Brigade, by this stage confined to a very tight area in Ranville and Le Bas de Ranville and the Germans were fiercely attacking, which meant there were constant storms of mortars coming down and a number of casualties occurring all the time. In the Field Ambulance itself, a large number, perhaps a hundred or two wounded, had been brought in and were filling the main building and outlying buildings including a barn, many of them desperately wounded. The surgeons were doing their best to cope with some of the worst wounded who would benefit most; for example, those with haemorrhage or thoracic wounds. The scene was one of noise, of wounded men, but nevertheless of organisation. People were going about ignoring all the mortar fire, though casualties were occurring within the Field Ambulance. Our own batteries of mortars were firing off from just about a hundred yards away so the noise was continual and heavy, and casualties were rolling in all the time.

Private James Baty
9th Battalion, Parachute Regiment
The medical officers picked a big barn which the French farmers had used for cutting up their meat, their animals, and they had a big marble slab there. We

used that for our operating table. Our MO, Doctor Bobby Marquis, he'd lost all his gear and he used a double-side razor blade to do all his operations. I know that's a fact because he operated on one of our friends who landed in a tree and got a branch right through his leg.

Sergeant Sidney Nuttall
3rd Airlanding Anti-Tank Battery, Royal Artillery

I had a job of going round bringing wounded in and I met some very, very brave people: conscientious objectors. They had volunteered as parachutists. They would not carry arms but they had volunteered for the Airborne Div and they'd dropped in to help the wounded. Now, I take my hat off to them. People talk about conscientious objectors and these were definitely genuine ones, they could not kill, but they were there.

Private Victor Newcomb
Medical Orderly, 224 Parachute Field Ambulance

I cannot recollect exactly how many COs [Conscientious Objectors] volunteered but it certainly made up in the end something like two-thirds of the strength of the Parachute Field Ambulance, which meant that it was in the region of 150 or so. I was nothing more than a stretcher-bearer, really, with a reasonable knowledge of first aid and treatment of wounds.

I never changed this view that war is a dehumanising activity and that the casualties of war are not necessarily to be blamed on the person who actually fires the bullets. The casualties of war are, to a large extent, innocent people who are caught in traps. I therefore didn't feel the slightest hostility towards German soldiers any more than I did to British soldiers. To me they were as much victims of the situation as British casualties or French civilians. As far as I was concerned there was no distinction. I have to admit I never had to face a situation which was an either/or. Do I treat this man or that man? Or, do I have to do something for a German in preference to a civilian? This sort of thing never occurred to me. I judged things on their merits and the person who seemed to have the greatest need of me got me.

Brigadier James Hill
Commanding Officer, 3rd Parachute Brigade

I arrived at the foot of the Le Plein feature and found the 9th Battalion and was told that they'd been successful and had silenced the guns in the Merville battery. Then I was seized upon by Doc Watts. He hustled me into his regimental aid post and he took a look at me and said, 'You look bad for morale.' So I looked at him and I said, 'You bloody fellow. If you'd been in four feet of water and had your left backside removed you wouldn't look good for morale. And it's your job to do something about it.' I learned afterwards that his reaction was, 'By George, I've got a difficult case on my hands. I'll put him out.' So he injected me and I was out for a couple of hours and while I was out he patched up my wounds.

Piper Bill Millin
HQ 1st Special Service Brigade
We got in a position to attack Le Plein and Lovat is standing at the crossroads there directing the attacks up the road. That's when all the casualties happened because the Germans by this time were well prepared. And when we went up the road, about fifty or sixty yards, to a quarry, all the wounded were in there and it seemed only a matter of time before one of the mortar bombs that the Germans were throwing in the air was going to fall in the quarry. Quite a few people had been killed; legs had been blown off; half a head away with a piece of shrapnel. It was depressing watching the wounded and of course they were getting alarmed at the mortar bombs bursting in the grass above the quarry. I got back to the crossroads and Lovat was there. I lay in the ditch looking at him and I thought, 'Goodness, thirty-two years of age.' Right enough he's old, as far as we were concerned. But what a responsibility, aged thirty-two, and all these people have been killed and seriously injured. And his face is all set.

Private Stanley Wilfred Scott
3 Commando
We come up the road to Le Plein and round the corner and there was a gun, a dirty great Russian thing on wheels with a shield, and when we come round that bloody corner, wallop, we got hit. We took about seven casualties straight away. D____ got it in the guts. He died in my arms. I couldn't do a thing for him; he was just looking at me. Les Hill got one in the head. Westley got hit in the wrist. Paddy Harnett got it across the arse. And Bud Abbott, he lost a foot.

I tried to help, 'cause I was carrying a first-aid kit as well; I done what I could for them. All Paddy Harnett kept saying was, 'Scotty, is my wedding tackle all right? Scotty, is my wedding tackle all right?' And I said, 'For Christ's sake, Paddy. You've got it through the arse, you haven't got it through anything else.' Anyway, I made a field dressing pad and I got it on him and I said, 'Hold it. Get your hand on it, hold it and really push in. Now, get out of it.'

Westley came up. I bandaged his wrist; he had a shattered wrist. I got that inside his battledress blouse. I had to take his gear off and I done the blouse up and I put a bandage round the outside and I said, 'You'll have to go, sir.' I had his Colt .45 and his compass but I gave them back to him like a bloody fool. I said, 'You'll need these, you'd better take them.'

Les Hill came back like a man in a dream, all blood coming down, and he had a Thompson and he was dragging that down the road and I looked at him and I thought, 'Well, he ain't going to go far.' I went to help him and they said to me, 'Let him go, Scotty.'

This is where Ozzy started getting his MM. He went out and got Abbott in, I think, and he went out to get D____. Ozzy dragged D____ back by his webbing straps and laid him in front of me. He was wearing one of these stupid bloody combat jackets, brown canvas things. I ripped all that open and he was just one mass of jelly, he must've taken the big part of the burst. I'd got this kit, morphine phials and all that. I got one out. I couldn't do anything; it was useless. He couldn't talk, he had blood coming out of his nostrils, blood coming out of his mouth, and he just went.

Sapper Bernard McDonough
591 Parachute Squadron, Royal Engineers
We was holding Varaville, because there was quite a contingent of Germans in that area. We encountered quite a lot of fresh German troops coming down a lane and I had to protect three entrances to this farm so as to ensure that they thought there was more Paras there than what there were. We did the cowboy-style effort: some of the chaps who'd been killed, we used their weapons and put them in the hedges and we kept running from one hedge to another to make them believe that there was more men there. When we finished up there was only about fourteen of us left.

Private Victor Newcomb
Medical Orderly, 224 Parachute Field Ambulance

Varaville was in a little bit of a flux because small groups of British troops were into it and out of it and small groups of German troops were moving into it and out of it at another point. It was, for the most part, in British hands and we did operate from there. As reports came in that there was a wounded man a hundred yards away or something, stretcher bearers were sent out to give them attention and bring them in, which we did, one or two.

One in particular I was sent out to, with three other people, was a parachutist who'd broken his leg by falling in a tree and on our way back, because of the confused situation, we were overtaken by a German patrol. It was kind of a no-man's-land, people were wandering around in small groups without any real cohesion, there was no front, and we came across each other by accident.

The German patrol, led by a lieutenant, overtook us, fired a couple of warning shots over our heads, recognised us as performing a medical task and therefore in fact didn't fire upon us. But when they caught up with us they insisted on taking us prisoner until they found that carrying a stretcher with a wounded man on it was not on. It was hampering them more than it was being of use to them.

So at one stage we found ourselves standing in the middle of the road with the officer trying to decide what to do about the situation. He said he wanted to be fair. He didn't feel he could release us for fear that we would betray his presence close by and yet he didn't want to be lumbered with a wounded man. So, in the end, apparently because I was the most vociferous spokesman with a very, very, light smattering of German, he was persuaded to leave me alone with the wounded man and take the other three with him. So this is how he solved his particular problem.

I walked back to Varaville and I collared one of my colleagues, a corporal, who came back to the stretcher with me, and the two of us attempted to take him back into Varaville. We didn't succeed in getting him back into Varaville because he was a very, very heavy man and it was beyond the power of two of us to carry him the distance it was. We therefore planted this poor man in a farmhouse and tied his foot to the kitchen stove, to stretch it as far as possible because he had a broken femur, and left him there and promised to come back with a jeep, if we could get one, or a four-man team. We gave him an injection to ease the pain. But unfortunately, when we got back to Varaville, we were ordered out in the other direction and I honestly don't know what happened to him. I assume he was taken to a German hospital but I've no way of knowing.

Captain David Tibbs
Regimental Medical Officer, 13th Battalion, Parachute Regiment
As the afternoon wore on, I was put in charge of a barn containing nearly a hundred wounded men. I did my best for them. It was filled with hay, which was in a way fortunate for them to lie on. But in the late afternoon there was a sudden moment of panic as somebody threw open the door to the barn and said, 'The Germans are here! They're just at the bottom of the road!' And one of the wounded, a sergeant, who up till that time had looked too ill to do anything, partially sat up, grabbed his Sten gun which was lying beside him and swore violently at this man and said in a broad Glaswegian accent, 'Stop your blethering, man. Or ye'll be the first to go!' I then noticed, to my horror, that not only was the hay a big incendiary risk but most of the wounded still had their weapons with them and they were quite prepared to fight and if the Germans did overrun us we wouldn't stand a chance. I myself was carrying a pistol. But while I was standing there, things settled down. The tank that was coming in with these Germans was knocked out and that particular scare was over.

Brigadier James Hill
Commanding Officer, 3rd Parachute Brigade
I was sitting on the top of the steps that led to an outdoor barn where I had my personal headquarters and I smelled to high heaven because I'd developed gangrene. I was very unapproachable, really. And I remember sitting on those steps on the evening of D-Day looking away to the north-west and seeing the arrival of an airlanding brigade into battle. It was a wonderful sight. Hundreds and hundreds of gliders coming in. So we knew we weren't going to be alone.

THE 6TH AIRLANDING BRIGADE

Major Napier Crookenden
Brigade Major, 6th Airlanding Brigade
The glider brigade was to take off from its airfields at 6pm and land at about nine o'clock in the evening. My brigadier – typical of Hugh Kindersley – went

Tarrant Rushton, Hampshire, on the afternoon of 6 June, as the 6th Airlanding Brigade prepares to fly out to Normandy that evening. On the runway are Hamilcar heavy-lift gliders, preceded by two smaller Horsa troop-carrying gliders. Halifax glider-tugs of 298 and 644 Squadrons, RAF, are parked either side.

across at three in the morning with the first wave of gliders carrying the general, his staff and the anti-tank guns. I had to go to Airborne Corps headquarters at Moor Park and wait there from one o'clock in the morning until news of the parachute landings came in and divisional headquarters, the general and staff, could pass me the message, 'OK, it's going well. Launch the glider brigade.'

I only got this message at twelve noon having sat there for hours, and at once telephoned all the take-off airfields for the gliders and set off down the Great West Road in a staff car to RAF Brize Norton in Oxfordshire where my aircraft were to take off. On the way, passing through Slough, I saw a paperboy selling a lot of newspapers with the banner headline, 'Skymen Land in Europe.' I can see it now. So I bought his whole stack, and my main contribution to D-Day after landing in Normandy, just about nine o'clock, was that I was able to go round my friends in the parachute brigades giving them the newspapers so that they could read about their own landings the same day.

Before we took off I was having a late meal in the officer's mess at Brize Norton when in through the dining room doors came Bill Collingwood, brigade major of the 3rd Parachute Brigade, my opposite number, his face covered in camouflage cream, his clothing rather torn and battered, very dirty, and limping badly. He had flown over to land at ten to one in the morning, but on jumping from his Albermarle aircraft he had been caught up in the strap which holds your parachute to the aircraft and he'd been suspended below the aircraft unable to cut loose. With great difficulty they pulled him in and by that time it was too late to drop the stick, the men inside, and he landed back in England. He knew we were taking off from Brize Norton and he'd made his way across England to Brize Norton in order to borrow spaces for himself and his men in one of our spare gliders.

Irene Gray
Civilian, Southampton

About teatime, I was, like all other women, busy in the home, fiddling about, and there was a sudden drone of aircraft in the distance. And as soon as you heard aircraft, of course, you were on edge, wondering. You didn't know if it was one of ours or one of theirs. But the noise increased in intensity to such a pitch that it was absolutely deafening, and I mean deafening. By now

Troops of the 6th Airlanding Brigade prepare to fly out as part of the second drop on the evening of D-Day.

everybody had gone out to their gates to see what on earth was happening. The sky was literally black with aircraft towing gliders. They were very, very low. Wave after wave.

Sergeant Mike Brown
Glider Pilot Regiment

We were under a glass canopy like a greenhouse and going out we flew over parts of England we had never seen before and I shall never forget the fields, field after field, of tanks, and then another field of guns, then another field of lorries. All that stuff that was accumulated. It was amazing. It gave you confidence. You could see so much going on everywhere. But at the same time we had to watch what we were doing. Flying a glider on tow was quite hard work. You had to keep the glider in position. There was no hydraulics. It was all pull and push. Levers.

Pilot Officer Ron Minchin
Australian Stirling bomber pilot, 196 Squadron, RAF

I think the planning by 38 Group was fantastic. We ended up with this great mass of aircraft, with gliders behind it, going out together across the English coast and into the Channel. And the sight when we got halfway across the Channel! Everywhere you could see, right to the horizon, on our left and right, there were aircraft. They weren't all with gliders and there were other groups, beyond 38 Group, taking American gliders, smaller gliders. We were all going to different areas once we'd got across the other side, there were various dropping zones, quite a lot of them, but the sheer weight of aircraft in the air was one of the most wonderful things. And down below us was a carpet, it seemed to us, of ships and the wakes of these ships. The Channel was being churned up all the way across; it was nearly white. When we saw how they'd organised it, to get us all together, we gave a lot more credit to air-vice marshals and things than we usually gave. It gave you a great deal of respect for the planners and it made you feel so much safer with all these people around you. In fact it wasn't until we got to the other side that we had trouble, when we were up against flak and we started to lose aircraft.

Sergeant Bob Rose
Glider Pilot Regiment

The nearer you got, it seemed, the more sea craft there were. You got the impression, 'Well, if this rope broke now, I'd hardly get wet. I'd ditch alongside one of these guys and I'd be quite safe in moments.' It was almost as if you could walk across. No matter where you looked, as far as the eye could see, you could see this armada. The other thing, of course, was the Typhoons and Spitfires, which were guarding us. They were flying underneath us and above us. And of course we didn't see one Jerry aircraft at all on the way over. Nothing.

Lieutenant Commander Patrick Bayly
HMS Mauritius (Royal Navy cruiser)

We were told to cease firing – I was the anti-aircraft officer right up in the top of the ship – and we looked northward. And there, spread from horizon to horizon, were hundreds of planes towing gliders carrying people. The whole of the RAF, it looked like, came low over our heads, went over the beach and dropped them all, God knows how many, on the front line. It really was the most remarkable sight I've ever seen. It was sad seeing some being hit and falling but very few compared to the actual numbers flying over. I had a marvellous position. I was in the highest point of the ship. We had a Russian admiral with us as well and we were both on the bridge absolutely marvelling at the whole scene.

Major Napier Crookenden
Brigade Major, 6th Airlanding Brigade

By quarter to nine we could see the French coast ahead of us, it was still light of course, and spread out below us was the spectacle of the whole invasion fleet. The warships and destroyers firing at the coast, you could see the flashes of their guns and puffs of smoke. Over the whole of the French coast, a great rolling cloud of smoke and dust; and the landing craft, smaller ones, scuttling to and fro, like water beetles, from the shore to the larger landing ships anchored off.

Then we were running down the line of the Orne River and Canal. Ahead of us, looking over the pilots' shoulders, I could see one of the tug aircraft winging down over Caen after releasing its glider with smoke pouring from his

The bridge of HMS *Holmes*, a Royal Navy frigate stationed off the Normandy coast, as the airborne armada passes overhead on the evening of 6 June.

starboard engine. And down to our left, to the left of the Orne River and canal, we could see our landing zone where the 5th Parachute Brigade had landed that morning and the first lift, the three o'clock lift, of gliders had also landed. The fields were covered with the parachutes of the 5th Brigade.

Over Ranville church, a church with a most characteristic separated tower, a famous landing mark for us, our pilot cast off. The roaring of the air stream from the tug ceased, he did a sharp left turn and another left turn and we were on our final run in. The second pilot put his head through the door and shouted out 'Brace! Brace!' We lifted our feet off the floor, put our arms round each other's shoulders and with a couple of major bumps were down: the perfect landing. In a minute or two we were out of the glider, unbolted the tail, swung it back, put the loading troughs against the sill of the glider, ran out our jeeps and trailers and were moving away to our brigade headquarters rendezvous, a little orchard.

Staff Sergeant Reg Dance
Glider Pilot Regiment
Some of the anti-invasion posts had been knocked down, some by gliders, some by blowing them up, but there were still quite a few left. I went down at quite a speed and aimed to hit one on my port wing – that would swing me round, then the starboard wing would hit the next one – and this is what we did. It took both wings off and that reduced my speed alarmingly and we just hit the deck and shot on like a cigar. Just at that moment another glider came down straight in front of me and levelled off and I hit the backside of it and knocked it right off. So it was an eventful landing but the only one hurt was myself. I got my nose split by the Perspex in front smashing up and cutting me.

Sergeant James Cramer
1st Battalion, Royal Ulster Rifles
We landed with a crash of splintered wood and we got out quick because you're very vulnerable when you first land. We had to kick the door open, we ran to the edge of the field, everybody was running like hell to get away from the gliders in case they were mortared, and then we saw the very tall figure of our divisional commander, General Gale. I'll never forget the smile on his face. 'Welcome to France, gentlemen,' he said. There were smashed gliders all over the place but the amazing thing is that we only lost one man out of the

battalion, by a German mortar explosion. Everybody else was safe. So we ran and formed up and marched towards the outskirts of Ranville, where we started to dig in.

Captain John Cadman Watts
195 Airlanding Field Ambulance
One of the Field Ambulance jeeps had arrived, so I hooked my trailer behind theirs and we rushed across country to the rendezvous with the result that we were the first lot there. And there the Germans, for some inscrutable Teutonic purpose, had dug a hole, about ten feet long, about six foot wide and about four foot deep, at the side of the road. I persuaded my glider passengers to get in the hole and I sat on the edge waving my feet.

The next chap to arrive, who later became a very eminent neurosurgeon, said, 'Hello. Is this the RV?' I said, 'Yes.' 'What do we do now?' I said, 'Well, you dig in, like we have.' And they were so inexperienced in strange circumstances that they got their silly entrenching tools out and went the other side of the road and started hacking away before they realised that in order to dig our hole we should have landed on D minus three. It was terribly amusing to realise that you could pull a chap's leg completely when he's out of balance and never done it before.

Captain David Tibbs
Regimental Medical Officer, 13th Battalion, Parachute Regiment
It was tremendous spectacle to see these coming in, the gliders circling round to find their way down safely to the ground and the planes passing on, and as they did so dropping these huge tow ropes, incidentally, on to the Germans. This was a tremendous morale booster. The extraordinary thing was how little ack-ack fire they encountered and how everything went silent, both the Germans and ourselves, who were watching this extraordinary spectacle, which was a tremendous boost for us but no doubt the very reverse for the Germans. The wonderful thing was that the great majority of these gliders came down exactly as planned. They were bringing desperately needed anti-tank guns and about 1,500 glider-borne infantry and a number of other weapons and communications equipment and another Field Ambulance.

Aerial photograph of Horsa gliders of the 6th Airborne Division on landing zone N between Ranville and Amfreville, east of the Orne River. Some have had their fuselages separated to facilitate unloading.

Warrant Officer George Oliver
Australian Stirling bomber pilot, 196 Squadron, RAF

So we dropped them there and turned around to fly home and just as we were about to cross the coast we noticed a flak gun down on the ground. There was a huge haystack there, they were trying to conceal themselves with this, and he was trying to pick us off as we went.

He had a good range on us, he knew exactly where we were, and the aircraft in front of me was set on fire. It was hit in the wing. We were just coming over the water by then and he seemed to climb away, we were only at about eight hundred feet, fairly low, but the wing was on fire and all of a sudden the wing just folded up and fell off and the aircraft of course then catapulted over and just plunged into the water. I didn't see anybody get out of it at all and I can remember saying to myself, 'Poor bastards.'

By the time we got back it was evening. Most of us had a meal and went to bed. I know we were all very relieved. We had heard on the radio that the invasion was going well at that time and I had a feeling of great satisfaction, inasmuch that 38 Group and 46 Group, we'd dropped the whole of the 6th Airborne Division into Normandy by the evening. Not without casualties.

Pilot Officer Ron Minchin
Australian Stirling bomber pilot, 196 Squadron, RAF

When we got back, six of the more senior pilots, our planes were loaded with containers of food and petrol and ammunition and we went back a third time, at night. We went back and dropped containers to the paratroopers that we'd dropped the night before and then returned. So it was quite a day.

LION-SUR-MER

Marine Raymond Mitchell
41 (Royal Marine) Commando

The Germans counter-attacked and the colonel decided to pull back to hold a more defensible line between the sea and a crossroads inland. We moved HQ to this orchard and the jeeps were well employed ferrying the wounded back to the beaches for evacuation. By that time it was about mid-afternoon, the main forces were pushing inland, but we were in a bit of a backwater with this pocket of Germans facing us.

Marine James Anthony Kelly
41 (Royal Marine) Commando

Captain Powell instructed me to go back to the beach with a message saying we'd been held up by what he thought was tanks and self-propelled guns. They'd got into a yard, like a farmyard, and the shells were going straight through the walls so he'd deduced that they must be armour-piercing shells which came from tanks. So off I went running down the lane. I remember he took the Bren gun off me. 'Leave that,' he said.

Fortunately, I didn't have to go right back to the beach because the Commando headquarters had moved up by that time. Major Taplin, I gave him the message, and he said to me, 'Well, go back and tell Captain Powell to hold on where he is for as long as he possibly can.' And he said, 'Good luck, Kelly,' because he knew me, I'd been in his troop, and off I went.

I went back up the lane and the Germans by that time had got the place really sorted out. Anything that was moving they were shooting at. The lane was now empty of troops, they'd all been deployed in firing positions and were engaged in fighting the Germans, so I was just running up the lane not knowing exactly where anybody was and there were bursts of firing coming down and hitting the brickwork just above my head.

This happened two or three times and on one occasion I dived into the side where there was a little opening of a trench and I just ducked into that for further cover. It turned out to be the air-raid shelter for a house close by and people were in it. French people, like. And I thought, 'What a precarious place to be at this time.' Of course they didn't know there was going to be an invasion in their area. I just said I was English, you know, and they gave me a quick drink of wine and I popped out again and made the rest of the run.

I ran right past a big gateway, it had pillars on either side, and it was a good job somebody popped out and shouted, 'In here!' otherwise I'd have ran straight into the Germans. That's where they'd taken refuge, a fairly large house, it was looking a bit worse for wear because the Germans were hitting it fairly regularly. I remember there were quite a few casualties lying in the courtyard. The signaller was there, a young lad, and I remember his body still twitching. He had a big radio set on his back.

So I ran in there and Captain Powell said, 'There's your gun, get over there,' and I headed in the direction that he'd pointed me. Another young officer said, 'In here, get in here.' This was another air raid shelter at the far side of the house, across into the garden. I got down on the steps where he indicated and I got my magazines out. He had binoculars and he was lying alongside me and it was very easy to comply with the fire control order that he gave me. A green field was stretching out in front of us and it came to a little hedgerow and a wooded area beyond it. 'They're all along that hedgerow,' he says. So all I had to use was the edge of the field and the bottom of the hedgerow as my aiming mark and it was quite easy to take aim at it. So I opened up with a few long bursts.

You could see clumps of them moving about and I kept firing. Then it died down and I switched the gun to single rounds, which was the drill to do. You fired bursts when you had a good target to shoot at but the Bren was always used to confuse the enemy – that was what we were taught – so that the enemy wouldn't know if it was a machine gun firing at them or a rifle. So you switched to single shots when you could and when I did it on this occasion it was just like being on the firing point in practice: the officer says to me, 'Very good; good lad.' A thing like that in the middle of a battle seemed a bit odd to me, but that's what he said. It was the first chance I'd had to look at him, and I didn't know him. Afterwards I found out that we'd all been split up so bad they were trying to make up one troop out of two. The various troops had taken such a battering on the beach that we were under-strength.

I think I was the only one who had a really clear field of fire so he kept supplying me with ammunition and loading the magazines for me and I kept up this steady rate of fire. But of course the Germans don't take that lying down – if they've got a troublesome point they try to eliminate it as much as we would – so it wasn't very long before I was getting mortared then and I realised I was the target. They came fairly close but I didn't take much notice of them except on one occasion when it burst really close. My reaction to it made me slide down these little shallow steps, down to the bottom, and the gun came with me and all the muck and dust. But I just got back up again and carried on.

During that time it seemed to go quiet and then it would rev up again in a different direction. Maybe they were trying to work their way round us. I didn't have the feeling that we were being overwhelmed at that time but they must've had us well in their sights because they shot Captain Powell through the mouth. He was always a man who stood up. On one occasion during the training in Scotland he'd said, 'Get down, you're too high up, you're too big a target,' and he'd stood on my back to press me into the ground further. But that's what he did and he was always shouting and moving about amongst the troops shouting encouragement and he was exactly the same on D-Day. He was walking around shouting and they shot him through the mouth and he must've still been shouting and bawling as it went right through and out the other side without touching his teeth. He always had his mouth open.

It must have been late afternoon, we must have been in this battle right through the day, I didn't know when it was going to end, but the order must have come through, 'Well, OK, you can pull out now'. I got told, 'Keep up a steady rate of fire now because we're running down the ammo.' I remember this young officer telling me this and he put three grenades on the top step and he says to me, 'Use them if they get too close.' That shocked me more than anything else. 'If he thinks that I'm staying here to throw those three things if they get that close – no chance!'

The only person I saw after that was Captain Powell. He was still there and he said, 'Right, stand by to move out now,' and I only remember him and I running. We were running through an orchard towards a big wall at the end and even though I was encumbered with the Bren gun I still made the wall before he did. It was quite a high one, about eight or nine foot high, I think, and made of these big rough stones. There was the odd crack around us as we were running but I didn't think the Germans were really shooting at us until I turned round when I got there and found myself by myself and a little panic crept in. 'Left on my own, what am I going to do?' I couldn't see Captain Powell and then I spotted him: he was lying on the ground about fifty metres or so back. I put the gun in the ball of a tree where the branches joined, aimed it back across the field and blasted away. The magazine must've been almost empty because it was only a burst of about ten rounds and I had no more ammunition left.

I ran out to Captain Powell and he was lying there groaning. I said, 'Come on, let's get out of here,' and I lifted him up and he was shouting at me and he wasn't very complimentary. He was a big, long, tall man, must've been about a foot taller than me, and big, long, lanky fellas are very awkward to handle. He had multiple wounds on him then, blood splattered all over him. He looked ghastly. And when I lifted him he didn't know I was just trying to help him and in my panic I suppose I was being awkward and the size of him was making it more difficult for me. I got him up and he was collapsing again and eventually he falls on the ground again and of course I'm on my knees with him then.

He said, 'For God's sake, leave me alone. You're doing far more damage to me than the Germans.' But of course it was told to me in the colourful language of the service of the time. You know: 'Go away and multiply.' His leg was broken, you see, and I was lifting him on his good leg and getting him to stand on the broken one. When I realised, I did get him up. And with the excitement and the things that were happening and the panic and the fear, all mixed up, I was sort of giggling and laughing and crying, like a frightened child, I suppose. Anyway, I got him to the wall and, of course, there was no way I was going to get him over that. Every time I let him go he slumped to the floor and I was nigh on exhausted myself.

There was a ladder. And I can only assume that the Germans, if they saw us, didn't shoot us because this is like the Keystone Cops and they were standing there laughing their heads off. So I got this ladder and I banged it against the wall. Then I had to lift this long man up to get him in a fireman's lift over my shoulders. When I eventually did that I got on the ladder and started to climb it, without any thought that the ladder didn't reach the top anyway and without any thought of what I was to do when I got to the top of the ladder. Who thinks straight in situations like that, except John Wayne or somebody like that? Anyway, I'd only gone about two or three steps and the thing broke and there we were in a heap on the floor again, and he was really telling me where to go and of course I think he was losing consciousness then as well.

Then a man named Mortlock appeared over the top of the wall and he hung his arms down. I had to stand Captain Powell against the wall again, by this time he must've given up all hope of ever getting any sense out of me, and I pinned him against the wall. Another chap joined Mortlock and they grabbed his wrists and I pushed at the bottom and over he went. I got over the wall on that bit of ladder, half was still left, I ran at it, jumped on it and got over. I threw my Bren gun over the wall first; I didn't leave my gun behind. And there in the garden was Captain Powell. I can only assume that Mortlock didn't know he was wounded; they must've jumped up and run and of course he didn't because he couldn't run. When I dropped down he was still there and I thought, 'God Almighty, I still haven't got shot of him. He's still there like an albatross around my neck.'

There was a wheelbarrow and I got Captain Powell into it with his legs stuck up towards the shaft. I put the Bren gun on his chest and I wheeled him down the garden path and had to turn round and pull it up a couple of steps into the rooms of the house and I wheeled him through and out through the front door. I came out into the street, into blazing sunshine and within seconds – where it came from I don't know – there was a jeep, which was converted into a very fragile type of ambulance. That pulled up and we put him in that and that was the last I saw of Captain Powell.

They're the things that amazed me about war. How they can be so dramatic and tense at times and then you can have idiotic things like that happening. There's no way I can describe the feeling I had when that jeep drove away, the loneliness I felt standing by myself in this road and not a soul around me. A bedraggled young marine standing in this street, clutching an empty Bren gun and watching his troop commander getting whisked away. Standing there bereft. Where was I going to go? What was I going to do? How was I going to link up again with the battle?

Then Sergeant Hazlehurst appeared from nowhere and had the audacity to ask me where I'd been. I said, 'I've got no ammo.' It took him about five seconds to produce it, much to my surprise. He hung these bandoliers around my neck and told me to get into a house just behind me. I went to the door, a big studded door. And the humiliation there! Being a Bren gunner I had a personal weapon, a Colt .45, so I took this pistol out and I fired at the door; you know, the way you see in the films. I fired one shot at it and there was a tap on my shoulder and when I turned round there was a priest standing there with his cassock and his robes on and a round flattish hat on his head. He shook his head and he reached forward and he turned the knob and opened the door. I slunk inside and I went upstairs to the bedroom and cried my eyes out. I just stood there and cried. I thought, 'I've made a complete and utter mess of the whole thing.' After all the training, I realised how immature, young, green, call it what you like, I was.

When I recovered a little bit, I filled the magazines and then I remember the training taking over. Don't break the windows, leave the curtains where they are; don't put the gun right up by the window, keep it well back. All those things started going through my mind again. I suppose I started functioning like a soldier again. It started to go dark then. And that was my D-Day. I didn't sleep that night; I sat on that bed, looking out the window, and the night passed.

Day's End

I remember the sergeant coming round, saying,
'This will be your arc of fire. Watch out, because Jerry
will come back. Don't think that it's all over; he'll be here.'

D-Day night was one of continued activity. Fighting carried on in many areas. Behind the front lines, exhausted units began digging in and feeding. Some men tried to sleep but many stayed alert in readiness for enemy counter-attacks or were kept awake as the *Luftwaffe* tried noisily to get at the beaches: Allied air superiority was less formidable in the dark. Supplies and reinforcements continued to pour ashore; wounded and prisoners were taken away.

Not all of the day's planned final objectives had been achieved. In the west, the Americans at Utah, assisted by their airborne divisions dropped inland, had made real progress in securing and extending the western flank, though casualties among the paratroopers were high. In the east, inland from Sword, the British Sixth Airborne had accomplished all of its D-Day aims: the only Allied division to do so. But while the Canadians had pushed far inland and the British 50th Division had reached the edge of Bayeux, all beachheads were less deep than had been hoped for and only Juno and Gold had linked up. Caen, the prize scalp, had not been taken. And the American grip on Omaha remained tenuous.

But the Allies were ashore. The essential plan had been a great success. By midnight more than 156,000 men had landed in Normandy.

The confusion of the battlefield, combined with conflicting sources, has caused estimates to vary considerably, but the day's cost for the Allies probably stood in the region of ten to twelve thousand dead, wounded and missing. The American share of that figure was most likely more than half.

The British and Canadian divisions that landed at Sword, Gold and Juno had three thousand casualties between them – approximately a thousand per division – and the Sixth Airborne may have suffered as many as 1,500 killed, wounded and missing.

The sixth of June was only the first day, of course. The Second Front had just begun. Securing the Normandy foreshore was to take ten days; a month of fighting would pass before Caen fell; eleven months were to pass before Berlin was reached and the Germans were finally beaten. Yet D-Day was the springboard to that final victory. D-Day secured for the Allies the vital toehold that made possible the liberation of north-west Europe and the defeat of Nazi Germany in the west.

Trooper Ronald Mole
Sherman tank gunner/wireless operator, 4th/7th Royal Dragoon Guards, inland from Gold Beach

Before we bedded down the first night, and it had been a heck of a long day, you had to scrub the gun, load up with about 80 gallons of diesel, replenish the 75-shells and boxes of Browning machine gun bullets. If you were a wireless operator, you had to do an hour's wireless watch. Others had to do an hour's guard. Obviously we couldn't make fires and I was so grateful to Mr Heinz and his products and his self-heating soup. This was a can with a little recess and you dug out the middle and this revealed a little fuse. You touched that with a cigarette and within thirty seconds you had a hot drink. We learned, of course, the hard way that if you didn't spike it with two holes before you lit it you got the lot down your uniform from the pressure inside, but we caught on very quickly. The biscuits we were given had surely been made of concrete but we made bully sandwiches and jam sandwiches or whatever.

Sergeant James Bellows
1st Battalion, Royal Hampshire Regiment, inland from Sword Beach

Sticking out the old RSM's pack was two French sticks. I said, 'Where did you get them, Jimmy?' 'Oh,' he said. 'I got them off the crew before I got ashore. I got false teeth, I can't chew bloody biscuits, can I?' I said, 'How about giving me a bit?' He told me what I could do. I said 'That's all right, Jim. I've got mushrooms and bacon for what I'm going to have.' So I got them out, this bacon and mushrooms, and I sliced some bacon off and put it in my mess tin and I opened up this tin of mushrooms. He relented. We had about the finest meal anybody had on D-Day, I think. Bacon, mushrooms, and real bread. That was lovely.

Sergeant Major Russell King
2nd Battalion, Royal Warwickshire Regiment, inland from Sword Beach
We posted sentries, naturally, and either myself or the company commander or both went round the sentry posts and made sure that everything was OK. We had hurried inspections of the lads, made sure that the grub was coming up. I don't think the lads got much sleep at all. I didn't seem to get much sleep anyway.

I remember the company HQ was in an old farmhouse and it had been evacuated that hurriedly, in fact, that they didn't seem to have taken a thing with them. There was a little enclosed courtyard and there was still stuff on the bloody tables and in the bedrooms. They just seemed to have taken off. And the thing I was most struck by in that part of France anyway was that every bugger seemed to keep rabbits. There was rabbit hutches all over. Everywhere you went there was little rabbit hutches. Mind, a lot of people were still there. There was an old couple in Benouville in fact and they had no intention of moving. I don't think they knew what it was all about, to be honest.

Driver Roy Hamlyn
282 Company, Royal Army Service Corps, attached to 3rd Canadian Division, inland from Juno Beach
We found our way along this road and we came to a cornfield. Being a country boy, I was bit shocked to think of what we were going to do to that cornfield because it was a splendid field, the corn was green and it had reached a height of two-foot-six or whatever, and through we had to go. The French farmer came on the scene and I don't speak French but I could understand exactly what his language was because we had to destroy his cornfield. He became a very, very excited man and I could rest assured that we were not very popular. The last thing that he wanted was an Allied invasion of his part of France. But unfortunately we had to destroy that lovely field of corn because it was earmarked as an ammunition dump and that was it.

Private Richard Atkinson
9th Battalion, Durham Light Infantry, inland from Gold Beach
Civilians didn't really want you there. They weren't too happy because you only brought death and destruction. It was beautiful lush farmland and there were cows, legs up in the air, they were all dead. All the livestock had been killed in the fields and whatnot. They did moan because we'd killed all their stuff and we were pinching their wine. The Germans hadn't done any of that to them. There was no love lost at this stage between us. We wrecked their houses; we killed their stock. We were in their farmhouses, not that you were allowed to sleep in the farmhouse, you slept on the vehicles round about it, but naturally you were rummaging, which you shouldn't have been but you did. By evening time we were into the farmhouses and taking the Calvados from the cellars.

Marine Dennis Smith
48 (Royal Marine) Commando, near Juno Beach
During the course of the night I was called to escort our intelligence officer, Lieutenant Smedley. He wanted to contact the mayor of the town. So we wandered through the town, he obviously had directions of where to find the mayor, and I went as his escort for the night. Very quiet it was. A few flashes of light here and there. We didn't know who we might meet, Germans or French people, but we eventually found the place and he asked me to sit by the gate and not let anyone in whilst he went indoors. Then he went and tapped on the door and a few words were spoken and he entered. Within half a minute he was out again and said, 'You must come inside. The mayor doesn't want you to be seen here.' So I went inside and stayed in the hall, just inside the doorway. I think at that time the French people thought it might only be a commando raid and that if we withdrew and they cooperated with us they would be in danger. That was the point of the intelligence officer explaining to the mayor that this was not a raid, we were there for good, we hoped.

Sergeant Edward Wallace
86th Field Regiment, Royal Artillery, inland from Juno Beach
Afterwards, of course, when they were liberated, they were all over you. Even now, if you go over there, they can't do enough for you. But deep down they knew what was going to happen to their townships and villages: that they

French civilians near Sword Beach show their identity cards to a British officer.

were going to be flattened. As you moved up through northern France, Belgium, and especially Holland, yes, you were really welcomed with open arms.

Lieutenant Eric Hooper
9th Battalion, Durham Light Infantry, inland from Gold Beach

I tell you one thing, I felt very, very sad about an incident there. There was a farmhouse that had been shelled and, when I got there, there was an old lady and a nun. The old lady was very, very distraught and in the conversation I found out that her two grandchildren were buried in the ruins and they wanted us to try and get them out. But we couldn't, we were under orders and had to be at a certain point at a certain time, and we had to go away and leave them.

Private Dennis Bowen
5th Battalion, East Yorkshire Regiment, inland from Gold Beach

We dug in by a little farm, by the side of the duck pond there. I remember the sergeant coming round, saying, 'This will be your arc of fire. Watch out, because Jerry will come back. Don't think that it's all over; he'll be here,' and we stood-to. I was completely petrified that these Germans would come storming back after we had been shooting and killing them and would attempt of course to shoot and kill us. But the men of the 5th East Yorkshires were not the slightest bit worried about them. They really were great old sticks.

Leading Telegraphist Alan Winstanley
Combined Operations Bombardment Unit, inland from Gold Beach

D-Day night, we actually slept under a tarpaulin at the side of a field. We hadn't time to pitch tents and things, the main thing was to get the W/T equipment set up and working. And as night fell in that little village we began to think, well, what happens overnight here? Are we suddenly going to get counter-attacked? Are there snipers around? There's all sorts of things go through your mind. Obviously it didn't happen as we're still here to tell the tale but it's one thing that goes through your mind. Even though you have someone on guard while maybe six or eight of you sleep, there's always the chance you could be surprised and overcome and the next thing you wake up dead, as it were.

Private Anthony Leake
8th Battalion, Parachute Regiment, near Ranville

We dug in for the night and strung anti-tank grenades across the road in case they sent any vehicles up. By this time we were very, very tired because we'd had no sleep since we were at the airfield: twenty-four hours, just about. Some of us were nodding off. Then there was some firing, we didn't know whether it was a false alarm or what, somebody said the Germans were coming but we didn't see any, I don't know what happened. But anyway we were too frightened then to sleep for the rest of that night.

Staff Sergeant Reg Dance
Glider Pilot Regiment, near Ranville

During the night we had one or two scares. People said, 'There's something moving out the front!' I kept peering and said, 'Well, don't fire, you'll give the position away.' I kept looking and I saw it was a cow. They were all dairy herds round there and of course cows don't go to sleep like we do, they keep eating all night long – munch, munch – and wandering around.

Piper Bill Millin
HQ 1st Special Service Brigade, east of Ranville

We moved to a farmhouse and Lovat took that over as his HQ. I dug in with a chap who had a PIAT gun and that evening we got out and took a walk along the gable end of the farmhouse. Everything was still and the firing had ceased. Everything was nice and quiet and there was the smell of the corn and the flowers and we're just walking along.

Suddenly, 'Swoosh!' and two mortars exploded in the cornfield and of course shrapnel came thudding into the wall of the farmhouse. I got right down and scrambled away back the way we had come and then another 'Swoosh!' and another two explosions. Well, I was in the trench by this time. The other chap was a big beefy man and I heard him running, his big thudding feet running along, and he fell into the trench beside me and I said, 'For Christ's sake, you're quite a hefty character!'

We'd arranged that he would go first on the gun so I could get my head down a little bit. But then he's still lying there, there wasn't no snoring nor sound of breathing in the darkness, so I felt the back of his head and his back and of course there's all blood. Obviously he'd been hit with several pieces of shrapnel in the back and one in the back of the head and he'd been dead all the time and I'd slept for about an hour.

Sergeant James Cramer
1st Battalion, Royal Ulster Rifles, near Ranville

Suddenly there was an awful crashing, explosions going off, in the field next to us. We jumped into our trenches thinking we were being mortared and to our relief it was the whole of the brigade's three-inch mortars. They had been brigaded, which meant that they had all been brought together, and they were all firing on a target: what we thought were explosions were our own mortars going off. So we had a very fitful night with all the noise. There were a lot of shots going on, explosions, and the *Luftwaffe* came over banging away at the beachhead.

Sergeant Reginald William Webb
Churchill Crocodile tank commander, 141st Regiment, Royal Armoured Corps, inland from Gold Beach

What one reads about D-Day night is that there wasn't much air activity but we thought there was a decent lot. We'd been two or three nights without any sleep and the ack-ack I recall near us was some Bofors and they were sending up a racket. And my crew always say – and I don't remember the truth of this, I must admit – that I went up to the officer in charge of the Bofors and asked him not to make so much noise because we couldn't get to sleep. I think we found some booze and I might have had a couple of drinks.

Lieutenant Richard Charles Bird
LCT crew, off Sword Beach

A bomber, a Heinkel, came over and everyone opened fire. And the Americans, oh, the Americans are very trigger-happy and there were a number of American merchant ships and they were all opening up with Oerlikons and God knows what. And of course, as it came over, their elevation kept getting lower and lower and lower until eventually the bullets were going just over our heads. And this plane crashed, oh, I suppose, not fifty yards from us. It just crashed and went under and nobody bothered any more about that.

We hadn't had any decent sleep for a long time, so we thought, 'This is a good chance to get a good night's rest, because in the morning we're going to be given all sorts of jobs to do.' I remember I'd just got off to sleep and the quartermaster who was on duty came and shook me. He said, 'I haven't told anybody, but there's a mine bobbing around our stern.' So I had to get dressed again and go and have a look over, and there, sure enough, was a damned great black thing. He said, 'What shall I do?' I said, 'Well, you can't do anything.' He said, 'Shall I push it off with a boathook?' I said, 'Yeah, but you got to be careful with it. I don't know what kind of mine it is. With contact it may go off.' Anyway, when it got closer, it was the wheel of this Heinkel, the tyre, just poking out.

Lieutenant James Lowther
Sherman tank commander, East Riding Yeomanry, inland from
Sword Beach
It must've been one o'clock in the morning or something when the night sky was alive with tracer bullets and anti-aircraft fire because the Germans were trying to bomb the beaches. There was an immense amount went up in the air and it all had to come down again and we lost two men killed and one wounded during the night by shrapnel or spent bullets or God knows what falling through their bivouacs. It was something we hadn't learned to expect in training. So whenever afterwards we stopped and harboured up at night, we dug a bloody great pit like an inspection pit and drove the tank over the top of it and slept underneath.

Captain Julius Neave
Sherman tank commander, 13th/18th Hussars, inland from Sword Beach
Tanks can't fight at night and the squadrons, when they had achieved as much of their objectives as they could, pulled into laagers, as we used to call them. Our HQ pulled into its own laager in a wheat field, and that's when we got our first prisoners. Two in particular were heard wandering about calling for 'Hans' and 'Rudi'. I can hear them now.

Corporal John Barnes
Sherman tank commander, 13th/18th Hussars, inland from Sword Beach
If they'd kept quiet and laid there they would've got away but they started to shout, as though they were trying to make us know there were lots of men

there. We stood them in the middle of where the tanks were and the squadron leader told them, 'Tell your mates to come in or we're going to shoot you here.'

We used to have little tins of soup and you'd flick the top off and put a light to them and you got hot soup and I looked at these Germans sitting there shivering and I said, 'Give 'em a hot soup,' and then we had a rapport. One said, 'Invasion. Tanks, no infantry. Infantry at the back.' I said, 'Yeah.' He said they were told that all they would see would be infantry and that it would take about two hours before tanks came. That's what he was crying for. And he was trying to tell us a lot of people were crying because they saw these canvas things coming and they'd thought there were infantry in there and they weren't worried until they came on the beaches, but suddenly up the beaches came tanks.

Trooper Kenneth Ewing
Sherman tank driver, Sherwood Rangers, inland from Gold Beach
We supported the Hampshire infantry and the colonel of the regiment asked our colonel if the tanks could stay behind them in the line for the night. Well, our colonel explained to him it was out of the question: normally all the tanks laagered up at the rear during the night because there was no protection. But after some discussion he said, 'All right, I'll agree to one squadron.'

Well, he went back and all the squadrons by this time had settled in for the night so they drew lots who was to go up and of course B Squadron lost the toss. So we went back into the line again and it was most unnerving because you were sticking out like a sore thumb. There was a huge tank sticking out there in the dark and you couldn't see anything. We used to take it in turns in the turret with the binoculars, but you couldn't see anything, it was non-productive. We spent a most uncomfortable night.

When dawn broke, the co-driver asked for a shell-case. Now, if you wanted to go to the toilet, the normal practice, if it was bad, was to use a shell-case. Well, the tank commander said, 'No, you're not. We've had a bad night; we've had a bad day before. You've got to get out.' So after much protesting he gets out the tank and a hedge was about twelve yards to our right and he gets in the bottom of the hedge and he squatted down to go to the toilet. The commander says to me, 'Keep an eye on him and make sure he's all right.' I said, 'OK.' I could watch him through the periscope.

Unbeknown to him, there was a German in the hedge behind him who was trying to give himself up. He didn't want to distract the chap's attention because he was frightened he might turn round and shoot him, you see. So while the chap's in the hedge, this German's poking his bottom with his finger to attract his attention. The chap thinks it's the hedge and he keeps trying to knock it away and after a couple of times he turns round to see what it was and there's this German with his hands up. Of course, his first reaction was to run, so he sets off to run and of course he trips himself up with his trousers obviously. The tank commander says, 'Oh, for God's sake. Go and get him in.' We sent the German back to the infantry.

Trooper Douglas Edwin Patrick Wileman
Tank fitter, 13th/18th Hussars, inland from Sword beach
One of the lads called out, 'Bloody hell, Jerries!' I had a Bren in my hands so I threw it down and fired it in their direction and they put their hands up immediately. Probably what had happened here was that, a short while before, the Airborne reinforcements had gone over and these Germans had realised they were on the wrong side of all these reinforcements dropping and they thought the best thing to do was to pack it in. But we had a heck of a job to get rid of these prisoners. In fact, our brigadier, when he saw us standing there wondering what to do with them, said, 'Get rid of those so-and-sos. We can't get rid of them any other way: shoot the buggers.' Fortunately, a party of about twenty Jerries were being marched down the road under an escort of about four men and we bunged our twelve on the back of the line, much to the annoyance of the infantrymen.

Lieutenant Herbert Jalland
8th Battalion, Durham Light Infantry, inland from Gold Beach
I remember the cries of *'Russki! Russki!'* very well. A lot of our men regarded them as traitors because they were Russian and should be shot as traitors. Some of them may have been shot but I think most of them were saved because the officers and NCOs saw to it that these people were prisoners of war and that was that.

Captured German soldiers being marched to the beaches.

Captain David Tibbs
Regimental Medical Officer, 13th Battalion, Parachute Regiment, near Ranville

Well, the evening wore on and at about half-past ten we learned that casualties could be evacuated. So carefully selected people, selected because they were near death but salvable if they were given proper help, were evacuated by jeep-ambulances across the bridges to join the main dressing station the other side of the river. This was a hazardous journey because they were liable to be mortared or sniped at all along this route. Anyway, evacuation had started and we were beginning to have real communications with the seaborne people.

Major Richard Gosling
147th Field Regiment (Essex Yeomanry), Royal Artillery, on Gold Beach

Just behind the sand dunes there was a German pillbox, which the Germans had used as sleeping quarters, and they turned it into a little first-aid post for us and we crawled into this. Very smelly it was of Germans. They'd been standing-to that morning and the remains of their breakfast was on the tables still and some red wine on the table and there was a letter from a French girl to one of the Germans. It was 'Hans chéri' – Dear Hans – 'Je vous attendrais' – I will meet you – 'derrière le pillbox' – behind the pillbox – 'à six heures du soir' – at six o'clock in the evening – 'le six juin' – on the sixth of June. And it was signed 'Madeleine'. So Madeleine was going to meet this German behind the pillbox at six o'clock that evening. So we all looked out and waited for Madeleine to come along. Madeleine never did.

Sergeant Desmond O'Neill
Cameraman, Army Film and Photographic Unit, on Sword Beach

There were hundreds of walking wounded and chaps on stretchers and we were told that we were going to be evacuated as soon as possible. Then they started putting us on DUKWs, which had brought troops ashore, and commenced taking us out to a big Liberty ship moored offshore. On the DUKW we had a lot of chaps – French commandos – who were wounded, badly wounded, two of them were blinded, and it was very uncomfortable for them going out because the waves were coming over the side and they were in a state of shock. But strangely enough, when they were being loaded on, they

BU 1190

Near Ouistreham, soldiers of 4 Commando stretcher a casualty back to an aid post.

didn't want to go. They nearly had to be forced to get on to the DUKWs and be taken away. After four, five years in England and now being back home in the motherland, to suddenly have to leave like that.

Lieutenant Eric Ashcroft
1st Battalion, South Lancashire Regiment, on Sword Beach

I was sent back to the field dressing station and it was at that stage that I saw many of the wounded on the beach area. I saw officers that had been blinded, walking wounded, stretcher cases, and all the documentation was going on. Labels, tags. Ones they were giving morphine had lipstick put on their forehead, I seem to remember: a capital M. The documentation went on meticulously by the Royal Army Medical Corps.

Towards nightfall we were collected by a Royal Army Service Corps DUKW vehicle, incredible vehicles which go on land and swim on water. Just about dusk we entered a fairly rough sea, we inflated our life jackets and we swam – that's the word used for the propelling of these vehicles – out to a Landing Ship Tank and this ship lowered its ramp and we went inside into brilliant light. The whole area was like entering a great hall. Around the sides were bunks and towards the end were green tents with lights in. They were the mobile operating theatres. And you could still smell the oil from the tanks: during the day the tanks had been carried across and the tank crews and the tanks had come out and the LST then became a mobile hospital.

We were then given sulfonamide. I was given trousers-down injections. Some of my fellows were taken for further dressings. I remember further dressings, further inoculations and further documentation and I was allocated a bunk. There must have been about three hundred people on this LST and the ones that were able were given a higher bunk and the ones who found it difficult were given a lower bunk. It was a hospital ship, really, and they were able to carry out quite sophisticated treatments right from the beaches. I want to emphasise the medical side of this, how efficient it was. Monty always said he'd look after the wounded and I remember thinking that that side had been taken care of.

Sergeant Major Russell King
2nd Battalion, Royal Warwickshire Regiment, inland from Sword Beach

I was surprised it hadn't been worse than what it was. I was pleased I was in one piece. Other than that, I was under the impression that it had been a lot

Soldiers wounded in the landings at Gold Beach arrive at a British port.

H 39199

easier than what I'd expected. Being stuck on the beach, hand-to-hand fighting: that's what everybody had expected, I think. Certainly when we'd got sorted out after a couple of days, I think everybody was rather pleased with the way it had gone. We hadn't had a great deal of casualties.

Lieutenant Charles Mills
Naval planning staff
One's feeling was one of absolute relief that it seemed to be happening without too much enemy interference. Of course there was opposition, as is well known; but at least from the messages that we were getting, the convoys seemed to be getting across and all seemed peace and quiet up to a certain point. And there's a curious feeling, I think I probably had it with the Algiers landing as well, that, when you've been mixed up with something, you can't understand why the enemy is not expecting it more than he actually is and is prepared for. Here we were at the beginning of June and I'd been mixed up with it since the previous September, and there's a tremendous feeling of relief when it actually happens.

Major Goronwy Rees
21st Army Group planning staff
As far as the British were concerned, we would have found it very difficult to replace any heavy casualties and one had to think all the time that it was human beings who were going to carry out these ideas – some of them seemed fairy tales – that one had made up. Of course they did this marvellously. I think, though, that anybody associated with the planning of that operation ought to feel extremely proud of themselves. I think it was one of the best-planned operations in military history.

Major David Warren
1st Battalion, Royal Hampshire Regiment
Security was the name of the game for that operation because there were so many people taking part in it, so many people that had to know eventually where the landing was going to be. It always seemed to me to be an incredible situation that we were able to keep it from the Germans, because, if they'd got to know, it would have been a very different story, I expect, to the landing. In our camp in the New Forest, I remember, one particular party that went for

the pay were having a little walk in Lyndhurst and there was a bookshop selling books and maps and they saw a map of Normandy right in the window. Of course this caused quite a stir because I think everyone felt rather edgy about the fact that if the Germans did get to know we were in for a real roughhouse.

Lieutenant Commander Lawrence Hogben
New Zealand officer, Royal Navy meteorological team

After the war Eisenhower became president and when he was inaugurating Kennedy, his successor, Kennedy asked him, 'Why was it that you succeeded rather than the Germans?' and Eisenhower said, 'I think we had better weather forecasters.'

The alternative date was 19 June and on the seventeenth all six of us forecast calm, smooth, fine weather. On this occasion, on the nineteenth, there was the worst gale that anybody can recall and one of the artificial harbours, the American harbour, was knocked down. Ours, at Arromanches, just survived. So this demonstrates that the forecasters were not infallible. If we had waited for the nineteenth, Ike would have said 'Go' and it would have been a total disaster.

Looking back, I'm happy that we succeeded in the way we did. I'm happy that the team succeeded, because it was a team. Even if it was the Royal Navy who made the right forecast both for the fifth and the sixth, this was because of our collaboration and discussion with the others. It was a team effort and, if anything like that happens again, it should be a team effort, as it was then.

Sergeant Major Russell King
2nd Battalion, Royal Warwickshire Regiment

I think the training had gone well actually. In fact it showed itself on that day in particular. The men did what they were told. They were taking cover better; everybody was using what cover they could. Certainly I think the training was paying off. They were being very sensible about what they were doing. I was really impressed: everybody seemed to settle in; there was no panic stations or anything like that. They did bloody well.

Bombardier Ralph Dye
Royal Artillery, attached to 48 (Royal Marine) Commando

People asked me afterwards what it was like and I said, 'Well, it was all in Technicolor'. I was right in the middle of the battlefield and everything we'd seen about the war up to that point had always been black-and-white photographs: war was fought in black-and-white. And here I was, on a summer's day – it was rather a grey, dreary sort of day – on a Normandy beach, and it was all in Technicolor. The next thing was, the machine-gun bullets were rattling off the hull. Clearly we hadn't taken the beach.

Sick Berth Attendant Norman Pimblett
LST crew

It was pretty traumatic. On D-Day, arriving at the beach, the noise, the gunfire, the amount of ships, was just something beyond your wildest dreams, you'd never seen anything like it. To see a guy with half his leg ripped off or something like that wasn't a nice thing. Bearing in mind that I was eighteen years of age, it wasn't something you expected to see. But you had a job to do and if you got on with it then life was that much easier. And I think, possibly, being younger you have more resilience. I don't think I could do that sort of thing now.

Private Douglas Botting
5th Battalion, Royal Berkshire Regiment (Beach Group)

I was frightened. Certainly I was frightened. I don't believe anyone who says they weren't frightened. It pulls you up with a jolt. I was fortunate because I was a young chap, I was only eighteen, and I had experienced chaps with me who really looked after me and taught me the right ways and really kept me alive, I think. I owe a lot to them.

Trooper Berkeley Meredith
Sherman tank driver, Staffordshire Yeomanry

Talking on your radio net, the tank commander is usually referred to in radiotelephony jargon as 'Sunray'. And I remember getting the voice of somebody whose tank commander had obviously been killed, coming up repeatedly saying, 'My Sunray is gone. What should I do?' Repeatedly saying this until he got an answer. I suppose the answer was 'Well, you must get on with it.' But I remember that voice because it was somebody who didn't know what to do in those circumstances and I could feel for him, obviously. There were a lot of greenhorns on D-Day.

Trooper Ronald Henderson
Sherman tank crew, 13th/18th Hussars
There was a chap who wasn't allowed to go, a chap from Birkenhead or Wallasey, because he wasn't quite old enough. He wasn't allowed to go with us and he was broken-hearted after all the training he'd done. But when you go and visit the graves in Normandy you see dozens of graves of seventeen-year-olds. I don't know what happened, they must've slipped through the net or given the wrong age. Boys of that age wanted to be in it. I wouldn't have missed it for the world.

Pilot Officer Ron Minchin
Australian Stirling bomber pilot, 196 Squadron, RAF
We were so young. I was, anyway. My rear-gunner was thirty-three, thirty-four when he joined our crew, and my navigator, who was about twenty-eight, he was an ex-foreman of a big factory, a furniture factory, I think, in London. They took more serious views of what was occurring than I did. And being the captain of the aircraft at such a young age you're dealing with older men in your crew and there's risk and you don't like risk. Tends to make you more concerned about your crew than with the outside factor of what's happening as far as your whole country is concerned. I don't think I really thought that much beyond being very taken by the tremendous sights that we saw. You're worrying about things at the time. You're frightened. When flak starts flying around you're more concerned about your own life, I'm afraid, than anybody else or anything else. I think a mature person's view would probably have been more thoughtful. I think all I was concerned about was surviving.

Major Allan Younger
Commanding Officer, 26th Assault Squadron, Royal Engineers
I knew I had a job to do and I was far more interested in making sure that nothing could go wrong with that job than worrying about whether it was a historic occasion.

Private Dennis Bowen
5th Battalion, East Yorkshire Regiment

I didn't know enough about politics, of course, at eighteen years old. But I knew at the back of my mind that there was something evil about the regime which the Germans were following and the method in which they were conducting their lives. I knew it was wrong and I knew that the only way we would alter it would be to defeat them in battle. It sounds a bit profound now for a bloke my age to say I thought like that when I was eighteen years old, but I did, probably because, as a child, I'd heard my mother and father talk about things which had been done which were wrong: styles of life; things which occurred; how people had been treated. I knew what the Germans were doing was wrong and I didn't want it to happen in England.

And I was very proud – still am – of the fact that I was instrumental in some small way in preventing that happening here or anywhere else in the world for that matter. I also knew that the French were, in my mind, oppressed; they were occupied by somebody in their country that they didn't want. The French couldn't get them out so we were going to do it for them. I was very proud to do that. It sounds as if I'm being heroic now but that is absolutely true, I really did think like that.

The following morning we were going forward again and there was a company in front of us and our job was to go through that company and continue with the advance. When we got up to that company there was a man there tending to a soldier who'd been wounded. As I went to walk past them to go to what was called the start line – what used to be called 'going over the top' in the First World War – this lad said to me, 'Will you help me? Will you help me?' I said, 'What's wrong?' He said, 'Will you look at him?' So I looked at this soldier that was laid there with him and I said, 'Well, he's dead.' He had four or five shots in him and a couple in the head. He was obviously dead. I said, 'There isn't anything you can do for this lad, he's dead.' And I remember this other lad saying, 'He can't be. He can't be dead. I promised his mother I'd look after him.' Oh, God. It struck me then that there was something wrong with war. I could quite happily have put my rifle down. I can only presume that when they went to join up his mother had said, 'He can't go,' and the other lad had said, 'He'll be all right with me, I'll look after him,' and there he was, dead. But that's the only time I had any hesitation about the fighting, the killing.

Sub Lieutenant Jimmy Green
LCA flotilla commander

We did what we had to do. We got our troops back into Europe. It was a great day and it was a great day to be remembered and I'm very fortunate to be part of it. But I'd had enough of the war by that time, I think. I was glad it was coming to a conclusion. I'd rather have been playing cricket on the village green than taking troops into a Normandy beach. But the fact that we could play cricket after the war was due to what we did on that occasion.

Captain David Tibbs
Regimental Medical Officer, 13th Battalion, Parachute Regiment

By midnight, although it was rather like the aftermath of the Battle of Waterloo with the Field Ambulance full of wounded, morale was high. During the night it was relatively quiet but we knew the dawn would bring a storm of fire again and further fighting and further casualties, as indeed happened. But we ended the day with great confidence that we were going to succeed. Obviously fear was by our side but with it was a great determination to see things through. I can only speak with the greatest of praise for the fighting men outside who were defending the perimeter and determined to hold everything they had obtained so far. We were very tired but in a way exultant, because we knew that we had got the better of the situation, and all the objectives that we had really wanted and were going for had been obtained, and if only we could hold on we should succeed.

Captain John Semken
Sherman tank commander, Sherwood Rangers

The terrible thing was that there we were, ashore, and it bore in upon us that we hadn't really given any thought to what happened next. For five months our sleeping and waking thoughts had been preoccupied with how the hell we were going to get ashore and what the hell was going to happen if we couldn't. Now it was all over and we hadn't really thought about what happened next.

Major John Howard
2nd Battalion, Oxfordshire and Buckinghamshire Light Infantry

We handed over the bridges around midnight to a battalion of the Royal Warwicks from Three Div and my orders then were to move and join my

Vehicles crossing the Caen Canal Bridge at Benouville, 9 June 1944. Two gliders of Major John Howard's coup de main force can be seen in the background.

battalion in a place called Ranville. We got to Ranville round about two o'clock. To my great delight, the first person I saw was my second in command, Brian Priday, and the missing platoon. They'd started off with about twenty-five men, they had four or five casualties on the way, but actually reached divisional headquarters with around a hundred because they were picking up Paras who'd dropped too far to the east.

Our job the next day was to move and capture a place called Escoville and D Company, my company, were the left forward company and we had a very tough time because we came up against 21 Panzer and my company was surrounded at one time. I went in with 110 men and came out with fifty-two which was really terrible after the success of the bridges, when I tell you that the casualties for the bridges operation, excluding the platoon that didn't get there, were two killed and fourteen wounded. A remarkably low casualty rate for the sort of operation we were doing. And it really shook us up what happened in Escoville that day, but that is another story.

Glossary

21st Army Group – the British and Canadian ground force assigned to the invasion of Europe

36 Grenade – standard British Army hand-grenade (also known as a Mills bomb)

88-millimetre – anti-aircraft gun used often in a ground artillery role (German)

ATS – Auxiliary Territorial Service (women's branch of the British Army)

AVRE – Armoured Vehicle Royal Engineers, a modified tank, armed with a Petard spigot mortar, developed primarily for breaking enemy defence fortifications

Avro Lancaster – four-engined heavy bomber (British)

Bangalore Torpedo – explosive charge placed on the end of a long, flexible pole and used to clear obstacles, especially barbed wire

Bren gun – light machine gun (British)

Crab – a modified Sherman tank equipped with a rotating flail of chains for clearing minefields

Crocodile – a modified Churchill tank equipped with a flame-thrower

D-Day – the term D-Day is forever associated with 6 June 1944 but was a standard military expression for the day any operation was to begin. The D derived simply from the word day in the same way as H-Hour stood for the time when operations were to start. D-minus-one means the day before D-Day and D-plus-one means the day afterwards

Dannert Wire – a type of coiled barbed wire

DCM – Distinguished Conduct Medal (British gallantry award)

DD tank – the amphibious Duplex-Drive Sherman tank, fitted with propellers and a flotation screen

DF – direction-finding, a radio receiver system for searching for and locating the source of enemy radio signals

DSO – Distinguished Service Order (British award for acts of gallantry and distinguished leadership)

DUKW – a six-wheel amphibious truck, known as a 'Duck'

DZ – dropping zone

E-Boat – small, fast, German torpedo boat

Flail – see Crab

Gammon grenade – a powerful hand grenade that could be primed to explode on impact (British)

GI – a US Army soldier

GOC – General Officer Commanding

H2S – an advanced RAF radar system used for navigation and night bombing

Handley Page Halifax – four-engined heavy bomber (British)

Hawker Typhoon – fighter-bomber (British)

Hawkins Grenade – anti-tank grenade (British)

HE – High Explosive

HMS *Ajax* – Royal Navy light cruiser

HMS *Arethusa* – Royal Navy light cruiser

HMS *Belfast* – Royal Navy light cruiser (now moored on the River Thames as a branch of the Imperial War Museum)

HMS *Bulolo* – Converted passenger liner and Royal Navy Flag Ship off Gold Beach

HMS *Diadem* – Royal Navy light cruiser

HMS *Dolphin* – Royal Navy submarine base at Gosport

HMS *Empire Javelin* – Royal Navy Landing Ship Infantry (LSI)

HMS *Glasgow* – Royal Navy light cruiser

HMS *Kingsmill* – Royal Navy frigate and Headquarters Ship off Gold Beach

HMS *Mauritius* – Royal Navy light cruiser

HMS *Obedient* – Royal Navy destroyer

HMS *Onslow* – Royal Navy destroyer

HMS *Prince Charles* – Royal Navy Landing Ship Infantry (LSI)

HMS *Seagull* – Royal Navy minesweeper

HMS *Squid* – Royal Navy landing craft repair base at Southampton

HMS *Urania* – Royal Navy destroyer

HMS *Virago* – Royal Navy destroyer

IO – Intelligence Officer

LBV – Landing Barge Vehicle, a converted barge or lighter used mostly for carrying stores

LCA – Landing Craft Assault, a small landing craft capable of carrying up to forty troops

LCA(HR) – Landing Craft Assault (Hedgerow), a converted LCA equipped with twenty-four spigot mortars

LCG – Landing Craft Gun, a converted LCT equipped with 4.7-inch guns

LCI – Landing Craft Infantry, a medium-sized landing craft capable of carrying around two hundred troops

LCM – Landing Craft Mechanised, a small landing craft capable of carrying one hundred troops, one small tank or two smaller vehicles

LCP – Landing Craft Personnel, a small landing craft capable of carrying up to forty troops

LCS(M) – Landing Craft Support (Medium), a small assault ship equipped to provide close fire support

LCT – Landing Craft Tank, a versatile landing craft, the regular version of which could carry up to six forty-ton tanks

LCT(R) – Landing Craft Tank (Rocket), a converted LCT equipped with more than one thousand rocket launchers

LSI – Landing Ship Infantry, the small assault version of which had a capacity of one hundred troops, while the larger version could carry twelve LCAs

LST – Landing Ship Tank, larger than an LCT, with a displacement of two thousand tons

MC – Military Cross (British gallantry award)

MG42 – machine gun (German) known to British troops as the Spandau

ML – Motor Launch

MM – Military Medal (British gallantry award)

MO – Medical Officer

MTB – Motor Torpedo Boat

Mulberry harbour – code name for the prefabricated artificial harbours towed across the Channel after D-Day

NAAFI – Navy, Army and Air Force Institute (British organisation running canteens, shops, etc., on British bases)

Oboe – British targeting system for blind bombing

OC – Officer Commanding

Oerlikon – Swiss-designed 20-millimetre automatic anti-aircraft gun

PE and PHE – plastic (high) explosive

Phoenix caisson – a prefabricated section of a Mulberry harbour

PIAT – Projectile Infantry Anti-Tank (a platoon-level British anti-tank weapon)

Pluto – code name (and acronym derived from Pipeline Under The Ocean) for the top-secret pipeline developed to pump fuel across the Channel after D-Day

RAMC – Royal Army Medical Corps

RCAF – Royal Canadian Air Force

RE – Royal Engineers

RSM – Regimental Sergeant Major

RT – Radio Telegraphy

RV – rendezvous

Scorpion – a modified Matilda tank equipped with a rotating flail of chains for clearing minefields

Shaped Charge – explosive charge shaped in order to focus the blast in a particular direction

Short Stirling – four-engined heavy bomber (British)

Snake – a long pipe of explosive pushed ahead of an AVRE into a minefield and detonated to clear a path

SOE – Special Operations Executive, the secret British organisation set up in 1940 to encourage resistance and carry out sabotage in enemy-occupied territory

SP gun – self-propelled gun

Sten gun – sub-machine gun (British)

Thompson / tommy gun – sub-machine gun (American)

TT – the formation sign of the British 50th (Tyne and Tees) Division

VC – Victoria Cross (highest British award for gallantry in the face of the enemy)

Very light – a coloured flare fired from a pistol

WAAF – Women's Auxiliary Air Force (British)

W/T – wireless telegraphy

Index of Contributors

Number in brackets denotes IWM Sound Archive catalogue number.
Page numbers in **bold** refer to photographs.

General Index

Page numbers in **bold** refer to photographs.